GW00646455

# THE ASCENDED MASTERS LIGHT THE WAY

## BEACONS OF ASCENSION

### JOSHUA DAVID STONE, Ph.D.

# THE ASCENDED MASTERS LIGHT THE WAY

## Beacons of Ascension

Joshua David Stone, Ph.D.

---

## THE EASY-TO-READ ENCYCLOPEDIA of the SPIRITUAL PATH
### ✦ Volume V ✦

---

Published by
Light Technology Publishing

Cover design by
Fay Richards

Published by

Phone (800) 450-0985 • (520) 526-1345
Fax (800) 393-7017 • (520) 714-1132
Mailing: P.O. Box 3540 • Flagstaff, AZ 86003
Shipping: 4030 E. Huntington Dr. • Flagstaff, AZ 86004
Website: lighttechnology.com

Printed by
Sedona Color Graphics
■ ■ ■ ■ PRINTING SPECIALISTS
2020 Contractors Road, Suite #2-5
Sedona, AZ 86336

# *Dedication*

I dedicate this book to the world's saints and spiritual masters of all the religions and spiritual paths that have graced this planet. Their unceasing devotion and dedication to God and to their brothers and sisters sets a spiritual example for everyone to follow. May all of humanity walk in their footsteps and build upon the foundation they have so sublimely laid down.

Also by Joshua David Stone, Ph.D.

*The Easy-to-Read Encyclopedia of the Spiritual Path*

# Contents

# 1

## *Shirdi Sai Baba*

*God is not attracted to outer appearances but
rather by the cleanliness of the inner self.*

Shirdi Sai Baba

Sathya Sai Baba is widely known across the world today as the extraordinary avatar he is, but not very many people know about his past life as Shirdi Sai Baba when his spiritual powers and love were as extraordinary as they are in his current incarnation. The present-day Sathya Sai Baba has said that in his past life as Shirdi Sai Baba he was an avatar who embodied the Shiva energy; in this present life he is embodying the Shiva and Shakti (father and mother) energies; in his next incarnation, which will complete the triple avatarship, he will embody just the Shakti energy.

In reading about the life of Shirdi Sai Baba, you will experience the awesome power of a master who is one with the Eternal Self. After experiencing that, I don't think any person's understanding of life can ever again be the same. Hold on to your seatbelts, for you are about to experience the awesome love and power of Shirdi Sai Baba.

Sai Baba first appeared in the small town of Shirdi in India in 1872 as a boy of sixteen. The people in the town considered him a fakir, a Moslem holy man with no worldly cares or attachments. After wandering for a short time, he decided to spend the rest of his life in the small town of Shirdi.

Early on, a holy man passed through the town and said about Shirdi Sai Baba, "Watch that young fakir. He's a jewel on a dunghill." Little did the holy man or the people of Shirdi know what a jewel he was! Shirdi Sai Baba was to spend the next forty-six years, until his death in 1918, in this town, and as his renown grew, more and more people from all over India flocked to see this avatar.

As a very young boy he had left home to follow a Moslem fakir who became his guru. When that fakir died he had joined a Hindu guru whom he called Venkusa. It was in about 1900 that Sai Baba's fame began to spread throughout India. There are some wonderful stories about the events in this saint's life.

One time some visitors to Sai Baba had to catch a night train back to Bombay, but there was a raging thunderstorm. Sai Baba looked up at the sky and said, "Hey, enough of that! Stop it now! My children have to go back." The storm stopped.

On another occasion a husband and wife had gone to see Shirdi Sai Baba, but while there, the wife came down with cholera. The doctors in the town said the case was hopeless and that she would die. Shirdi Sai Baba gave her some virbhuti (sacred ash) to eat. Within thirty minutes she was doing better, and in a short time she was completely healed.

Another time a Hindu devotee was standing outside of Shirdi Sai Baba's mosque but wouldn't go in because he worshiped only Rama. He told his friends he would not bow down before Shirdi Sai Baba for this reason. All of a sudden, he went rushing inside and prostrated himself before Shirdi Sai Baba. When asked why he had changed his mind, he said that he'd seen Sai Baba standing there in the form of Sri Rama.

The interesting thing about Shirdi Sai Baba was that Moslems, Hindus, and persons of all other religions revered him and considered him their guru. That was unheard of at the time. Shirdi Sai Baba performed Moslem practices and Hindu practices, so no one knew which religion he identified with. Shirdi Sai Baba once referred to himself as a reincarnation of Kabir, the poet-saint of the fifteenth century who also embraced both Moslem and Hindu disciples. He convinced everyone that he was fully identified with whichever particular deity a given person worshiped.

A blind man went before Sai Baba and said, "I can't see." Sai Baba laid his hands on the man's head and his sight was restored. A blind woman made a passionate request to see Baba with her eyes. Her sight was immediately restored; however, upon leaving the mosque, her blindness returned because all she had asked for was to be able to see Baba, so by cosmic law, Sai Baba could give her only that.

A Hindu man's son had an extremely high temperature for six days, and he prayed to Sai Baba from another city. Sai Baba materialized in the room, gave him virbhuti, and said his son would be fine. Then he dematerialized.

Another devotee of Sai Baba had had several children but they had all died in infancy. He went to Sai Baba and told him of his misfortune, praying that one child would live. Sai Baba immediately said, "Why ask for one? I'll give you two!" The man had two sons and two daughters.

Sometimes it would be necessary to explain to an extremely sick person that a miraculous healing was not in the person's destiny and in the long run would only cause more suffering. Sai Baba would promise, however, to bring the person back in a new birth if he or she so wished.

A very attractive Moslem woman visiting him in the mosque took off the veil covering her face as she bowed before Shirdi Sai Baba. One of the devotees sitting beside him was thinking to himself that he would like to get another look at the beautiful woman. Sai Baba swung his stick around in a flash and smacked his devotee.

Sai Baba was completely omniscient, omnipresent, and omnipotent, no matter how far away on Earth his devotees lived or were traveling. Sai Baba said in this regard, "I am not confined to Shirdi or to this body. I am everywhere you think of me."

Once Shirdi Sai Baba complained of a severe pain in his abdomen. He ordered his devotees to wind a cloth around his stomach and tighten it, and the pain finally passed. It came to be known that a female devotee had been experiencing painful childbirth and had prayed to Baba to relieve the pain. Sai Baba, of course, took the pain on himself.

Very often Shirdi Sai Baba asked for small amounts of money from certain devotees. When asked about this he said that he asked only those whom God told him to ask; in exchange, he would give them ten times as much. By accepting alms he was, by cosmic law, taking responsibility for those people. In the later years of Sai Baba's life an enormous amount of money was received from devotees. It was said that he made as much as the governor of a province. The authorities decided that they should tax Sai Baba. The only problem was that by the end of every day, everything that Sai Baba had received he had given away to the poor. When he died he had the equivalent of sixteen dollars to his name.

On one occasion he told a devotee to take care of his physical body for three days. He said, "I am going to Allah. Take care of this body for three days. If I return I will look after it myself. If not, bury it in that open land over there and put up two posts to mark the place." Sai Baba lay dead for three days and then returned and continued his life.

One time a devotee who was very poor was embarrassed because all he could offer Shirdi Sai Baba was a few almonds and sugar crystals when all the other devotees were offering so much more. To his amazement, when he took out his offering it had multiplied, and it was enough to feed all twenty-five devotees assembled in the mosque.

In 1911 a plague epidemic occurred in India, and Sai Baba began developing welts all over his body. Not a single person in all of the town of Shirdi was affected by the plague, for Shirdi Sai Baba had taken on the karma himself and manifested it through his own body in order to save the town.

Another time Shirdi Sai Baba put his hand in the fire and severely burned it. His devotees grabbed him and pulled him out of the fire. In another part of India, a child sitting on her mother's lap had fallen into the fire and Sai Baba had pulled her out, saving her life and burning his hand in the process. Sai Baba never failed to protect his devotees wherever they were if they called to him.

Sai Baba often referred to God as the Fakir. For example, when a devotee was bitten by a poisonous snake and ran toward him, Sai Baba said, "Don't come up, Brahmin! Go back, get down!" (He was referring to the poison, although the devotee didn't realize it.) A moment later Sai Baba said, "Come up, now. The Fakir is gracious to you. You will recover."

One of Shirdi Sai Baba's main devotees received permission to bathe his head, for Sai Baba said that putting water on his head was as good as bathing his whole body. The devotee wanted to wash his whole body, however, and disobeyed Sai Baba's command, pouring all of the water in a large copper vessel over Sai Baba's head, expecting to completely drench him. To his amazement, Sai Baba's head was wet but the rest of his body remained completely dry.

This same devotee had a dream a year later in which Shirdi Sai Baba appeared and sprinkled rice on his bed in some sort of blessing. When he awoke there was rice all over his bed. He couldn't understand how this was possible since the door to his bedroom was bolted shut. He asked about it and Sai Baba said, "Do I need to open doors to get into rooms? I have neither shape nor size; I am omnipresent."

A man had offered half his salary to the Lord Dattatreya (an incarnation of Brahma, Vishnu, and Shiva) and if he got a particular job he was seeking. He got the job but then forgot to keep the vow he had made. Years later he went to see Shirdi Sai Baba who immediately asked for fifteen rupees, the exact amount he owed the Lord Dattatreya.

One time some militant fundamentalist Moslems who didn't approve of Shirdi Sai Baba's openness to all religions armed themselves in front of his mosque, refusing to let devotees in to worship. A devotee who had come to worship prayed to Sai Baba from outside the temple. Shirdi Sai Baba walked outside and called him into the mosque. The armed militants were completely immobilized. Then they quickly dispersed in the face of such awesome power.

Another time there was a fire on the farm of one of his devotees, and it was starting to spread. His devotees prayed for his help. Shirdi Sai Baba walked over to a stack of leaves and sprinkled some water on them, saying, "The fire will die down now." And so it happened as he said it would.

On another occasion the villagers wanted to have a fair celebrating Rama's birthday, but there was no water supply, for the well was completely dry. Shirdi Sai Baba said, "So you want plenty of water, do you? Here, take this and drop it into the well and wait and see." The term "this" referred to a platter containing dry leaves and prasad (consecrated food) and alms that had been collected that day. The devotees poured it all into the well and the water instantly rose to fill the well.

A devotee's three-year-old daughter fell into a well once, and when the villagers rushed to the well they found the young child suspended in midair as if some invisible force were holding her up. Shirdi Sai Baba was very fond of the child, who often referred to herself as Sai Baba's sister.

Another devotee was about to take his medical exams when an astrologer told him that his stars were in a terrible configuration and that he wouldn't pass them. The man was dejected and went to see Sai Baba who said, "Keep aside your horoscope and have faith in me." The man passed his exams.

A young woman who was dying of tuberculosis asked to have darshan (a visit with a holy man) with Shirdi Sai Baba. He gave instructions for her care, but on the eighth day of a water fast she died. Meanwhile, Sai Baba had overslept for the first time the devotees could remember. Three or four hours later, the woman who had been dead woke up. The family was in a state of shock. She said that after she had died she was being forcibly led away by a dark man when she prayed to Sai Baba. Baba immediately appeared with his staff and freed her. Then he took her to his mosque and sleeping quarters. She had never been there in person but described it in perfectly accurate detail.

Sometimes Shirdi Sai Baba's cures were quite astounding. One time a devotee was suffering from a terrible bout of malaria. Sai Baba told him that if he would feed cooked rice and curds to a black dog near the Laxmidevi Temple, he would be cured. The devotee had total faith in Sai Baba so he prepared the food and went to the temple. Sure enough, there was the black dog. He fed the dog and was cured.

In 1913 the new headmaster at the primary school in Shirdi was concerned about the low academic standing of the boys and girls. It was a new job for him and he was worried about his reputation. The students had the answer; they all went to see Sai Baba and received the virbhuti ash and his blessing. On the day of the exam, not a single pupil failed, and never in the school's history had such high scores been achieved. The headmaster started believing in Sai Baba.

A man who had had all his savings stolen was brokenhearted. He told his story to a passing fakir who told him to make a pilgrimage to Shirdi Sai Baba and to take an offering of food once the money had been returned. The next week the man who had stolen the money felt remorse and returned all of the money, begging for forgiveness.

A man whose business was deeply in debt owed 30,000 rupees which was a monumental amount of money in India at that time. He was in utmost trouble and anxiety when he had a dream that reminded him to rely on Sai Baba instead of on worldly means. Filled with remorse, he tearfully prayed to Sai Baba for forgiveness for his lack of faith and asked for help. As the day for repayment neared, he still had no possible means of obtaining the money. He had just one more day to go when the son of a deceased friend called him to ask how he could invest 30,000 rupees. He shared with him his financial predicament and the son of his friend gave him the money to invest in his business.

A father took his son for darshan with Sai Baba because the son was about to take a major exam in college. Sai Baba said that he would pass and would rank one hundred fourteenth in his class. That is exactly what occurred.

Once a devotee took a group of people on a pilgrimage to another place in India. On the way, he lost the tickets and they were all stranded. The devotee prayed to Sai Baba for help. Sai Baba appeared in a dream of the devotee's son and told him to send money to his father. When the son awoke from the dream he was startled by the realness of the dream but decided not to act. The next night Sai Baba appeared again in a dream and told him the same thing. That time the son acted, and the father was pleasantly surprised.

Two devotees who went to see Sai Baba purchased two pictures to take home with them for their altars. On their trip home one of them realized he should have bought a third picture for his brother. On returning home and unpacking their bags, they found three pictures.

A young man who could not go with his family and friends to see Shirdi Sai Baba vowed that unless he received Baba's darshan at home he would not accept him as his guru. Meanwhile in Shirdi, Sai Baba was having darshan with an unknown gentleman. When Sai Baba asked him for a favor, the gentleman said, Of course. Sai Baba gave him a package of virbhuti and told him to travel by train to a certain place on his way home. No matter who asks you for an inch of space on the seat next to you, give him this packet of virbhuti. The gentleman did exactly as he was ordered. Sure enough, the young man had gotten on the crowded train at the last minute and asked the gentleman, "Can you give me an inch of space to sit, please? I am feeling giddy." The gentleman said, "Do please sit down!" He then handed the packet of virbhuti ash to the young man and explained Baba's instructions to him. The young man had received his darshan in absentia.

A woman devotee had received darshan from Sai Baba, and he had given her a four-anna coin. The woman used the coin in her worship rituals every day as an attunement to Sai Baba. One day she accidentally used the coin to buy food from a vendor. Upon arriving home and realizing what she had done, she felt heartbroken and immediately prayed to Sai Baba. That evening the woman vendor knocked on her door and said, "You gave me a coin from your puja. I don't want to keep it."

An elderly devotee was hiking up a mountain to attend a special fair. It was an extremely hot day and he became weak and dehydrated. He prayed to Sai Baba for help. All his friends had hiked onward but he was too weak to move. Meanwhile back in Shirdi, Sai Baba remarked to his devotees that this particular gentleman was in trouble. All of a sudden the elderly man noticed a man carrying a load of wood and asked him where he could get some water. The man said, "Right below the rock you are sitting on." The elderly man lifted the small rock and water came shooting into the air. The man carrying the wood was Shirdi Sai Baba.

There was a devotee who suffered from asthma. In order to prevent his devotee from eating curds which were bad for the asthma he materialized himself in the form of a cat and lapped up the curds. The asthmatic devotee saw the cat eating his curds and proceeded to smack it twice with two hard blows. Baba later showed the devotee the marks on his body resulting from the blows he had received.

In respect to his dying, Sai Baba said, "Though the spirit may depart from my Earthly tabernacle, know this for certain, that my bones will assure you from my samadhi and not only I, but my samadhi will speak to you. It will communicate with whosoever takes refuge in it." In other words, Sai Baba would continue helping his devotees even after the death of the physical body.

One time a band of robbers raided a train on which a devotee happened to be traveling. He immediately started chanting Sai Baba's name, and the people in his compartment started chanting along with him. A big burly man suddenly  materialized and stood in front of their compartment, protecting it. When the train arrived at the station, it was discovered that every compartment in the entire train had been robbed except that one.

Once a devotee was sent away to another city by Sai Baba, even though he wanted to stay. Sai Baba appeared to him in his hotel room in the other city, and the man asked why Sai Baba had sent him away. Baba said, "Your mind was restless while you were in Shirdi. I wanted to steady your mind, so I sent you away. It was your belief then that my existence was confined to the three-and-a-half-cubit length of my body. Now look carefully for yourself and see that I am as much with you here as I am in Shirdi!"

Sai Baba often appeared to devotees in various forms other than his own. On one occasion a devotee's daughter was afraid to walk alone at night to her home. Sai Baba appeared as her father and walked her home. On arriving at the house, Sai Baba said that he would not be coming inside and that she should go in by herself. The next day the daughter berated her father for not coming inside and discovered that her actual father had never left the house the entire night.

A female devotee went to see Sai Baba and he asked for six rupees but she was very poor and had no money. She went home in tears. When she told her husband what had happened, he said that Sai Baba did not want real money, he wanted the symbolic money of the six enemies of man — kaama, krodha, moha, mada, lobha, matsarya (lust, anger, attachment, passion, greed, and jealousy). The next day she returned to Sai Baba and he immediately requested the six rupees. She confidently said she had already given them to him, for she had renounced the six qualities the previous night in her meditation and prayers. Sai Baba said, "Have you really?" The woman said confidently, "Yes I have!" Sai Baba said, "And you won't take them back?" The devotee understood completely and said she wouldn't.

## Summation

On his death bed, Shirdi Sai Baba told his devotees that he was about to leave his physical body, but that he would return in eight years in a city in southern India as Sathya Sai Baba.

Sathya Sai Baba is the Cosmic Christ and the embodiment of Shiva and Shakti and Lord Dattatreya (Brahma, Vishnu, and Shiva), all in one body. Sathya Sai Baba has all the power of Shirdi Sai Baba and even more, for he now carries with him the full power of the Shakti (Divine Mother) energy also. Humanity is indeed blessed to have him gracing this planet. He has said he will return for a third incarnation, after two years on the spiritual plane, in about 2025, when he will be Avatar Prema (Love) Sai Baba.

Sai Baba says you can keep whatever religion you are comfortable with, for he is in all religions and in all forms of God. You can call upon him for help and he will not fail to respond to every sincere need.

Sai Baba exemplifies what consciousness on Earth is like when you are one with the Eternal Self and the monad. Let it be clearly understood that this is not unique to Sai Baba. It is the destiny of every human to become fully merged with the Eternal Present and the living God. His life and example can be an inspiration to strive for your highest potentials so you may be of greater service to humankind.

# 2

## Sri Rama and the Ramayana

*Know that the chanting of my name destroys all*
*sins in this world if the chanting is done with*
*one-pointed devotion and complete*
*dependence upon me.*

Sri Rama

The life and teachings of the avatar Sri Rama are contained in a wonderful book called the *Ramayana* which was written by the great poet-saint Valmiki. It is one of the four *Itihasa* of the Hindu religion, the other three being the *Mahabarata* (which contains the *Bhagavad-Gita*, the story of Krishna), the *Yoga Vaistha*, and the *Harivamsa*.

Rama lived over twenty thousand years ago. Valmiki wrote his story as a lyrical tale out of the compassionate understanding that many of the common people had not developed sufficiently abstract minds to be able to study the Vedas and Upanishads which are the more serious texts of ancient Hindu teaching. The *Ramayana* contains the essence of the technical Vedic scriptures, yet a child can still enjoy the story. It is a textbook of morals and ideals for people of all ages to aspire to, and it is not just for Hindus but is a book for the whole world, just as are the stories of Jesus, Krishna, Buddha, Moses, and Sai Baba. The name Rama means God; Sai Baba actually goes by the name Sai Ram, and Gandhi chanted "Ram" throughout his life.

The *Ramayana* is allegorical, even though Rama was a great avatar who did live in ancient India. It has been recorded in Hindu scripture that Vishnu has incarnated ten or twelve times onto the Earth; Rama was one of these incarnations, as was Krishna, but Vishnu's greatest incarnation is in the form of Sai Baba, who is also Brahma and Shiva, all in one body. Sai

Baba has said that Rama was the embodiment of righteousness, whereas Krishna was the embodiment of love. Rama was also the embodiment of every social and domestic virtue; he was an ideal king, husband, father, and brother. He lived like a normal man even though he was, in truth, a spiritual avatar incarnate on the Earth. His wife, Sita, became the ideal of womanhood. She was put to severe tests, and she always demonstrated purity, courage, love, patience, and the ideal of womanly virtue.

## The Story of the Ramayana

There lived a noble ruler named Dasaratha who was a great king and a hero to his people. He had three devoted wives, and one of his many sons was Sri Rama. His sons were all considered to be part of Vishnu, but Sri Rama embodied all the divine virtues. One of his brothers, Lakshmana, was especially devoted to him.

When Rama was sixteen years of age, one of the sages of the court asked the king to send Rama and Lakshmana with him to slay the demons who were creating disturbances and problems for the other sages and priests. The king agreed and Sri Rama, with his great skill in archery and the blessing of the sage, killed all the demons. Sri Rama was blessed by all the sages for his great service to them.

The brothers were taken to Mithila, the capital where the renowned King Janaka reigned. There Rama demonstrated his great strength and skill by lifting and stringing the wondrous bow of Lord Rudra, a task many mighty princes had failed to accomplish. The king had promised that any great prince who was able to perform the miraculous task would receive his lustrous daughter, Sita, in marriage, so Rama and Sita returned home and loved for many years.

Finally, the old king, Dasaratha, wanted to step down from his throne and pass it on to Sri Rama. Everything was set for the ceremony when the cruel queen, Kaikeyi, found out from the maidservant what was about to occur.

Dasaratha owed the queen two boons which he had promised her. The cruel queen asked to collect on these promises, and the king could not refuse. What she requested was that Rama be banished for fourteen years and that her own son, Bharata, be installed as crown prince instead of Sri Rama. Realizing his father's predicament, Rama left with Sita and Lakshmana for the forest.

While living in the forest, Sita was abducted by the evil king of Lanka, Ravana, who tried to talk Sita into becoming his queen. However, since she was totally absorbed in her love for and service to Rama, Sita was imprisoned. With the help of Hanuman, a being who is half man, half monkey and who embodies the divine quality of selfless service, Rama found

Ravana, and a great battle took place between the opposing armies. Ravana was killed and Sita was rescued.

At first Rama refused to accept Sita, for he assumed she had long been the concubine of Ravana. To prove her innocence and purity, Sita entered into the bonfire, and Agni, the god of fire, came out with Sita, declaring her to be unsullied and pure. He requested that Rama take her back as his wife. Rama's joy knew no bounds at this turn of events. He returned to his city, and since fourteen years had passed, Rama and Sita were crowned king and queen. So began a long and prosperous reign. Everywhere in the city and province there were great joy, health, and happiness.

I have not, in truth, done justice to the beauty of the story, but this is its essence. Please read it for yourself, for it is the eternal companion of almost all Hindu families, even to this day.

## The Metaphysical Meaning of the Story

Ravana, the evil king, symbolizes the negative ego and lower self; his ten heads represent the ten senses. Sita symbolizes peace. Rama represents righteousness and knowledge. His killing of Ravana is symbolic of killing the negative ego and mastering the senses. Reuniting with his wife, Sita, signifies the attainment of peace and the recovering of his soul which had become lost on account of desire. Knowledge is achieved through union with Rama, who is the embodiment of the Supreme Self. Sri Rama's victory represents the goodness and righteousness of God overcoming evil, maya, and illusion.

Swami Vivekananda has made the following statement about the Ramayana: "Rama, the ancient idol of the heroic ages, the embodiment of truth, of morality, the ideal son, the ideal husband, the ideal father, above all, the ideal king, this Rama has been presented before us by the great sage, Valmiki. No language can be purer, none chaster, none more beautiful and at the same time simpler, than the language in which the great poet has depicted the life of Rama."

## Quotations from Sri Rama

Sri Rama's teachings in the *Ramayana* are so profound that I have selected some passages that best communicate his wisdom:

It is the shadow of the Paramatman [God] that you see reflected in all the living beings as Jivatman [Eternal Self, or soul].

Paramatman alone is real; this world is unreal. The latter appears as real in man's vision, hearing, and thoughts, but it lasts only as long as the things seen in a dream last.

This Atman [Eternal Self] is certainly different from the body, senses, mind, and prana. It is blissful, supreme, non-dual, permanent, formless, sinless, and pure. The moment this realization comes to you, you are liberated.

If you constantly think of the Atman, your mind will be purified and your ignorance will be uprooted along with the past tendencies, just as your ailments will completely disappear by your taking medicine daily. When the mind is pure, you will get unalloyed bliss.

When one realizes the truth of the unity between the Jivatma [soul of man] and the Paramatma [God], whether by instruction from a guru or from spiritual texts, then every moment the source of ignorance, along with the cause and effect, will mingle with Paramatma. The state mentioned above is called moksha [liberation]. The self is ever free.

Those who take shelter under me in this world, meditating on me and repeating the mantra of my sacred name, will surely get my vision, even unasked, as I know they have no other refuge.

As a result of the spiritual disciplines you have undergone, you are even now liberated from all worldly desires. After your death, you will attain union with me.

Just as even people possessing eyes cannot see things clearly in the night, but they can see their steps well when a light is brought, so also in those having devotion toward me, the self becomes self-effulgent.

Those who have devotion toward me will get knowledge and renunciation and they will attain liberation from the round of births and deaths.

Know that the chanting of my name destroys all sins in this world, if the chanting is done with one-pointed devotion and complete dependence upon me.

The mistaking of the body for the Self is called maya. This maya is responsible for the creation of samsara.

On account of false imagination, much as a rope is mistaken for a snake, so also the pure Supreme Self is mistaken for this universe by the power of maya. If we think deeply, the universe disappears and Brahman [God] alone remains.

In this effort, man will have to face many enemies like kama, or desire; krodha, or anger; lobha, or greed; and moha, or delusion. Of these, anger is the most fearful for it will try to put all sorts of obstacles in one's struggle to attain moksha [liberation].

I clearly see that such men are rare who do not become dejected when faced with danger, or overcome by delusion, who do not become proud when their selfish end is attained and who are not perturbed by the glances of women. We can seldom find such men.

The world is transitory, having not a grain of happiness in it. I do not desire death nor do I covet life; I have no eagerness for kingdom, wealth, enjoyments, and desires, for I have relinquished egoism which is the root of all these.

Neither should you find fault with anyone. Control your mind, speech, and body, and never be perturbed. Daily do service to your guru with devotion after purifying your body and mind. Do not be slack in doing good actions even for a single day.

Do not be overjoyed if you get a fortune; neither should you be dejected if you lose it. Your mind should be well balanced. I, Rama, am the life of all souls. Your mind should be fixed on me alone.

What I have advised you is the knowledge that can be obtained only by the study of Vedanta. He who studies this with great faith and devotion to me and my words will surely attain union with me.

As long as you identify yourself with this body, you will feel miserable. Atman is not the body, sense, or ego. It is due to ignorance that you are affected by these worldly sorrows.

When you dream of something it seems real as long as the dream lasts. Similarly, to a man who always thinks of the senses and the pleasures derived therefrom, this world seems real.

But if these good deeds are done with a sense of ego, they only bind you to this world. So to gain knowledge you should work without the least trace of pride.

Pure knowledge is that which kills all desires and attachments. Any work with a particular motive behind it should be given up. It only binds you to the cycle of birth and death. It is harmful for your attaining real knowledge.

# 3

## Mahavira and Jainism

*Jainists are "conquerors of mortal bondage."*

The founder of Jainism was the spiritual master Mahavira who was born in India in 599 B.C. At the age of thirty he gave up his life as a wealthy prince and became a religious ascetic. In this regard, his life closely mirrors that of Gautama Buddha. He traveled throughout India seeking liberation from the cycle of reincarnation.

He practiced the transcendence of duality, which was also taught by Krishna — remaining evenminded through pleasure and pain, sickness and health, cold and heat. He believed that through extreme self-denial and through the practice of ahimsa (nonviolence) toward all living things, he could achieve moksha (liberation).

Legend has it that he attained nirvana after thirteen years of such practice. Then, again like Buddha, he dedicated the rest of his life to becoming a leader among men and a teacher of monks. He apparently had extraordinary success, and his disciples became known as Jains.

Jainism is based on the achievement of the three jewels: right faith, right knowledge, and right understanding. Jainism arose as a protest against the caste system of Hinduism, along with its ritualism and impersonality.

Mahavira was referred to as "the Conqueror" because of the control he demonstrated over the world, his body, and his desires. Jainism adheres strongly to the concepts of reincarnation and the law of karma. Mahavira differed from Buddha in that Mahavira never gave up his identification with the ascetic path, whereas Buddha trod that path but then moved toward the Middle Way.

The yati (ascetic) had to take the Five Great Vows:

To injure no creature,

To speak the truth,

To abstain from stealing,

To renounce all worldly goods, and

To practice sexual self-control.

The most important of these was harmlessness. It applied to animals, insects, and even to plants. A Jainist could not be a farmer because of the danger of killing insects. The Five Great Vows were too stiff for most people so the Jains provided a less strict spiritual practice which was called the Twelve Vows. Those who adhered to the Twelve Vows promised

Not to take human or animal life,

Not to be unfaithful to their spouses,

Not to lie, steal, or cheat,

To give alms,

To practice self-denial,

To guard against evil,

To meditate regularly,

To avoid needless travel, and

Not to be greedy.

Because of their extreme belief in pacifism, Jains work, even to this day, in the areas of finance and commerce. They are lawyers, brokers, money-lenders, and bankers. Their wealth has allowed them to build beautiful and lavish temples which are some of the most beautiful in the world.

Jainism began as a conscious effort to reform Hinduism, but it became a new religion instead. Mahavira was very much against the caste system and taught that all his followers were equals. He was also very much against the animal sacrifice of those ancient times and believed that kindness was preferable. Jainism is a religion of love and compassion above all else.

Jainism has a similarity to Buddhism in that it doesn't accept the existence of a supreme diety or the gods of the Hindu religion. Mahavira believed that each person should find his salvation within himself. He is quoted as saying, "Man! Thou art thine own friend. Why wishest thou for a friend beyond thyself?"

It seems to be a kind of existentialism, yet it includes the concepts of reincarnation, liberation, and potential immortality for the soul. Mahavira believed that the world was his home, not just India or any particular country. He divided souls on Earth into three categories:

Those who are not yet evolved,

Those who are in the process of evolution, and

Those who have evolved to the point of liberation.

The name Jainism comes from the Sanskrit word for saint, "jinah," which derives from "jayati," meaning "he conquers"; thus, they are conquerors of mortal bondage. Jainism teaches that there have been twenty-four jinahs in the present world cycle. One of the jinahs, Rishabha, is said to have lived millions of years ago. They consider their religion to be eternal and believe that it is revealed and revived in every century.

Legend has it that in his time, Mahvira attracted over fifty thousand monks and over five hundred thousand lay followers. Today Jainism has about one and one-half million followers and is considered one of the world's great religions. The Jains reject the Vedas of Hinduism and use their own scripture. They believe in the eternity of the soul, and there are thought to be multitudes of souls, or life-monads, which are all independent and eternal.

Practicing the ideals of Jainism results in the soul's getting lighter in color and rising on the scale of universal being. The goal of the Jains is to achieve liberation and then to "float like a bubble to the ceiling of the universe." Since the universe is eternal, they don't see any need to speculate on who created it, so strangely enough, they could be called atheistic. Some of the monks are so extreme in their devotion to ahimsa (nonviolence) that they sweep their paths as they walk and wear cloths over their mouths so as to avoid killing insects. They are all vegetarians, of course, as they believe killing any animal or insect builds up evil karma. Mahatma Gandhi's parents were believed to be greatly influenced by the Jains, and Gandhi's strong commitment to nonviolence could have had its roots in Jainism, even though Gandhi was strongly influenced by Hinduism and the *Bhagavad-Gita* and very much believed in the Hindu gods.

# 4

# *The Life and Teachings of Sri Sankara*

*The world is filled with attachments and aversions
and is like a dream; it appears to be real as long
as one is ignorant but becomes unreal when one
is awake.*

Sri Sankara

Sri Sankara, also known as Sankaracharya, was a Hindu avatar born in approximately 788 A.D. to a Brahmin family in southern India. He was so precocious that at the age of ten he had memorized most of the Hindu scriptures. By the time he was sixteen he had completed all his writings.

His parents had been praying for a child for a long time when one night in a dream Sri Sankara's father, Sivaguru, heard the Lord speaking to him. "Hail devotee! I am deeply moved by thy prayers and penances. Choose now: would you have a hundred sons devoid of brains and character who would live long or only one son who would live a shortened life?" Upon making his request he heard an inner voice that said, "I myself shall be born as your son." A local astrologer doing the child's chart suggested that they name him Sankara, which means "the giver of auspiciousness to all living things."

By the time the boy was three he was the master of many languages, including Sanskrit, and by the age of five, he had mastered most arts and sciences. When he was five his father passed away; Sankara was spiritually initiated at that time and he began his study of the four Vedas and other religious texts. Tradition has it that by the age of eight he had mastered the Vedas and the other principal branches of knowledge with effortless ease. At that time he left home to search for his guru, who was to be the well-known sage and Self-realized being, Govinda Bhagavatpada. Through divine dispensation and because his mother agreed to allow him to follow the path of a sanyasin (a renunciate), Sankara was permitted to live on Earth until the age of thirty-two.

When he was still only eight years old, the Lord spoke to Sankara, saying, "Sankara, thou art myself manifest amongst men that thou mayst preach to them the doctrines of the Brahman set out in the Vedanta sutras of Vyassa. [Vyassa wrote down the *Bhagavad-Gita* and was a past life of Buddha.] Do write the bhyasya of the sutras and instruct worthy men in the wisdom of Vedanta. Nay, you shall be the supreme world teacher, establishing the Vedanta doctrine in the world." So Sankara set down a commentary on the Vedanta sutras of Vyassa, which is the true doctrine of the Upanishads, the wisdom teachings of the Vedas and bible of the Eastern world.

Sankara's mission was to stamp out the seventy-two misguided religions of the age known as the Kali Yuga and to reestablish the six Vedic religions for the world's well-being. He achieved great spiritual and mystical heights and surpassed all the saints and scholars of his time in his understanding of the nature of God, man, and the universe. He traveled across the vast subcontinent four times, spreading his gospel. He started principal monasteries at the four cardinal points of India and organized the large number of wandering monks into ten tightly knit orders. He died at the age of thirty-two, as it had been prophesied in the Himalayas.

Sri Sankara's philosophy was based on the belief that the purpose of life and of worship is to become perfect, to become divine, to reach God, and to be God on Earth, even though reaching for that goal requires constant struggle. The sole reality is Brahman, Brahman being absolute existence, absolute knowledge, and absolute bliss — sat, chit, and ananda.

God was considered to be impersonal, to have no attributes that come and go but to be permanent infinite essence, completely changeless and without any unfulfilled desires. It was thought to be impossible to grasp God (Brahman) with the finite mind. The soul of each human (atman) was seen as being part of Brahman.

The physical universe was considered maya that causes the illusion of individuality. It is this ignorance that makes humans feel they are separate from Brahman and that causes them to project and superimpose onto reality their egos, the sense of separate individuality and division.

Sankara saw man as having three states of consciousness: waking, dreaming, and dreamlessness.

| State | Coat | Sheath |
|-------|------|--------|
| Waking state ..... | Physical body .. | Sheath of food |
| Dream state........ | Subtle body ..... | Sheath of vital airs, the mind, and self-consciousness |
| Dreamless deep-sleep state.......... | Causal body ..... | Sheath of bliss |

The appearance of a world filled with many separate forms and objects is illusion. The reality underlying all the apparent diversity is Brahman, which is all bliss and all goodness. Brahman is achieved through renunciation, discrimination, and self-control which lead to true devotion which, in turn, leads to a transcendental consciousness.

The purpose of life is moksha, or liberation, which is achieved through incarnation into a physical body. The world is seen to contain both good and evil, but the absolute reality of Brahman is beyond good and evil, pleasure and pain, success and failure. In other words, the absolute reality is beyond duality. The only true statement is "I am Brahman" or "I am God."

The goal of life is to overcome maya and ignorance and, hence, realize the atman and Brahman. To achieve this it is necessary to master the five senses, the mind, the emotions, and the body; it is necessary to destroy the negative ego and material desire. When the self finally merges with Brahman, the devotee goes into a trance called nirvikalpa samadhi, the state of nonduality.

## Quotations from Sri Sankara

Sankara formulated a complete system of philosophy and theology which regenerated India during the time he lived. The following are some quotations from his writings:

Just as a piece of rope is imagined to be a snake and an oyster to be a piece of silver, so is the atman [soul] determined to be the physical body by an ignorant person.

Atman is verily one and without parts, whereas the body consists of many parts, and yet the people see these as one. What else can be called ignorance but this?

Action cannot destroy ignorance, for it is not in conflict with ignorance. Knowledge alone destroys ignorance, as light destroys darkness.

The impression of "I am Brahman" created by uninterrupted reflection destroys ignorance and its distractions as medicine destroys disease.

All beings are, by nature, pure consciousness itself. It is due to ignorance that they appear to be different.

Faith, devotion, and the yoga of meditation — these are mentioned by the Vedas as the immediate factors of liberation in the case of a seeker. Whoever abides by these gets liberation from the bondage of the body, which is the conjuring of ignorance.

Lust at the sight of a young woman springs from ignorance and delusion. Reason points out time and again that bodies are only the combination of flesh, blood, and fat.

Never boast of your wealth, friends, and youth; time may steal away all these in the twinkling of an eye. Giving up attachment to this world, which is full of illusion, try to realize Brahman soon and merge into it.

The knowledge of one's identity with the pure self negates the notion of the identity of the body and sets a man free even against his will from the belief that he is a human being.

The world, which is full of attachment, aversion, and the like, is like a dream. It appears to be real as long as one is ignorant. With the dawning of knowledge, the world becomes unreal.

The yogi endowed with complete enlightenment sees, through the eye of knowledge, the entire universe in his own eye and regards everything as the Self and nothing else.

The right knowledge, the subject of Vedanta, produces the conviction that the self is Brahman. One becomes perfectly free from the bondage of this transmigratory existence when one achieves it.

He is a knower of the Self to whom the ideas of me and mine have become quite obsolete.

The intense desire for the realization of the atman, after renouncing all other desires, is alone the means for the attainment of the atman.

Among things conducive to liberation, devotion alone holds the supreme place. The seeking after one's real nature is designated as devotion.

Everyone in all the three worlds strives for happiness and not at all for misery. The two sources of misery are the sense of I-ness in the body and the sense of mine-ness arising therefrom, in the objects of one's own consciousness.

Brahman alone is true, and the world is false; the jiva [soul] is Brahman only and not different from it.

# 5

## *Sri Ramakrishna: His Life and Teachings*

*You should remember
the heart of the devotee is the abode of God.*

Sri Ramakrishna

There have been at least ten truly great Hindu masters, and Sri Rama-krishna was definitely among them. He was born in 1836 in Kamar-pukur, India. As a young boy he grew indifferent to his studies and became deeply absorbed in the stories of Rama and Krishna. As he grew older, his passion to realize God became stronger and stronger. For a period of his young adulthood, Ramakrishna longed for the sight of Kali. Then he experienced an intense twelve-year search for the realization of the Divine Mother aspect of God.

Paramahansa Yogananda once said that if a person wants to realize God, he must want God as much as a drowning man wants air. This perfectly describes Ramakrishna. A vision of the Divine Mother was his all-consuming desire. On one particular day he felt he could no longer bear the separation he felt from the Divine Mother. He was in the temple of the Divine Mother when he spotted a sword and decided to kill himself. At that moment the Divine Mother revealed herself to him and he fell unconscious to the floor. Ramakrishna felt a steady flow of divine bliss when he awoke. His main concern after that experience was to stabilize it so he could live in that state all the time. He doubled his prayer and meditation practices.

After that, Ramakrishna focused his attention on the incarnation of Rama. He put himself in the place of Hanuman, the monkey god who was the selfless and devoted servant of Rama. He gave himself completely to the practice, even to the point of living on nuts and fruits and acting like a monkey at times. As the result of that practice he had a vision of Sita, the beloved wife and devotee of Rama.

Ramakrishna's family worried about him because of what they perceived to be his occasional odd behavior. They decided that he should get married. Ramakrishna just flowed with divine providence and in an ecstatic state of meditation prophesied where they should go to find his bride. He was married in May of 1859, and from that day onward he worshiped his wife as the very embodiment of the Divine Mother, although his understanding of marriage was quite different from that of the average worldly person.

One day, near one of the temples on the banks of the Ganges, Ramakrishna encountered a woman who was a sanyasini, a female spiritual renunciate, and yogini. She exclaimed, "My son, you are here! Knowing that you were somewhere on the banks of the Ganges, I have been searching for you for so long, and now I have found you." Her name was Yogeswari. Ramakrishna accepted her as his spiritual guide and passed through the tantric spiritual practices. To Ramakrishna, all women were incarnations of the Divine Mother, whom he worshiped until the end of his life.

One of the interesting things about Ramakrishna was that he was never satisfied with just one system of spiritual practice. During this twelve-year period, he also went through phases of worshiping Krishna and Radha, Krishna's wife, and had divine visions and full realizations of both beings.

Then one day, in the garden of one of the temples, he met an itinerant monk named Totapuri who asked Ramakrishna if he would like to learn Vedanta. Ramakrishna went into the temple and asked the Divine Mother in meditation. The Divine Mother said to him, "Yes, my son, go and learn of him. It is for this purpose that he has come here."

On the first day Ramakrishna practiced advaita spiritual practices he went into nirvikalpa samadhi, the enlightenment experience, and remained in that state, dead to the world, for three days. Totapuri, his teacher, was amazed, for it had taken him forty years of strenuous practice to achieve that state of consciousness. Totapuri remained with Ramakrishna for eleven months, during which time Ramakrishna became a Jnani, a knowledge yogi, in addition to his previous training as a Bhakta, a devotional yogi.

After Totapuri had left, Ramakrishna had another experience of samadhi that lasted for six full months. At that point, the Divine Mother said to him, "Remain on the threshold of relative consciousness for the sake of humanity." Because of that command, he came out of the enlightened state in which he had been merged with the Eternal Self.

Ramakrishna then went through a period of studying and realizing God through the Sufi teachings of the Islamic faith. After three days he had a vision of the prophet Mohammed and realized God in that form.

Then he even delved into the Bible and studied Christianity, receiving a vision of Jesus Christ. Ramakrishna firmly believed that all forms of religion were valid pathways to God.

In 1879 Ramakrishna took on his first disciples and for the next seven years, pearls of great wisdom flowed from his mouth. He never read books; he was completely uneducated in a left-brained sense. However, divine knowledge poured through him, and all of that knowledge came from union with the Eternal Self.

He was the embodiment of the mystic path through life. It was for this reason, I believe, that Ramakrishna attracted his premiere disciple, Swami Vivekananda, who was exactly the opposite of Ramakrishna, being left-brained and having been college educated.

Ramakrishna left his physical body in 1886.

## Quotations from Ramakrishna

He is born in vain who, having attained the human birth, so difficult to get, does not attempt to realize God in this very life.

Repeat God's name and sing His glories and keep holy company; and now and then visit God's devotees and holy men. The mind cannot dwell on God if it is immersed, day and night, in worldliness, in worldly duties and responsibilities. It is most necessary to go into solitude now and then and think of God.

You should always discriminate between the real and the unreal. God alone is real, the eternal substance. All else is unreal — that is, impermanent. By discriminating thus, one should shake off impermanent objects from the mind.

The point is to love God even as the mother loves her child, the chaste wife her husband, and the worldly man his wealth. Add together these three forces of love, these three powers of attraction, and give it all to God. Then you will certainly see Him.

One cannot have the vision of God as long as one has these three: shame, hatred, and fear.

A man must work. Only then can he see God. One cannot develop love of God or obtain His vision without work. Work means meditation, prayer, affirmation, and the like. The chanting of God's name and glories is work too. You may also include charity, sacrifice, and so on.

God cannot be realized if there is the slightest attachment to the things of the world. A thread cannot pass through the eye of a needle if the tiniest fiber sticks out.

Do not let worldly thoughts and anxieties disturb your mind. Do everything in the proper time, and let your mind be always fixed on God.

You should remember that the heart of the devotee is the abode of God. He dwells, no doubt, in all beings, but He especially manifests Himself in the heart of the devotee. The heart of the devotee is the drawing room of God.

Do all your duties, but keep your mind on God. Live with all — with wife and children, father and mother, and serve them. Treat them as if they were very dear to you, but know in your heart of hearts they do not belong to you.

He who has surrendered his mind, heart, and soul to God is a sadru [spiritual seeker]. He who has given up lust and gold is a sadru. He looks upon women as his mother and accordingly worships them. A sadhu always thinks of God and serves all, knowing that God is in everything.

# 6

## The Holy Mother, Sri Saradamani Devi

*Repeat the name of God always
in the innermost core of your heart, and in all
sincerity take refuge in God.*

The Holy Mother

Ramakrishna was one of the great God-realized beings of all time; Swami Vivekananda was a great yogi and teacher and an instrument of Ramakrishna from the spiritual world; Sri Saradamani Devi embodied the female principle, the mother principle, for the world and was also used by Ramakrishna in the continuation of his mission after his death. Vivekananda and the Holy Mother were the male and female, the yin and yang instruments used to carry on Ramakrishna's work. Neither of them attained the supreme exalted position that Ramakrishna had reached, but because they allowed themselves to be used as instruments by him, their work was greatly enhanced and they became, in and of themselves, Lights to the world.

The Holy Mother was born to pious Brahmin parents on December 22, 1853. Her father was a very righteous man and a sincere devotee of Rama. Her mother was kind, religious, and an excellent and organized householder. One day her mother was sitting under a tree when she had a vision of a small girl coming down from the tree. The girl clasped her about the neck and she lost consciousness. She had the premonition that the girl had entered her womb.

Her father, meanwhile, in another part of the city, took a nap after his meal and had a vivid dream of a girl with a beautiful golden complexion embracing his neck with her arms. When he asked who she was, she said, "You see, I have come to your family." Later, her parents shared their experiences with each other and were convinced that a deity would be born into the family.

They named her Saradamani, or Sarada for short. They went on to have five more children. As a young child, Sarada had an imaginary playmate who used to help her in her work but who disappeared when other people came around.

In a nearby city, Ramakrishna was going through his spiritual practices and was demonstrating signs of being God-intoxicated. His family, not understanding this, thought he was insane. Their solution was to find him a bride. They were looking all over for the right bride when Ramakrishna, in a state of samadhi, said, "Go to Ramachandra Mukherjee's house at Jayrambati and you will find the girl there." In a state of omniscience, Ramakrishna had picked out the ideal spiritual mate for himself. At the time of the betrothal, however, Sarada was only six years old, and Rama-krishna was twenty-three. Such an arrangement was very common in India; the actual marriage does not take place until the girl attains maturity. Ramakrishna, in the God-realized state of samadhi in which he lived most of the time, saw all women as the embodiment of the Divine Mother of the universe. He also worshiped the Divine Mother in his spiritual practices. Sarada became the outer representation of his inner worship.

Because of Ramakrishna's total focus on the Eternal Self, they never sexually consummated their marriage. Ramakrishna had prayed at an early age that his wife would be able to accept such an arrangement, and to his amazement, she was easily able to do so.

Ramakrishna became her teacher and guru in both spiritual and worldly matters because she was so young. He trained her in cultivating detachment from the world and deep devotion to God. As she matured, she became more introverted and worked very hard at all her household duties and spiritual practices. She was different from Ramakrishna in that he was truly the embodiment of the archetypal renunciate, whereas her path was to practice the same philosophy as a householder. Swami Nikhilananda, in his book *Holy Mother*, describes Ramakrishna's attitude toward his wife and women in general by quoting Ramakrishna's teacher, Totapuri, who stated, "He alone is established in the realization of Brahman who sees the same Self in both men and women. He who sees a difference between the sexes may be an aspirant, but he is far from having experienced Brahman."

On one occasion, Ramakrishna was sleeping next to his Sarada when he awoke and looked at her with his worldly eyes. He said, "O mind, this is a woman's body; people regard it as a most covetable object and are ever eager to enjoy it. But if a man embraces this body, he becomes entangled in the world and cannot realize God. Now, oh mind, don't be a hypocrite. Your tongue must not say what you do not feel at heart. Be truthful and tell me what you want – this body or God. If you want the body, it is right here in front of you. Take it." Ramakrishna immediately chose God and went into samadhi.

To Ramakrishna, Sarada was the ideal of Indian womanhood. She was a devoted wife, renunciate, teacher, and loving mother to all. Such a state of consciousness developed over time, as she lived in the presence of an exalted, God-realized saint and his disciples from such a young age. Ramakrishna was training her for her future mission all along. At the age of eighteen, Sarada was initiated by Ramakrishna as the embodiment of the Divine Mother incarnate on Earth. Ramakrishna, in a sense, set the mold which the Holy Mother was in the process of moving into and filling. She was trained by Ramakrishna in the use of different mantras to create different states of samadhi.

Ramakrishna, as he evolved, would sometimes spend days in exalted states of samadhi and so depended on the Holy Mother to take care of and feed his physical body. Being a renunciate, he could not deal with worldly matters at all. She tells how he once touched a coin, and it was as though he had been stung by a horned fish. The Holy Mother looked at Ramakrishna as God incarnate (which, in truth, he was) and to serve him was to worship God. Ramakrishna always treated her kindly and as an equal. To her, Ramakrishna was teacher, father, mother, companion, husband, and God.

Ramakrishna watched over the Holy Mother's development and made sure she meditated. She would get up every morning at 3:00 a.m. to begin her spiritual practice. Later in life, she taught her disciples the great need for firmness and determination in order to achieve spiritual progress. The Holy Mother never let her spiritual practices interfere with her daily duties, however; in this regard she was different from Ramakrishna, for they had different missions. She once said to her devotees that "through spiritual realization, the mind becomes pure, and through that pure mind, one obtains enlightenment."

Ramakrishna said, "Why should you worry? I shall leave you many children, all pure as gold, the likes of whom women do not get, even through the prayers and austerities of millions of lives. So many people will call you Mother that you will find it hard to look after them all." Ramakrishna's prophecy turned out to be true.

Ramakrishna finally passed away chanting the name Kali, Kali, Kali. The next day the Holy Mother began to remove her ornaments, as is the custom for Hindu women upon a death, when Ramakrishna materialized himself right in front of her eyes. In Swami Nikhilananda's book, he is quoted as saying, "Am I dead, that you are acting like a widow? I have just moved from one room to another." She put her jewelry back on. The Holy

Mother did mourn greatly the loss of her husband, guru, and teacher and went into a withdrawn state for a period of time. She continued her spiritual practices and once spent two days in a superconscious state which transformed her profoundly.

Her future mission began when Ramakrishna appeared to her one day and told her to formally initiate a new disciple. He gave her the name of the disciple and even the mantra she should use. She resisted at first, but did as she was instructed and Swami Yogananda became her first disciple. (This is not the same person as Paramahansa Yogananda.)

Her public spiritual ministry began in 1898 and culminated in 1920. During that time she fully expanded into the embodiment of the Holy Mother that Ramakrishna had envisioned for her. She became the spiritual mother for all the disciples of Ramakrishna. She would often say, "If one is without kindness, how can one be called a human being?"

Along with Swami Vivekananda, she became Ramakrishna's spiritual successor. She would give spiritual initiations and allow the disciple to choose his ideal, or personal god. To the Holy Mother, Ramakrishna was the supreme spirit and incarnation for these modern times. However, sometimes disciples would choose another deity, and that was fine with her. She, like Ramakrishna, saw that all paths lead to the same place.

The Holy Mother did not look for disciples. She allowed them to come to her. She gave the responsibility for her disciples to Ramakrishna, who happily accepted them. She and her disciples practiced japa, which is the repetition of the name of God.

To her disciples and all others, she demonstrated unconditional love, devotion, forgiveness, and compassion. She also imparted the spirit of renunciation, sexual and sensory control, nonattachment, and transcendence of ego. She regarded all disciples as her children. She came to see herself as the Divine Mother of the universe. Ramakrishna often overshadowed her in his subtle body.

She would tell disciples in times of trouble, "Do not be afraid, the master is behind you, and I am too, as your mother." For the Holy Mother, the purpose of life was to "realize God and remain immersed in contemplation of him. God, alone, is real, and everything else is false. God is one's very own, and this is the eternal relationship between God and creatures. One realizes God in proportion to the intensity of one's feeling for him."

She saw Ramakrishna as the "embodiment of all deities and all mantras. One can worship through him all gods and goddesses." Ramakrishna practiced many different religions and realized God in all of them. The Holy Mother taught that the teachings of all the saints are true, not just those of Ramakrishna.

When asked how one attains Self-realization and Brahman, she said,

"The path leading to Brahman is very difficult. It is quite natural for a man to forget God. Therefore whenever the need arises, God becomes incarnated on Earth and shows the path by practicing spiritual discipline himself. This time, too, God has shown the example of renunciation."

The Holy Mother also taught that lust and attachment to money must be renounced along with attachment to the physical body. People with desires are born over and over again. She said, "One should desire desirelessness. Desire is the obstacle to liberation!"

On death, she said, "The thought that is uppermost in the mind before one loses consciousness determines the course of one's soul after death." She prescribed steady effort in meditation, prayers, japa, and devotions. In respect to japa, she recommended her disciples repeat the name of God fifteen or twenty thousand times a day. Love of God and humanity was seen as essential to spiritual progress.

In respect to food, the Holy Mother said, "All food should be offered to God. As your food is, so will your blood be. From pure blood, you will get bodily strength and a pure mind. A pure mind begets ecstatic love for God."

About truth, she said, "The Master used to say that truthfulness alone is the austerity of the present age. One attains to God by holding to the truth." To householders, she advised a practice of inner renunciation without running away from the world, which could be achieved by the repetition of God's name and dedication to self-control. The cultivation of good company was also highly recommended.

Self-surrender was considered the ultimate state of spiritual growth before God bestowed final liberation. Letting go of the ego led to the union of the individual soul and the universal soul. Until the "I-consciousness" was transcended, desires would still arise.

On Tuesday, July 21, 1920, the Holy Mother passed away. Three shrines now stand as memorials to her. She had said, "I am the mother of the virtuous. I am the mother of the wicked. Whenever you are in distress, say to yourself, I have a mother."

## Quotations from the Holy Mother

Always try to discriminate. Try to realize that the outside object that is attracting your mind is impermanent, and turn your attention to God.

Don't relax your spiritual practice simply because you do not get his vision. Does an angler catch a big carp every day the moment he sits with the rod? He has to wait and wait, and many times he is disappointed.

The mantra purifies the body. Man becomes pure by repeating the name of God, so repeat his name always. If you do good action, that will counteract your past evil actions. Past sins can be counteracted by meditation, japa, and spiritual thought.

God is one's very own. The more intensely a person practices spiritual disciplines, the more quickly he attains to God.

He who has a pure mind sees everything as pure.

The mind is rendered pure as a result of many austerities. God, who is purity itself, cannot be attained without austerities.

Repeating the name of God once, when the mind is controlled, is equivalent to a million repetitions when the mind strays from God. You may repeat the name of God for the whole day, but if the mind be elsewhere, that does not produce much result. The repetition of the name must accompany concentration.

As the wind removes the cloud, so the name of the Lord destroys the cloud of worldliness that overcasts the mind.

I tell you one thing. If you want peace of mind, do not find fault with others. Rather, see your own faults.

One should not hurt others even by words. One must not speak even an unpleasant thought unnecessarily. By indulging in rude words, one's nature becomes coarse. One's sensibility is lost if one has not control over one's speech.

Even the injunctions of destiny are canceled if one takes refuge in God. Destiny strikes off with her own hands what she had written about such a person.

One's love of God depends entirely upon one's inner feelings. Love of God is the essential thing.

Our essential point is love. It is through love alone that the spiritual family of Sri Ramakrishna has grown and developed.

The goal of life is to realize God and to be always immersed in His thought.

# 7

## *The Life and Teachings of Swami Vivekananda*

*Stand up, be bold, be strong.*
*Take the whole responsibility on your own*
*shoulders, and know that you are the creator of*
*your own destiny. All the strength and succor*
*you want is within yourself. Therefore,*
*make your own future.*

Swami Vivekananda

Swami Vivekananda was only seventeen years of age when he first met Sri Ramakrishna who immediately recognized his future messenger. Ramakrishna grasped Swami Vivekananda and said, "Ah! You have come so late. How unkind of you to keep me waiting so long! My ears are almost seared listening to the cheap talk of worldly people. Oh how I have been yearning to unburden my mind to one who will understand my thought! Lord, I know you are the ancient sage, Nara, the incarnation of Narayana [Vishnu], born on Earth to remove the miseries of mankind." The only problem was that Vivekananda, being so left-brained and young, thought Ramakrishna was crazy!

But Vivekananda was a sincere seeker of God, and on his next visit to Ramakrishna, he asked him if he had ever seen God. This was a question he had asked many different spiritual teachers, but no one had answered in the positive. When Ramakrishna was asked, he said, "Yes, I have seen God. I see Him as I see you here, only more clearly. God can be seen. One can talk to Him. But the problem is what people care for God. People shed torrents of tears for their wives, children, wealth, and property, but who weeps for the vision of God? If one cries sincerely for God, one can surely see Him." Vivekananda was amazed.

During Vivekananda's second visit, Ramakrishna, in an ecstatic state of meditation, put his foot on Vivekananda's body and, with his eyes open, the walls, room, temple, and garden began to disappear into the void. Vivekananda thought he was dying. He cried out, "What are you doing to me? I have my parents, brothers, and sisters at home." Ramakrishna laughed and said, "All right, everything will happen in due time."

On Vivekananda's third visit, Ramakrishna touched him on his third eye and Vivekananda lost consciousness. Ramakrishna asked questions during this trance state about his purpose and mission, and the answers Vivekananda gave only confirmed what Ramakrishna already knew. He told the other disciples that Vivekananda had attained perfection even before his birth.

Ramakrishna had a vision about Vivekananda and himself; I would like to quote the following description of it from Swami Nikhilananda's book, *Vivekananda: A Biography.*

> Absorbed one day in samadhi, Ramakrishna had found that his mind was soaring high, going beyond the physical universe of the sun, moon, stars, and passing into the subtle region of ideas. As it continued to ascend, the forms of gods and goddesses were left behind, and it crossed the luminous barrier separating the phenomenal universe from the absolute, entering finally the transcendental realm.
>
> There Ramakrishna saw seven venerable sages absorbed in meditation. These, he thought, must have surpassed even the gods and goddesses in wisdom and holiness, and as he was admiring their unique spirituality he saw a portion of the undifferentiated absolute become congealed, as it were, and take the form of a divine child. Clamoring upon the lap of one of the sages and gently clasping his neck with his soft arms, the child whispered something in his ear, and at this magic touch the sage awoke from meditation.
>
> He fixed his half-open eyes upon the wondrous child, who said in great joy, "I am going down to Earth. Won't you come with me?" With a benign look, the sage expressed assent and returned to deep spiritual ecstasy. Ramakrishna was amazed to observe that a tiny portion of the sage, however, descended to Earth, taking the form of light, which struck the house in Calcutta where Vivekananda's family lived. When he saw Vivekananda for the first time, he at once recognized him as the incarnation of the sage. He also admitted that the divine child who brought about the descent of the rishi was none other than himself.

For five years Vivekananda tested Ramakrishna, not being able to let go of his left-brained education and see fully the realization that Ramakrishna had achieved. Ramakrishna never asked Vivekananda to let go of his reason, for this was part of his greatest gift as well as being his greatest curse. In Djwhal Khul's terminology, Ramakrishna was the mystic and Vivekananda the occultist and teacher.

Ramakrishna had great love for Vivekananda even though Vivekananda was quite disrespectful in the early stages of their relationship. One time Ramakrishna asked the Divine Mother in meditation about this disrespect and the Divine Mother said, "Why do you care about what he says? In a short time he will accept your every word as true."

Vivekananda was continuing his college education and visiting Ramakrishna on a regular basis. Ramakrishna kept a close watch on Vivekananda's practice of discrimination, detachment, self-control, and regular meditation. On one occasion, Ramakrishna was going to transfer many of his spiritual powers to Vivekananda. Vivekananda asked if it would help him to realize God. Ramakrishna said no, but that it would help him in his future work as a spiritual teacher. Vivekananda replied, "Let me realize God first, and then I shall perhaps know whether or not I want supernatural powers. If I accept them now, I may forget God, make selfish use of them, and thus come to grief." Ramakrishna was greatly pleased with his disciple's reply.

Vivekananda did long for an experience of nirvikalpa samadhi and had asked Ramakrishna many times for his help in achieving this exalted state of enlightenment. Ramakrishna insisted that he had to be patient and keep up his spiritual practices. One particular night Vivekananda was meditating when he felt a light burning at the back of his head. The light grew in intensity and finally burst. Vivekananda fell unconscious. When he awoke, he could feel only his head, not the rest of his body. He was consumed by an ineffable peace. Ramakrishna later said, "Now the Mother has shown you everything. But this realization, like the jewels locked in a box, will be hidden away from you and kept in my custody. I will keep the key with me. Only after you have fulfilled your mission on this Earth will the box be unlocked, and you will know everything as you have known it now." Ramakrishna predicted that Swami Vivekananda would shake the world with his spiritual powers. Ramakrishna did not want Vivekananda to stay in nirvikalpa samadhi before his task in the world was complete.

Vivekananda was almost an extension of Ramakrishna. It was nearly as though Ramakrishna were going to complete his mission through the teaching abilities of Vivekananda. They were complements of each other, Ramakrishna having great mystic and experiential powers and Vivekananda having the education and left-brained teaching abilities that Ramakrishna had never been trained in.

When Ramakrishna was dying, he took hold of Vivekananda and passed an electrical current into his body. Vivekananda lost outer consciousness. When he awoke he found Ramakrishna crying and saying, "Oh Naren, today I have given you everything I possess. Now I am no more than a fakir [renunciate], a penniless beggar. By the powers I have transmitted to you, you will accomplish great things in the world, and not until then will you return to the Source whence you have come." Vivekananda had become a channel for Ramakrishna's powers and a spokesperson for his message.

Two days before Ramakrishna died, Vivekananda was standing before Ramakrishna's dying physical body. He suddenly had a doubt in his mind about whether Ramakrishna was truly an incarnation of God. (This parallels the Christian story of "doubting Thomas.") He said to himself that he would accept Ramakrishna as an incarnation of God if Ramakrishna would declare himself to be so.

Vivekananda never spoke this thought out loud, but Ramakrishna turned to him and said, "Oh my Naren, are you still not convinced? He who in the past was born as Rama and Krishna is now living in this very body as Ramakrishna." Ramakrishna had affirmed that he was one with the Vishnu aspect of God, as Rama and Krishna were also incarnations of Vishnu. Vivekananda was convinced.

After Ramakrishna's physical death, Vivekananda became the spiritual teacher for Ramakrishna's order of disciples that still exists to this day. Vivekananda traveled throughout India and was then guided to go to America to attend a parliament of religions in Chicago. After many trials and tribulations, Swami Vivekananda made it to the Parliamentary Convocation of the World's Religions and spoke a number of times. His talks were an immediate success, and he was the star of the entire convocation. *The New York Herald* wrote, "He is undoubtedly the greatest fixture in the Parliament of Religions. After hearing him, we feel how foolish it is to send missionaries to this learned nation." Swami Vivekananda was then only thirty years old.

Swami Vivekananda was the first Eastern master to come to the United States and spread the Hindu teachings. Integral to these teachings was the Hindu belief that "all religions are pathways to God, hence, all religions are true." Vivekananda spent three years on lecture tours around the United States where he was a tremendous success. He also spent three months in London where he was also very successful. He then returned home and was honored by a united India.

Vivekananda believed that religion was the heart of India's national life and that politics, economics, trade, industry, and commerce were all, in truth, subsidiary to it. India had much to learn from the West in terms of material sciences, but in philosophy and religion the country was far more highly developed.

Vivekananda noted four qualities that impressed him most about the Western nations: Western nations' concern for the masses; the high culture of the women in America; the power of organization in the West; and the material prosperity of the West.

Swami Vivekananda traveled throughout India and was hailed as a prophet of modern India. He also gave himself to training Eastern and Western disciples so they could carry on his work.

Swami's health began to disintegrate because he was pushing himself so hard. He made one last trip to the West to see how the teachings of Vedanta, which he had started, were spreading. New Vedanta centers had sprung up in Santa Clara, San Francisco, Oakland, and Alameda, California. It was Vivekananda's mission to teach the Vedas and Upanishads to the masses.

On his return to India, Swami Vivekananda died at the age of thirty-nine, nine years after he had spoken at the Parliament of Religions. His gift was the opening of not only Western eyes to the great teachings of the Vedas, but also the reopening of the eyes of many Hindus in India who had forgotten their own rich heritage. The aim of the Ramakrishna movement, according to Vivekananda, was to spread the Vedanta teachings in all countries and to apply them practically to all national problems at home in India.

An interesting sidenote is that Swami Vivekananda has again incarnated on Earth; Sai Baba has prophesied that he will come to visit him.

## Quotations from Swami Vivekananda

Vedanta recognizes no sin, it recognizes only error; and the greatest error, says the Vedanta, is to say that you are weak, that you are a sinner, a miserable creature, and that you have no power and you cannot do this or that.

Truth, purity, and unselfishness: wherever these are present, there is no power below or above the sun to crush the possessor thereof. Equipped with these, one individual is able to face the whole universe in opposition.

Be thankful that you are allowed to exercise your power of benevolence and mercy in the world and thus become pure and perfect. Be grateful to the man you help; think of him as God. Is it not a great privilege to be allowed to worship God by helping our fellow men?

This is the gist of all worship — to be pure and to do good to others. He who sees Siva [God] in the poor, in the weak, and in the diseased really worships Siva, and if he sees Siva only in the image, his worship is but preliminary. He who has served and helped one poor man seeing Siva in him, without thinking of his caste, creed, or race, or anything, with him Siva is more pleased than with the man who sees him only in church or temples.

Never talk about the faults of others, no matter how bad they may be. Nothing is ever gained by that. You never help one by telling about his faults, but you do him an injury and injure yourself as well.

Get up and set your shoulder to the wheel. How long is this life for? As you have come into this world, leave some mark behind. Otherwise, where is the difference between you and the trees and stones?

Faith, sympathy, fiery faith and fiery sympathy . . . faith, faith, faith in ourselves, faith, faith in God — this is the secret of greatness.

Never quarrel about religion. All quarrels and disputes concerning religion simply show that spirituality is not present. Religious quarrels are always over the husks. When purity, when spirituality goes, leaving the soul dry, quarrels begin, and not before.

Sincerity of conviction and purity of motive will surely gain the day, and even a small minority armed with these is surely destined to prevail against all odds.

Those who want to help mankind must take their own pleasure and pain, name and fame, and all sorts of interests, and make a bundle and throw them into the sea and then come to the Lord. This is what all the masters said and did.

What good is it if we acknowledge in our prayers that God is the Father of us all, and in our daily lives do not treat every man as our brother?

Give up jealousy and conceit. Learn to work unitedly for others. This is the great need of our country.

# 8

## *Paramahansa Yogananda and the Self-Realization Fellowship*

*Mankind is engaged
in an eternal quest for that "something else"
he hopes will bring him happiness, complete and
unending. For those individual souls who have
sought and found God, the search is over.
He is that something else.*

Paramahansa Yogananda

Paramahansa Yogananda is one of the most beautiful, pure, and devoted spiritual masters who has lived on this planet in the twentieth century. If you have never read his book *Autobiography of a Yogi*, you have missed an important experience; it is one of the top ten books of all time. Although born in India, he speaks like a Westerner in his writings and, in my opinion, sets forth some of the clearest, most integrated, most balanced teachings available. His book *Man's Eternal Quest* is literally one of the best books I have ever read.

I have an intimate connection with and understanding of Paramahansa Yogananda, for I took the Kriya initiation and accepted him as my teacher for a long period of time. I have read all his books and practiced all his techniques.

He is such a wonderful being that it is my great pleasure to give you a small glimpse into his life and teachings.

Paramahansa Yogananda was born on January 5, 1893, in Gorakhpur in northeast India, near the Himalaya Mountains, and was named Mukunda Lal Chosh. Early in life he had recollections of a past life when he had lived as a yogi in the Himalayas. When he was still a child, his parents became disciples of the great spiritual master Lahiri Mahasaya, the premier disciple of the great Babaji, the Yogi Christ. From that time on Lahiri Mahasaya took an interest in the young boy.

At an early age he caught the Asiatic cholera which basically meant death, in those days. His mother told him to bow to a picture of Lahiri Mahasaya, even though he was incredibly weak. Yogananda did so and a blinding Light filled his body and the entire room. He was miraculously healed.

Yogananda focused his prayers on the Divine Mother aspect of God. Upon the death of his biological mother, he felt crushed. From within a lifeless state of grief, he heard the Divine Mother speak to him, saying, "It is I who have watched over thee, life after life, with the tenderness of many mothers. See in my gaze the two black eyes, the lost beautiful eyes thou seekest!"

Fourteen months after her death he was told by his brother, Ananta, that his mother had left him a message. In his autobiography, he quotes the letter: "Let these words be my final blessing, my beloved son, Mukunda! The hour is here when I must relate a number of phenomenal events following your birth. I first knew your destined path when you were but a babe in my arms. I carried you then to the home of my guru in Banaras. Almost hidden behind a throng of disciples, I could barely see Lahiri Mahasaya as he sat in deep meditation. While I patted you, I was praying that the great guru would take notice and bestow a blessing. As my silent devotional demand grew in intensity, he opened his eyes and beckoned me to approach. The others made a way for me; I bowed at the sacred feet. Lahiri Mahasaya seated you on his lap, placing his hand on your forehead by way of spiritually baptizing you. He said, 'Little Mother, thy son will be a yogi. As a spiritual engine, he will carry many souls to God's kingdom.' "

The letter went on to tell of another experience she had had. A strange spiritual master knocked on the front door one day and told her that she would die soon. He also told her that a silver amulet would materialize in her hands during her meditation the following day. She was told to have her oldest son give this silver amulet to Yogananda one year after her death which would be the time when he would be ready to renounce all worldly hopes and endeavors. When the amulet had served its purpose, it would just disappear again. Everything occurred exactly as the spiritual master had prophesied.

As a youth, Yogananda's ardor for God and love for the Himalaya Mountains was tremendous. He tells of many meetings with the great saints of India who had miraculous powers. It was everything his family could do to prevent him from leaving home and school. When the time for his high school graduation exams was approaching, he was not prepared because of his total preoccupation with Godly matters. He prayed to the Divine Mother for help. After the prayer, one of the brightest students in class offered to tutor him. Then he realized he wasn't prepared for his Sanskrit exam. Walking to class that day, in the weeds he found two loose sheets of Sanskrit verse. He had them interpreted and the poem helped him to pass the exam.

In the time that followed, Yogananda was praying in anguish to find his guru. After much prayer and meditation, he heard the Divine Mother say, "Thy master cometh today!" As he was walking through the street with a friend later that day, he saw a Christ-like man in the robes of a swami. As he walked past the swami, he found that he could no longer walk in any direction except back to the swami. The swami said, "O my own, you have come to me! How many years I have waited for you!" It was the great God-realized yogi Sri Yukteswar Giri, the disciple of Lahiri Mahasaya.

Sri Yukteswar was a strict disciplinarian, so only truly committed disciples stuck with him. The fruits gained by those who persevered were great, but even Sri Yukteswar said that Yogananda's style would be more loving and less severe than his own. In fact, in the beginning there were some battles. Then Yogananda made a deal with him. He told Sri Yukteswar that he would completely surrender and do whatever he was told, no matter what, as long as Sri Yukteswar promised to reveal God to him. Sri Yukteswar finally agreed.

One of Sri Yukteswar's first commands was that Yogananda go to college. Yogananda assented, although he very much disliked worldly schooling. But Sri Yukteswar told him that he would be going to the West where a college degree would give him more credibility which would be useful in his future mission. Sri Yukteswar then initiated him into the spiritual science of Kriya Yoga.

The spiritual powers of Sri Yukteswar were quite amazing, as were those of his former guru, Lahiri Mahasaya. Sri Yukteswar told a story of having once lost a lot of weight. Then he told Lahiri Mahasaya that he was ready to gain all the weight back; with Lahiri Mahasaya's blessing he had gained fifty pounds by the next day.

One time Yogananda went against Sri Yukteswar's will and decided he wanted to go to the Himalaya Mountains and realize God in unbroken solitude. He left the ashram and began searching in the Himalaya Mountains for a spiritual master named Ram Gopal, also a disciple of Larhiri Mahasaya, who had realized God in the isolated caves there. His trip was plagued with problems. By the grace of God he did finally find Ram Gopal, and the first thing he said to Yogananda was, "Young yogi, I see you are running away from your master. He has everything you need. You should return to him. Mountains cannot be your guru. . . . Are you able to have a little room where you can close the door and be alone? . . . That is your cave!" Yogananda's life-long obsession with the Himalaya Mountains was suddenly banished, and he humbly returned to the ashram. Before leaving, however, Yogananda asked Ram Gopal to give him the experience of samadhi. Ram Gopal told him that his nervous system was not yet ready for that experience; too much cosmic current would burn up his body. He was told that Sri Yukteswar would give him the experience soon, but that he needed to continue his spiritual practices to prepare himself. Soon after, on his return to the ashram, Ram Gopal's prediction came true when Sri Yukteswar, during meditation with Yogananda, gave him a thump on the chest above the heart and Yogananda had his experience of samadhi and cosmic consciousness.

Yogananda had been in college for two years and it was time for a series of major exams. He had only a week before they started and he hadn't studied at all or even attended all his classes because of his intense focus on spiritual pursuits. He went to Sri Yukteswar with his problem and was told to cram for the next week and he would be helped. There was no way he could do two years' worth of work in a week, so he was guided to just open each book at random and study only those pages that lay exposed. Yogananda passed all his courses.

On one occasion, he received a postcard from Sri Yukteswar saying that he was in Calcutta and needed to be picked up at the train station at 9:00 a.m. on Wednesday. Wednesday morning while Yogananda was sitting in his room, Sri Yukteswar physically materialized in front of him and said that he had been divinely commanded to give Yogananda that experience.

Yogananda was officially initiated as a monk in the swami's order and was then given the name Yogananda. "Yoga" means divine union, and "ananda" means bliss – thus, bliss through divine union. At another initiation almost twenty years later, he was given the title Paramahansa, "parama" meaning highest and "hansa" meaning swan, the mount of Brahma, and also meaning "I am He."

Paramahansa Yogananda began a school for elementary and high school grades which he called Yogoda Satsanga Brahmacharya Vidyalaya. His students were taught yoga, meditation, and physical development as well as all the normal academic subjects.

One time, Yogananda went to visit the wife of Lahiri Mahasaya (Sri Yukteswar's guru and Babaji's premier disciple) who told him some wonderful stories about Lahiri Mahasaya. She said, "It was years before I came to realize the divine stature of my husband. One night, in this very room, I had a vivid dream. Glorious angels floated in unimaginable grace above me. So realistic was the sight that I awoke at once. Strangely, the room was enveloped in a dazzling light. My husband, in lotus posture, was levitated in the center of the room, surrounded by angels. In supplicating dignity they were worshiping him with folded hands. Astonished beyond measure, I was convinced that I was still dreaming.

" 'Woman,' Lahiri Mahasaya said, 'you are not dreaming. Forsake your sleep forever and forever.'

" 'Master,' I cried, 'again and again I bow before you! Will you forgive me for having considered you as my husband? I die with shame to realize that I have remained asleep in ignorance by the side of one who is divinely awakened. From this night, you are no longer my husband but my guru. Will you accept my insignificant self as your disciple?' " She was accepted and given an experience of samadhi. He never slept in her room again, and she says that he never slept, day or night, ever again. An interesting sidenote is that Yogananda said he slept only four hours a month.

The reverend mother told another story about a time when she had fallen into delusion and become angry with her husband, saying, " 'you spend all your time with disciples. What about your responsibilities for your wife and children? I regret that you do not interest yourself in providing more money for the family.'

"The master glanced at me for a moment, then disappeared right before my eyes. Awed and frightened, I heard a voice resounding from every part of the room: 'It is all nothing, don't you see? How could a nothing like me produce riches for you?'

" 'Guruji,' I cried, 'I implore pardon a million times! My sinful eyes can see you no more. Please appear in your sacred form.'

" 'I am here.' This reply came from above me. I looked up and saw the master materialize in the air, his head touching the ceiling. His eyes were like blinding flames. 'Woman, seek divine wealth, not the paltry tinsel of Earth. After acquiring inward treasure, you will find that outward supply is always forthcoming.' "

Sri Yukteswar tells a story about a time when he was a disciple of Lahiri Mahasaya. His best friend, Rama, had come down with Asiatic cholera. He prayed to Lahiri Mahasaya to heal him, and Lahiri Mahasaya said he would. The only problem was that Rama was getting sicker and sicker, and the doctors finally gave up on him. Sri Yukteswar was in a panic. Rama died, and Sri Yukteswar was grief-stricken.

Lahiri Mahasaya then told Sri Yukteswar to drop seven drops of castor oil into Rama's mouth. Sri Yukteswar couldn't understand why, since he had already told Lahiri Mahasaya that Rama had been dead for over thirty-six hours. Lahiri Mahasaya said, "Just do as I say."

He returned to the dead body. Even though rigor mortis was starting to set in he put the drops in his dead friend's mouth. Rama shivered violently and sat up. Sri Yukteswar had just been given a lesson in having greater faith in the word of his guru.

Lahiri Mahasaya made a prophecy to Sri Yukteswar that fifty years from his death, an account of his life would be written because of the interest in yoga arising in the West. Fifty years from Lahiri Mahasaya's death, Paramahansa Yogananda's autobiography was completed.

Some years later, Yogananda was invited to address a religious congress in America, much as Swami Vivekananda had done earlier in the century. That initiated the fifteen-year saga of Paramahansa Yogananda's mission to spread the creedless teachings of Kriya Yoga to the West. Before leaving, he prayed to God fervently, wanting to be sure it was the path he was supposed to take. All of a sudden there was a knock on the door and there, standing before him, was the great Babaji himself. Babaji said, "Yes, I am Babaji. Our Heavenly Father has heard your prayer. He commands me to tell you, 'Follow the behests of your guru and go to America. Fear not. You shall be protected. You are the one I have chosen to spread the message of Kriya Yoga in the West. Long ago I met your guru, Sri Yukteswar, at a Kumbha Mela; I told him then I would send you to him for training.' "

Paramahansa Yogananda lectured and taught all over the United States during the next fifteen years. His lectures and teachings were an extraordinary success. During that period he initiated over one hundred thousand people into Kriya Yoga.

There are so many wonderful stories about him and his work. On one occasion Swami Kriyananda and another disciple were putting wet plaster on a wall when Yogananda came by. They chatted with him for half an hour even though they knew the plaster would dry out within five minutes and cause them hours of extra work. They didn't care, however, because having a darshan with their master was more important. To their amazement, when they returned to their work the plaster was as wet as they had left it thirty minutes earlier.

A disciple who was driving back to the ashram from out of town stopped and ate two hamburgers, even though Yogananda had recommended that his disciples be vegetarians, because he was in a hurry and couldn't find anything else to eat. The next day, Yogananda told him that in similar circumstances in the future, it would be better to eat nothing at all than to eat hamburgers.

Paramahansa Yogananda had warned a particular disciple not to hitch-hike. The disciple did so anyway and was picked up by three criminals. He asked to get out of the car and they wouldn't let him. They drove to a house in the country and one of the criminals got out and started knocking on the door, calling to the people inside. No one answered for a long time and so they all got scared and drove off, letting him out of the car. When the disciple saw his master the next day, Yogananda lovingly scolded him for hitchhiking and told him that he had prevented the people inside the house from hearing the knocking; if he hadn't, the disciple would have been in big trouble.

Another disciple was working on some scaffolding when he fell from a height of twenty feet which would probably have killed him. As he was falling, he called out to his guru. Witnesses say that an invisible force pushed him back up to safety.

At one time, a famous artist was commissioned to paint a portrait of Lahiri Mahasaya. When Yogananda saw the painting, he found that he didn't like it and asked the man how long it had taken him to learn to paint. The man replied twenty years and angrily told Yogananda that he would like to see him do it and in half the time it had taken him to learn to paint. Yogananda said he would do it in one week. Paramahansa Yogananda had never painted in his entire life, but he practiced for the next week, tuning into God at a more refined level during each session, until he had completed his portrait of Lahiri Mahasaya. When the artist saw it, he was forced to admit that it was better than his own.

Paramahansa Yogananda wanted to know about the great God-realized being, Ramakrishna. He started to meditate and Ramakrishna materialized right in front of him on the bed. They sat side by side holding hands and exchanging telepathic communication.

On another occasion Paramahansa Yogananda went to visit Therese Neumann, who at the age of twenty had been in an accident that blinded and paralyzed her. She received a miraculous healing in 1923 through prayers to St. Therese of Lisieux and since that time has not consumed any food or liquids except for one small consecrated wafer each day. Neumann was born on Good Friday in 1898; in 1926, stigmata, the sacred wounds of Christ, began to appear on her head, breast, hands, and feet every Friday while she experienced the passion of Christ. Yogananda later said that in a past life she had been Mary Magdalene. She is here to show that it is possible to live on just God's Light.

Fifteen years after having left his beloved guru and country, Yoga-nanda returned because he had received a message that his guru would be passing into the spirit world soon. They had a glorious reunion, and it was at that time he was given the name Paramahansa. Sri Yukteswar passed on while Paramahansa Yogananda was lecturing throughout India. Yogananda was deeply saddened by not being present at his guru's death. Then on June 19, 1936, Sri Yukteswar resurrected himself and materialized to Yogananda in full physical form in his Bombay hotel room. Sri Yukteswar explained that he had become a World Savior on an astral planet called

Hiranyaloka, or Illumined Astral Planet. There, he was aiding advanced souls in attaining liberation from astral rebirths. At that time Sri Yukteswar apologized to Yogananda for being a little too severe in his discipline. Yogananda wouldn't accept that, of course.

Yogananda finally met Mahatma Gandhi when he went to visit him at his ashram and initiated him into Kriya Yoga.

After that, Yogananda returned to the West to continue his work. Many ashrams and centers were opened all over California and, of course, he founded the Self-Realization Fellowship.

If you have never been to the Lake Shrine Temple in the Pacific Palisades, do try to go there, as it is one of the most beautiful spots in all of Los Angeles. There is a bookstore there that carries all his books, tapes, pictures, and information about lessons and the science of Kriya Yoga.

# 9

## *Sri Anandamayi Ma,*
## *the Joy-Permeated Mother*

*Man is no other than the Eternal Self
but he wrongly thinks of himself as a separate
individual centered in his body and
identified by a particular name.*

Sri Anandamayi Ma

Sri Anandamayi Ma first came to the attention of people in the West through Paramahansa Yogananda's book *Autobiography of a Yogi*. Upon first meeting Anandamayi Ma, Yogananda was aware of the high state of samadhi she was in. He told of having met many men who were God-realized, but never had he met such an exalted female saint.

When Yogananda asked her to tell him something of her life, she replied, "My consciousness has never associated itself with this temporary body. Before I came onto this Earth, Father, I was the same. As a little girl, I was the same. I grew into womanhood; still I was the same. When the family into which I had been born made arrangements to have this body married, I was the same and, Father, in front of you now, I am the same. Even afterward, though the dance of creation changes around me in the hall of eternity, I shall be the same."

These are not just idle words; that is exactly how she lived. She was uneducated; all her knowledge and wisdom came directly from inner revelation. I don't think she ever read a book, yet her beautiful teachings could have come right out of the Vedas and Upanishads.

She lived completely in the Eternal Self; it was almost as though she had no ego. I am not talking about the negative ego here, but about the part of a person that takes care of the physical body, telling it when to sleep, eat, or watch out for physical danger. Sri Anandamayi Ma was so totally identified with the Atman, or Eternal Self, that in her adult life she wouldn't eat unless one of her devotees fed her. She was just the Self, immersed in spirit, so her husband and devotees took care of her physical body.

This is not necessarily the right path for most people, but I do feel that it was the example she was supposed to set for humankind. Often, she would stay in a divine trance for days, scarcely breathing or even blinking. In her general demeanor, she was like a child saint. Her only interest in life was union with God and that was where she lived. She frequently described herself as a detached onlooker voluntarily performing in a play in the theater called Earth life.

She was born on April 30, 1896, in Bangladesh and given the name Nirmala Sundari, which means "immaculate beauty." She attended only two years of school because her family was so poor; thus, she is a living testament to the fact that wisdom is not based on booklearning. She had no formal religious education, either. She was very mystically inclined, even as a child, and was often seen talking to plants and invisible beings. Her parents arranged for her to be married at the age of thirteen to a man by the name of Bholanatha, a name for Shiva, but they did not live together until five years later.

From an early age, Sri Anandamayi Ma was joyful and a hard worker. When her husband first tried to approach her sexually, he got such a violent electrical shock that he put the thought out of his mind. They never consummated the marriage sexually. Even at that relatively young age, Sri Anandamayi Ma had no sexual desire; her consciousness was already attuned to God. On a few occasions throughout their marriage her husband had sexual thoughts about her and when he did, she went immediately into a death trance. Bholanatha would feel so frightened he would start repeating the name of God over and over again, and that was the only thing that would bring her out of the trance. As they grew into adulthood, she became his guru.

She herself never had a guru and was completely unaware of any religious scripture, but she obviously had been a Self-realized yogi or yogini in a past life. She would go into trance, however, and start repeating mantras and yoga postures. She was a channel for an inner voice, a teacher of some kind, and she also had many inner visions. During one period of her life, she was able to heal people miraculously with just the touch of her hand. Her spiritual practices would go on for hours at a time, spontaneously directed by her inner guidance. Soon she was chanting long Sanskrit stanzas she had never studied with her conscious mind.

Friends and relatives who were not spiritually inclined thought she was crazy or possessed, so they asked an exorcist to help her. When the exorcist touched her, he fell writhing to the ground in pain. Sri Anandamayi Ma removed the pain, and the family never tried that again. Sri Anandamayi Ma was not crazy, she was God-intoxicated. In that respect she was much like the great Ramakrishna.

Her spiritual practices grew in intensity. During this phase she was hardly aware of her physical body and the need to sleep or eat. In 1922 she spiritually initiated her husband in accordance with the rules of the scriptures, even though she had never read the scriptures. For the following three years, Sri Anandamayi Ma remained in almost complete silence. After that, news of her exalted status began to spread and she attracted her first disciples.

Her disciples became convinced that her body was possessed by divine forces and people began to call her the Bliss-Permeated Mother. She lived so completely in the Eternal Self that when she referred to herself, she would say "this body" or "this little daughter of yours."

She never participated in animal sacrifices and said the true meaning of such a rite was the sacrifice of one's own lower, animal nature. She would never eat fruit unless it had fallen from a tree in a natural way; if someone had picked it from a tree she would not eat it. She had a divine vision of how all the chakras work and gave a detailed explanation that even advanced scholars on the subject couldn't match. Sri Anandamayi Ma did not see herself as a guru, although she did do a great deal of counseling and teaching when disciples and people in need asked questions. The clarity of her understanding was remarkable, especially considering that she never studied any religious materials.

Once on a spiritual pilgrimage, they were passing through a particular area in a jungle when Sri Anandamayi Ma went into a trance and said that the area in which they were walking was hallowed ground. They told the authorities later and when excavations were made, several temple ruins were discovered.

In the later years of her life, she had serious health problems, but she lived in such a transcendental and nondualistic reality that she was able to say, "For this body there is no cause whatever for inconvenience or discomfort. This [ill health] is also a fine play."

In Dr. Alexander Lipski's book, *Life and Teaching of Sri Anandamayi Ma*, he tells of an Italian devotee, Miriam Orr, who described Sri Anandamayi Ma in the following manner: "Mother is not a human being like all the others. She is divine Light clad in a human form."

## The Teachings of Sri Anandamayi Ma

Sri Anandamayi Ma never condemned anyone, for she saw all people as souls — tarnished with egoistical tendencies, but still souls. She was universalistic in her acceptance of all religions, and within her own heart, she abhorred the caste system.

The essence of her teaching is that there is only one God who is Brahman, and all people are, in truth, Atman, the Eternal Self. Realizing God is the cure-all for worldly suffering and human imperfection. Happiness can't be found in the world; permanent happiness and peace can be found only in God. If people seek to find happiness in fame, money, power, or human love, they are just binding themselves to the wheel of rebirth. Everything in the world is achieved through will power. When people don't own their power in service of God, they become victims of their moods, cravings, desires, and impulses.

Sri Anandamayi Ma saw the average man as being like a cow tied to a post with a rope. Within the limits of the rope, the cow has freedom, but if the cow can break free from the post he will have total freedom. Similarly, a person can cut the rope of delusion and false happiness through spiritual practice and perseverance.

She saw prayer as a means of overcoming karmic debts from this life or past lives, although she discouraged people from spending too much time dealing with past lives, for the Eternal Self is existent through eternity.

She guided her disciples to understand that all situations come from God and to accept those situations with equanimity and evenmindedness. A person's responsibility is to remain steady and calm under all circumstances. All suffering was seen to be a guide toward spiritual liberation. Everything that happens was considered a product of karma. All human attachments needed to be given up or eventually they would be taken away to remind the person of his true home.

Sri Anandamayi Ma also warned her disciples not to spend excessive time mourning and grieving over loved ones, for it can be an obstacle on the path for both the deceased and the survivor. The deceased is kept Earthbound by the thoughts of the mourner, and the survivor is indulging in too much worldly attachment. Instead, people should cry in yearning for God. Suicide was considered to be a completely negative action for anyone concerned with spiritual growth. A soul's spiritual evolution as well as where that soul goes were believed to be strongly affected by what is being thought at the time of death.

She was constantly directing her devotees to concentrate on God, to practice being the Divine Presence, and to maintain their spiritual practices. In the beginning, sadhana (spiritual practice) takes a great deal of effort because of the pull of worldly programming, but when the first glimpses of God's bliss are obtained, spiritual enthusiasm ensues. Worldly attractions begin to decrease as God's magnetic pull is felt. As development of identification with the atman (the Self) occurs, selfishness begins to disappear. Desire for God is the most important spiritual practice. She said a person must crave God as a shipwrecked sailor longs for the shore.

One of the most important spiritual practices was the repetition of the name of God and the visualization of the form of God. She also recommended listening to lectures and talks by Self-realized beings, studying sacred writings, and singing devotional songs. Which of the many names of God is used is completely unimportant, for all names and forms refer to the one God.

As a person develops in his or her spiritual practice, all people, animals, plants, minerals, and objects come to be seen as God, and He becomes the only reality. The quest for an outer guru eventually leads to the inner guru who is the atman, or Eternal Self; that guru will not be found until the seeker has achieved freedom from all anger, greed, delusion, pride, and egoism.

Sri Anandamayi Ma told a delightful and profound story of a guru who noticed his disciple was having a problem meditating. The guru asked the disciple whether there was anyone or anything he was really interested in, and the disciple said his main interest was his buffalo. The guru guided the disciple to single-pointedly meditate on the buffalo. The next day when the guru knocked on the disciple's door, there was a period of silence. The disciple then replied in a deep voice that he couldn't leave the room because his horns could not pass through the door.

She described how a person can sit and play cards, watch movies, make money, pass exams, and concentrate for hours on worldly things; that worldly concentration just needs to be shifted to God. She said the greatest obstacle to Self-realization is the negative ego. The remedy is to "always bear this in mind: everything is in God's hands, and you are His tool to be used by Him as He pleases." This kind of surrender leads to seeing everyone and everything as the Eternal Self. Man must learn to get rid of all pride, worldly desire, passion, and the sense of "I am" and "I do."

Although immersed in spirit herself, she strongly recommended serving others by giving to the poor, feeding the hungry, nursing the sick, and doing service as a religious duty. Such actions lead to direct perception of the person being served. The one served and the act of service become one. All is the Self. All suffering was seen to stem from alienation from one's Self. Suffering was believed to be caused by perceiving duality; when only oneness is seen, then pain and suffering end.

She made an interesting statement when she said that all people are, in fact, renunciates but most people have given up God instead of giving up worldly pleasures. She saw the path of the householder as an equally valid path; she recommended seeing and serving one's wife or husband and children as God and considering one's home as a temple or ashram. She recommended that at the age of fifty-five or sixty, people should withdraw from worldly activities and spend their remaining years focusing on God.

To prevent moral and spiritual decay in society, she recommended that young men and women live celibate lives and receive spiritual training from their gurus before setting out to get married and raise a family. Young people should first be taught self-control, evenmindedness, unselfishness, and God-centeredness.

Her concept of a good diet applied also to the mental and emotional food people allow into their consciousnesses. They should abstain from diets of lust, greed, hatred, envy, anger, and jealousy. The ultimate criterion for any decision must be, "Will this action lead me toward God-realization or not?"

## Quotations from Sri Anandamayi Ma

The following quotations are from a book entitled *Anandamayi Ma, the Mother Bliss Incarnate* published by the Shree Shree Anandamayee Charitable Society.

God's name is He Himself; the name and the named are identical.

The more one thinks of one's Ishta [beloved  Deity], the firmer will one's faith in Him grow.

God, Himself, appears as the guru. He has to be invoked, full of faith.

There is nothing in this world, yet everyone is madly pursuing this nothing – some more, some less.

Man is no other than the Self, but he wrongly thinks of himself as a separate individual centered in his body and identified by a particular name.

All sorrow is due to the fact that many are seen where there is only one.

Duality is pain. So long as man does not wake up to his identity with the one, the round of birth and death continues for him.

Sense enjoyment acts like slow poison. You are driven thereby toward death. Therefore, it is man's duty as a human being to get into the current that leads to immortality.

Your sole duty is to remember that He alone is, and that everything is His doing.

Invoke Him and be constantly intent on realizing Him.

Householders should emulate the ancient rishis [sages] who were married men living with their families and leading a life dedicated to God.

Love and serve your consort and children as divine manifestations. Perform all work as God's service. Do not allow your mind to wander here and there. Endeavor to make it one-pointed. Have one single end in view.

Control your desires for sense objects. Be moderate in eating and sleeping. As a pilgrim on the path to God, you should be content with such food and sleep as will help you to remain fit for the onward march.

Whatever may be your shortcomings, don't be depressed, don't lose hope. Try to improve yourself.

Exert yourself to the limits of your power, however feeble. He is there to fulfill what has been left undone.

By God's grace one is born as a human being. Try to make the best of this opportunity. Everything is possible for man.

A spiritual traveler must not allow his mind to be distracted by anything. He should proceed with determination toward his goal.

It is but the Self that calls itself, and none other than the Self that realizes itself.

Relative happiness, that is to say, happiness depending on the fulfillment of any worldly desire, ends in grief.

You will have peace only if you rise above worldly desires.

Unconditional surrender to Him is the best solace for man.

Among all creatures, man alone has been endowed with the capacity to realize God.

Who am I? This realization is the purpose of human life.

It is the will of the Almighty that prevails. By living in harmony with His will and becoming an instrument in His hands you should try to realize Him.

# 10

## *Giri Bala, the Woman Who Never Ate*

*Dear little one, I am
the guru sent here by God to fulfill your
urgent prayer. He was deeply touched by its very
unusual nature. From today you shall live by the
astral Light. Your bodily atoms shall be recharged
by the infinite current.*

Guru of Giri Bala

It was the great Paramahansa Yogananda who brought to the world's attention Giri Bala, previously an unknown saint of India, in his classic book, *Autobiography of a Yogi*. He tells of meeting Giri Bala, the only woman in the world who had not consumed any food or liquids in more than fifty-six years. Therese Newman, the Catholic stigmatist who ate only one blessed wafer a day, was similar, but they differed in the fact that Giri Bala achieved her ability through practicing certain meditative and yogic exercises given to her by her guru, whereas Therese Neumann's ability existed because of personal karma resulting from many lives dedicated to union with God.

Giri Bala's story is a fascinating one. At a young age, she possessed an insatiable appetite. When she was nine, a marriage was arranged, and her mother often scolded her for her greedy appetite, warning her of potential embarrassment after her marriage. Sure enough, her mother's prophecy came true and her mother-in-law shamed her unmercifully because of her gluttony. One particular day when that scene occurred again, she exclaimed, "I shall soon prove to you that I shall never touch food again as long as I live." The mother-in-law teased her even more after that comment.

Giri made an iron resolution from that moment forward to live up to her promise. She went to a secluded spot and prayed to God to send her a guru who could teach her to live by God's Light alone, needing no physical food. She immediately felt an ecstasy come over her and she set out to travel to the holy river, the Ganges.

As she left the riverbank, her guru materialized right in front of her. This is what he said, as quoted in Paramahansa Yogananda's *Autobiography of a Yogi*: "Dear little one, I am the guru sent here by God to fulfill your urgent prayer. He was deeply touched by its very unusual nature. From today you shall live by the astral Light. Your bodily atoms shall be recharged by the infinite current."

Giri Bala was initiated into a specific Kriya Yoga technique that frees the physical body from the need for gross physical food. The technique included the use of a mantra and certain breathing exercises. She practiced the technique with total commitment and never ate again. She said she had never been sick in her entire life and was not at all emaciated. She has no bodily excretions. She was strictly commanded by her guru never to divulge the secret technique she had been taught. The reason she set that example was to prove that a human is, in truth, spirit and to prove that a human can live by the eternal Light of God.

She had not eaten from the time she was twelve years and four months old until the time when she met Paramahansa Yogananda, when she was sixty-eight years old. Her nourishment comes from air, sunlight, and cosmic power that enters through the medulla oblongata.

Early in her life, an investigation was performed to prove whether or not she was telling the truth. She agreed to go to the palace of the leader of her province and be locked in a small cell in his home for two months. She happily agreed and was not given any food during the entire period. At a later time she spent twenty days there, and then there was a third test of fifteen days. The tests proved without a doubt that she was telling the truth.

# 11

## The Life and Teachings
## of Ramana Maharshi

*Self-realization is nothing to be gained afresh; it is
already there. All that is necessary is to get rid of
the thought "I have not realized."*

Sri Ramana Maharshi

Ramana Maharshi was one of the great spiritual teachers of modern India. He lived from 1879 until 1950. When he was seventeen years old he had a profound experience of realizing the Eternal Self without the help of a guru. From the time of that experience he remained in the consciousness of the Self for the rest of his life. In a book entitled *Bhagavan Sri Ramana, A Pictorial Biography* by Sri T.N. Venkataraman, Ramana Maharshi tells of his experience:

I was sitting alone in a room on the first floor of my uncle's house. I seldom had any sickness, and on that day there was nothing wrong with my health, but a sudden violent fear of death overtook me. There was nothing in my state of health to account for it, and I did not try to account for it or to find out whether there was any reason for the fear. I just felt, "I am going to die" and began thinking what to do about it. It did not occur to me to consult a doctor or my elders or friends. I felt that I had to solve the problem myself, then and there.

The shock of the fear of death drove my mind inward and I said to myself mentally, without actually framing the words, Now death has come. What does it mean? What is it that is dying? This body dies; and at once I dramatized the occurrence of death. I lay with my limbs stretched out stiff as though rigor mortis had set in and imitated a corpse so as to give greater reality to the inquiry.

I held my breath and kept my lips tightly closed so that no sound could escape, so that neither the word "I" nor any other word could be uttered. Well then, I said to myself, This body is dead. It will be carried stiff to the burning ground and there burnt and reduced to ashes. But with the death of this body, am I dead? Is the body I? It is silent and inert, but I feel the full force of my personality and even the voice of the I within me, apart from it.

So I am spirit transcending the body. The body dies, but the spirit that transcends it can not be touched by death. That means I am the deathless spirit.

All this was not dull thought. It flashed through me vividly as living truth which I perceived directly, almost without thought process. I was something very real; the only real thing about my present state and all the conscious activity connected with my body was centered on that I.

From that moment onward the I, or self, focused attention on itself by a powerful fascination. Fear of death had vanished once and for all. Absorption in the Self continued unbroken from that time on. Other thoughts might come and go like the various notes of music, but the I continued like the fundamental note that underlies and blends with all other notes.

Whether the body was engaged in talking, reading, or anything else, I will still be centered on I. Previous to that crisis I had no clear perception of my Self and was not consciously attracted to it. I felt no perceptible or direct interest in it, much less any inclination to dwell permanently in it.

Sai Baba, in his writings, speaks of this Eternal I. When a person says, I think, or I feel, the thinking or feeling varies, but the I always remains the same. When another person says, I think, or I feel, his feeling and thinking might be different from yours, but the I in them is the same as the I in your feelings and thoughts. That I is the Eternal Self. Language depicts the nature of true reality, but most people do not see it.

The essence of Ramana Maharshi's teachings is that the Eternal Self, the Eternal I, is the true identity of a human being, not the physical body. Self-realization, which all are striving for, is nothing more than realizing this and getting rid of the small "i" that says he is something other than what he really is.

Below is a quotation from *Maharshi's Gospel* by T.N. Venkataraman. In this passage, Ramana Maharshi is having a question-and-answer session with a disciple.

Disciple: How can I attain Self-realization?

Maharshi: Realization is nothing to be gained afresh; it is already there. All that is necessary is to get rid of the thought "I have not realized." Stillness or peace is realization. There is no moment when the Self is not. So long as there is doubt or the feeling of non-realization, the attempt should be made to rid oneself of these thoughts. They are due to the identification of the Self with the not-Self. When the not-Self disappears, the Self alone remains. To make room, it is enough that the cramping be removed; room is not brought in from elsewhere.

D: Since realization is not possible without vasanaksaya, how am I to realize that state in which the vasanas are effectively destroyed?

M: You are in that state now!

D: Does it mean that by holding on to the Self, the vasanas should be destroyed as and when they emerge?

M: They will themselves be destroyed if you remain as you are.

D: How shall I reach the Self?

M: There is no reaching the Self. If the Self were to be reached, it would mean that the Self is not here and now but is yet to be obtained. What is got afresh will also be lost. So it will be impermanent. What is not permanent is not worth striving for. So I say the Self is not reached. You are the Self, you are already that.

The fact is, you are ignorant of your blissful state. Ignorance supervenes and draws a veil over the pure Self, which is bliss. Attempts are directed only to remove this veil of ignorance, which is merely wrong knowledge. The wrong knowledge is the false identification of the self with the body, mind, etc. This false identification must go, and then the Self alone remains.

Therefore, realization is for everyone; realization makes no differences between aspirants. This very doubt whether you can realize and the notion "I have not realized" are themselves the obstacles. Be free from these obstacles also.

There is nothing to do to achieve God, for you already are God. That is how God created you. It is your true identity. It always has been and always will be. Your lesson is to own this fact, see it in others, and demonstrate it on Earth. You either believe the material world is real or you see beyond appearances to the Eternal Self living in all things.

The spiritual practice Ramana Maharshi used was a method of self-inquiry based on asking "Who am I?" Ramana Maharshi explains this in a book called *The Spiritual Teaching of Ramana Maharshi* (Shambhala Publishing):

When other thoughts arise, one should not pursue them but should inquire, "To whom did they arise?"

It does not matter how many thoughts arise. As each thought arises, one should inquire with diligence, "To whom has this thought arisen?" The answer that would emerge would be, "To me." Thereupon, if one inquires, "Who am I?" the mind will go back to its source, and the thought that arose will become quiescent. With repeated practice in this manner, the mind will develop the skill to stay in its source.

Ramana Maharshi says this process will bring all thoughts back to the heart which is the source of all thoughts and, hence, back to the Eternal Self. Any thoughts not of the Eternal Self would be termed ego, the little i, or illusion. His practice involves never letting the mind move in that direction but keeping it always on the Self. The Eternal Self has no sense of a separate individuality of the body consciousness and little i.

A married or unmarried person can realize the Self, for it is what everyone has been all along but only thought he was something else.

Remaining in this state of consciousness was Ramana Maharshi's whole practice. The guru was seen as the embodiment of the Self. All happiness was said to stem from the realization of the Self. Ramana Maharshi saw the process of self-inquiry as the only direct way for a person to realize the unconditioned, absolute being he really is.

The cause of all misery is not life outside but rather the illusionary ego within. All unhappiness is due to the ego. The realization of the Self brings bliss. Ramana Maharshi saw spiritual practices (sadhana) as a means of transcending a nonexistent limitation. The only spiritual practice he felt was necessary was to eliminate the ignorance that says you are someone other than who you really are and that says your brothers and sisters are beings other than who they really are.

The essence of the Vedas, he said, was to teach the nature of the imperishable atman, the Eternal Self, and to teach that "thou art that." To keep the mind constantly turned within and to abide thus in the Self is correct Self-inquiry. The Self alone exists, and the Self alone is real. The Self alone is the world, is the I, is God.

All that exists is but a manifestation of the Supreme Being. The personal Self is not realized unless the mind is quiet, for the Self is beyond and behind the mind. The human is wrapped in seven sheaths, or bodies, and the Eternal Self is at the very core. The problem is that people identify themselves with the sheathes and bodies (thoughts, feelings, sensations, instincts) instead of with the true identity at the core. The mind of the enlightened one never exists apart from the Self, the Absolute, Brahman, God.

The aspirant must learn to become more introverted rather than being always extroverted in order to realize this truth. A devotee was once leaving Ramana Maharshi and asked for his blessing. Ramana Maharshi replied, "You do not go anywhere away from the presence you imagine. The body moves from place to place, yet it does not leave the One Presence, so no one can be out of sight of the Supreme Presence. Since you identify one body with Sri Bhagavan and another body with yourself, you find two separate entities and speak of going away from here. Wherever you may be, you cannot leave me."

There is only one being in the infinite universe, and that is God incarnated as the Self in all beings including animals, plants, and rocks. When your consciousness is in the Self, you don't live in just one physical body, you live in all physical bodies. That is why what you do to others is what you are doing to yourself; you literally *are* the others you are acting upon. God is acting upon God. This is the true understanding of the law of karma.

It is possible to live in this state of consciousness and still perform all necessary daily activities and duties; but the activities are performed from God's point of view rather than from the point of view of the separative, body-identified ego. Renunciation means the renunciation of the ego and, hence, attachment to material existence. The spiritual practices of meditation, prayer, yoga, repetition of the name of God, and so on, ripen the mind for the embracing of the full realization and help the mind to remain there and realize the truth more fully.

# 12

## *Swami Sivananda
and the Divine Life Society*

*You have come to this Earth
to attain spiritual perfection. You have come
here to attain supreme and unalloyed bliss. The
purpose of this human birth is the achievement
of divine consciousness. The goal of life
is Self-realization.*

Swami Sivananda

Swami Sivananda is one of the great spiritual saints of India. His books on yoga and on the multifaceted scriptures of India are among the best books I have read on those subjects because he writes in an exciting tone that is filled with devotion and he includes useful, practical, spiritual information.

Swami Sivananda was born on September 8, 1887, in southern India into a family of devotees, saints, and philosophers who worshiped Shiva. Even as a boy he showed signs of desire for a life of renunciation and he radiated love for his fellow humans. In high school he was at the top of his class and he won scholastic prizes every year.

He chose to become a medical doctor, and in his first year in medical school he could answer questions that even students in their final year could not answer. Again, he topped his class in all subjects. Needless to say, Swami Sivananda had an absolutely brilliant mind and he had more energy and enthusiasm for living than any other saint I have ever studied.

He was a master of the spiritual paths and spiritual texts of all Eastern religions. He not only understood them but was also able to teach them clearly in his lectures and writings. He was brilliant, and his brilliance was blended with spirituality and desire for selfless service.

After graduating from medical school he traveled to Malaya and doctored the poor for ten years. God came to Sivananda as an all-consuming aspiration to realize Him as the Self of all; God came to Sivananda in the form of the sick.

While in Malaya he was put in charge of an entire hospital and his integrity, positive disposition, and hard work won him praise and promotion.

One day a wandering sadhu gave him a book by Swami Satchidananda about the soul's path to God which ignited any last vestiges of his spirituality that remained dormant. He began to study the teachings of Sankara, the Theosophical movement, the Bible, and the vast Indian scriptures such as the Vedas, the *Bhagavad-Gita*, and the *Ramayana*.

He left Malaya in search of a life of renunciation as a sanyasin. He traveled to many different religious centers and studied with many great yogis, mahatmas, and spiritual teachers. He finally found his guru, Paramahansa Viswananda Saraswathi, who gave him initiation on the banks of the Ganges River on June 1, 1924. His guru named him Swami Sivananda Saraswathi.

As well as having a brilliant mind, Swami Sivananda felt an unbelievably intense devotion to God. He practiced all the various yogic paths and studied the scriptures unceasingly until he finally achieved nirvikalpa samadhi. Along with his ongoing spiritual practices, he decided to open a medical dispensary to help the poor, the sick, the devotees, and the mahatmas. People began to come to him in large numbers for his spiritual teachings as well as for medical help so he started teaching classes and holding meetings for the singing of bhagvans (devotional songs). Once he was even invited to sing in the ashram of Sri Ramana Marharshi and his devotees.

In 1936 Swami Sivananda founded the Divine Life Society on the right bank of the Ganges River. The small organization was eventually to grow into a worldwide organization. The free spiritual literature that was given out attracted a steady stream of devotees to Swami Sivananda. He has written over three hundred books. His teachings are universal, holding in the highest regard all religions and all spiritual paths that lead to God. He calls his type of yoga the Yoga of Synthesis.

After the opening of the Divine Life Society, Swami Sivananda traveled extensively throughout India and Ceylon disseminating spiritual knowledge. He went to schools, public meetings, cities, and villages teaching his universalistic, eclectic spirituality. He was a fiery and dynamic speaker and was well received wherever he went. He never accepted any money from the organizers but instead asked them to print large numbers of pamphlets in different languages for wide circulation. He never became anyone's guru and never accepted the title of sadguru or avatar. He never sought fame, but his profound devotion to God, his humility, and his service to humanity through his teachings, his ashram and his books have made him renown. There are over three hundred branches of the Divine Life Society throughout the world.

He initiated thousands of students into the order of sanyasins (renunciates). He founded Yoga-Vedanta Forest University, the Sivananda General Hospital, and a temple of all faiths. His ashram eventually grew into a spiritual colony which included a press to print his many books.

He taught the messages of the sages and saints of all religions to help humanity achieve peace, bliss, and liberation. He taught that all people could realize God, regardless of their stations or situations in life. The central core of his teaching was the path of yoga and Vedanta. He acknowledged one of his main teachers to be the great avatar Sri Sankara, who revolutionized the teachings of Hinduism. (See the chapter about him in this book, page 19.)

The basic tenet of his teaching is adherence to the ideals of truth, nonviolence, and purity which is the essence of all yogas, all religions, and all spiritual paths.

The ashram publishes a monthly journal called *Divine Life*, which has been in publication since 1938. During World War II Swami Sivananda established nonstop chanting for world peace and a thrice-daily worship service. He also opened the Sivananda Ayurvedic Pharmacy, which offers ayurvedic herbal preparations from the Himalayas, and in 1957, the Sivananda Eye Hospital. Even though Swami Sivananda achieved mahasamadhi in 1963, the entire ashram with all its services has continued to function to this day. Senior monks now run the facility under the directorship of the president, Sri Swami Chidananda.

The Divine Life gospel can be summed up in six words: "Serve, love, give, purify, meditate, and realize." The teachings are intended to help seekers realize their true selves and transcend ego. The teachings say that each soul is potentially divine and that everyone's goal is to manifest that divinity by controlling his internal and external natures and by being good and doing good. Anyone who feels himself to be compatible with those goals is welcome to be a member.

The following is Swami Sivananda's message to aspirants:

> You have come to this Earth to attain spiritual perfection. You have come here to attain supreme and unalloyed bliss. The purpose of this human birth is the achievement of divine consciousness. The goal of life is Self-realization.

Man is not a sensual animal. Man, in his essential nature, is an ever free, ever pure, ever perfect, immortal, spiritual being. Feel this. Feel that you are the immortal self, that you are satchidananda. Remember the words Ajo nityah saswatogam puranah – you are the unborn, the eternal, the imperishable, the ancient. To live in this exalted consciousness is to experience indescribable joy every moment of your life, to experience a limitless freedom in the spirit. This is your birthright. This is the aim of your life. This is the goal. To realize this through a life of truth, purity, service and devotion is the chief purpose of the Divine Life Society.

Fear dominates in this era of nuclear weapons for mass destruction. Hatred rules the policies of vast sections of the so-called enlightened and civilized mankind. This age of advancement has been exposed to be, in reality, an age of degeneracy in the views and values, the ideals and morals, of the greater masses of mankind. At this juncture in time, cultured men and women all over the world look to the sacred land, India, for Light and knowledge. It is your noble task to spread this Light of spiritual knowledge and spiritual idealism to all corners of the globe.

See God in all faces. Serve all. Love all. Be kind to all. Be compassionate. Feel everyone to be your own. Serve your fellow beings in the spirit of worship offered to the divine which indwells them. Service of man is truly the worship of God.

Know well that the heart of the Vedas, the heart of the Bible, the holy Koran, the sacred Gathas, and all the world's scriptures are, in truth, one, and they sing in unison the sweet message of love and concord, goodness and kindness, service and worship.

Discard the barriers of name and form. Seek the oneness at the heart of all beings. Include within your spiritual embrace the entire humanity. Live for peace. Live for universal love. Live the life divine.

To behold the Atman or the Self in every being or form; to feel the Brahmic consciousness everywhere, at all times, and in all conditions of life; to see, hear, taste, smell, and feel everything as the Atman: This is my creed. To live in Brahman, to melt in Him, and to merge and dissolve in Him is my creed. Whilst dwelling in union with Brahman, to utilize the hands, mind, and senses and the body for the service of humanity; to sing the Lord's name for elevating devotees of God; to give instructions to sincere aspirants; and to disseminate knowledge far and wide through books, pamphlets, leaflets, magazines, and platform lectures. This is my creed.

Purify your mind. Develop sattvic [harmonious] qualities such as nobility, courage, magnanimity, generosity, love, straightforwardness, and truthfulness. Eradicate all evil qualities such as lust, greed, anger, avarice, likes and dislikes, and other negative traits which stand in the way of ethical perfection and Self-realization.

Ethical perfection is a prerequisite to Self-realization. No amount of practice can be of any value to the aspirant if he ignores this side of sadhana (spiritual practice). Love all. Prostrate yourself before everybody. Become humble. Talk loving, sweet, endearing words. Give up selfishness, pride, egoism, and hypocrisy. Regenerate your lower nature.

The one Brahman or the Supreme Self appears as the divine universe in all the planes or degrees of its manifestation and therefore, the aspirant has to pay his homage to the lower manifestation before he steps into the higher. Sound health, clear understanding, deep knowledge, powerful will, and moral integrity are all parts of the process of realizing the ideal preached by Vedanta.

I insist on all-round discipline of the lower self. The teachings of Vedanta are not in conflict with Hatha, Bhakti [devotional], Raja [mental], or Karma [selfless service] Yoga. All these are blended together as elements constituting a whole.

Honor those who are bad characters. Serve the rogue first. Treat him as a future saint, as a saint himself. This is the way to purify your heart and to elevate him also. I take special delight in serving such people carefully. I always keep around me any number of people who would abuse me, vilify me, insult me, and even try to injure me. I want to serve them, educate them, elevate them, and transform them. I address them in the most respectful terms. Acclaim the rogue or the thief as a saint and publicly honor him. He would be ashamed to continue his evil doings.

## Preliminary Spiritual Experiences

More and more dispassion and discrimination,
More and more yearning for liberation,
Peace, cheerfulness, contentment,
Fearlessness, unruffled state of mind,
Lustre in the eyes, good smell from the body,
Beautiful complexion, sweet, powerful voice,
Wonderful health, vim, vigor, and vitality.
Freedom from disease, laziness, and depression,
Lightness of body, alertness of mind,
Powerful jatharigni, or digestive fire,
Eagerness to sit and mediate for a long time,
Aversion to worldly talks and complaint of worldliness,
Feeling the presence of God everywhere,
Love for all creatures,
Feeling that all forms are forms of the Lord,
That the world is the Lord Himself;
Absence of ghrina, or dislike for any creature,
Even to those who despise and insult,
Strength of mind to bear insult and injury,
To meet dangers and calamities . . .
Indicate that one is advancing on the spiritual path.

# 13

## The Life and Teachings of Mahatma Gandhi

*What I want to achieve, what
I have been striving and pining to achieve these
thirty years, is Self-realization, to see God face to
face, to attain liberation.*

Mahatma Gandhi

Without a doubt, Mohandas Karamchand Gandhi was one of the most extraordinary men of the twentieth century. One of the things that made him so extraordinary was his humanness. In his early life he had a great many problems; as a child he was so shy that the moment class was over he would run home so he would not have to talk to anyone, and he was only an average student. For a time he tried to study medicine but was completely overwhelmed by the difficulty of the classes and had to drop out. He finally studied law, and upon passing the bar and presenting his first case worth more than ten dollars, he felt so frightened he was unable to speak and had to pass the case over to another lawyer. He had been married at the age of thirteen and struggled greatly during his early years.

As he grew older, one of the experiences that began to change his life was the reading of the *Bhagavad-Gita*, the teachings of Sri Bhagavan Krishna, the Christ of the Eastern world. He said that the first time he read it, the words went straight to his heart, and it became his spiritual reference book throughout all the lessons he faced during the rest of his life. The teachings guided his conduct, and he referred to them daily.

It was during his experiences in South Africa that he first translated the sublime ideals into action in the world. Gandhi had clearly stepped onto the path of making Self-realization his supreme goal in life.

It was during these early days that Gandhi began to struggle with the idea of taking the vow of the Bramacharya which has to do with gaining mastery over the sexual energies in order to channel them into spiritual pursuits instead of into lust and carnality. Gandhi struggled with this for some time. He tells how he failed many times in this regard, but in 1906, at the age of thirty-seven, he made the vow and found great freedom and enlightenment in having done so because it served as a sort of shield against the lower self, which had been pushing him around a great deal. He did discuss the taking of the vow with his wife who was in full agreement. Many times Gandhi said that it was his wife who had truly taught him the nature of love in its highest form; the Bramacharya vow was the renunciation only of the carnal aspect of their relationship.

For Gandhi the vow was also more than that. It was a vow that related to his diet and to controlling the other passions of his lower self and negative ego. The perfect realization of the vow of the Bramacharya in all areas of his life meant the realization of Brahman (God). Even twenty years later, he spoke of the need to maintain strict vigilance at all times. It is not possible to achieve this self-mastery without absolute control over the mind.

He found that eating a vegetarian diet that included natural, wholesome foods helped to avoid exciting the lower passions and negative emotions. As a part of the vow he also gave himself to fasting, which he saw as an indispensable part of the overall regime. Bramacharya meant control of and mastery over all the senses, for the first time in his life. As another ingredient in this transformation, he tried to simplify his life.

The vow of the Bramacharya began to transform his entire nature. He began an intensive process of purification of all aspects of his being as he released all impure thoughts, feelings, foods, passions, and energies. It was this vow that lead him to the development of his political and social philosophy of Satyagraha.

## Satyagraha

Satyagraha is the political and social philosophy of passive resistance. The word also means "holding on to truth"; the idea of living the truth was the keynote of Gandhi's entire life. Integral to this philosophy was an overriding belief in nonviolence – nonviolence on not just a physical or a political level, but also on a mental and an emotional level. Satyagraha is the path of love integrated with every citizen's right to practice civil disobedience.

This was a revolutionary concept in the field of politics and social action. Saints practiced nonviolence, but not politicians. Gandhi defined his theories on civil disobedience in the following way: "Disobedience, to be civil, must be sincere, respectful, restrained, never defiant, must be based upon some well understood principle, must not be capricious and, above all, must have no ill will or hatred behind it."

Gandhi said that although it might appear useful, violence is only temporary in its success; in the long run it creates permanent damage. His method was much like that of Saint Francis of Assisi (who was also Kuthumi) who said

> Where there is hatred, let me sow love,
> Where there is injury, pardon,
> Where there is doubt, faith,
> Where there is darkness, light,
> Where there is sadness, joy.

This is exactly what Gandhi believed. The only difference was that he was going to apply the theory to a realm of experience to which it had never before been applied. Gandhi tested the theory against an extremely hostile government in South Africa for seven years, and it was a great success.

A noted historian, J.B. Kripalani, once said to Gandhi, "Mr. Gandhi, you may know all about the Bible or the *Bhagavad-Gita*, but you know nothing at all about history. Never has a nation been able to free itself without violence."

Gandhi replied, "You know nothing about history. The first thing you have to learn about history is that because something has not taken place in the past, that does not mean it cannot take place in the future."

Integral to the philosophy of Satyagraha is an attitude of selflessness and a recognition that you and the attacker are one. In truth, the philosophy of Satyagraha is the philosophy of Sri Bhagavan Krishna. Krishna told Arjuna that he had to fight in life, for that was his spiritual responsibility. He must fight for unconditional love, and if he were thinking only of God, he would create no sin.

Satyagraha was love in action. The key to understanding Mahatma Gandhi, as he came to be called because it means "great soul," was to observe how he walked his talk. There is a cute story about him that has to do with a mother who took her child to see Gandhi because the child was eating too much sugar. The mother asked Gandhi to tell the child to stop, but Gandhi told the mother to bring the boy back in one week. The mother followed his direction and came back in a week's time. Gandhi then told the boy, "Stop eating sugar." The mother asked why he hadn't just said that a week earlier when she and her son had first been there. Gandhi said, "I first had to stop eating sugar myself." This sums up the essence of Mahatma Gandhi!

To Gandhi, life was an experiment in truth. He would live his truth, and new insights and ideals would arise which he would then put into motion. In the field of politics and social action he was truly on virgin territory. He said, "Satyagraha is gentle, it never wounds. It must not be the result of anger or malice. It is never fussy, never impatient, never vociferous. It is the direct opposite of compulsion. It was conceived of as a complete substitute for violence." Gandhi saw violence as being only for animals. For humans to partake in such action was to reverse the course of evolution.

Gandhi never hated people, he hated only injustice and he fought it at every step. Gandhi was also very much against the caste system in India and the mistreatment of the "untouchables." One time he went to a Hindu temple where lower-class Hindus were not allowed to enter. He himself would not enter the temple and said to the crowd, "There is no God here. If God were here, everyone would have access."

Gandhi was much like Mother Teresa, an advocate of the poor and downtrodden. When he traveled on a train he would always take third class, in which the poor were forced to travel. When asked why he traveled third class he replied, "Because there is no fourth class." This, again, is the essence of who Mahatma Gandhi was. He always taught by example.

I am particularly happy to include this chapter about Gandhi because of the importance I place on being politically active, conscious, and aware. God's Divine Plan is to bring Heaven to Earth. People on this world have introduced the concept of separation of church and state, which has separated God from His creation.

The world will change only when soul-consciousness pervades all aspects of society, including politics. The reason people have such a low opinion of politicians, and the reason there is so much corruption in politics is because of this separation. Imagine how the world will change when ascended masters of the first ray are governing the countries of the world.

The Spiritual Hierarchy is Earth's spiritual government. What if they just descended and took over the governing of Planet Earth? That is the eventual plan. Many spiritual people dissociate themselves from politics, voting, political action, letter-writing, and so on, but how is the world going to change if spiritual people don't get involved?

I would like to share with you what Gandhi had to say on the matter. This quote is from a wonderful book called *Gandhi, the Man* by Eknath Easwaran:

> To see the universal and all-pervading spirit of truth face to face, one must be able to love the meanest of creation as oneself. And a man who aspires after that cannot afford to keep out of any field of life. That is why my devotion to truth has drawn me into the field of politics; and I

can say, without the slightest hesitation, and yet in all humility, that those who say that religion has nothing to do with politics do not know what religion means.

During one phase of Gandhi's work, the government of India imposed a law forbidding Indians to make salt so the British could collect all the revenue. Gandhi's form of civil disobedience came to him in a dream. He decided to go on a march of two hundred forty miles to the ocean with seventy-eight of his trusted followers to collect salt. By the time they reached the ocean many thousands of people had joined them. The night of their arrival they all prayed together to be able to resist violence if they were attacked by the British police. Tens of thousands of people joined him at the beaches to collect salt and there was nationwide rejoicing. When Gandhi went before Lord Irwin, he took some salt from his pocket and put it into his tea, saying, "This is to remind us of the famous Boston tea party." Even Lord Irwin laughed.

They finally came to arrest Gandhi in the middle of the night. He said, "I am at your service. I am ready now." He brushed his teeth, prayed briefly, and went off to jail. Gandhi could not be imprisoned, in reality, for he saw imprisonment as a state of mind, not a set of bars. The physical prison was called Yeravda, so Gandhi referred to it as Yeravda Temple.

On the subject of anger, Gandhi said, "I have learned through bitter experience the one supreme lesson – to conserve my anger; and as heat conserved is transmuted into energy, even so our anger controlled can be transmuted into a power which can move the world."

Almost singlehandedly, Gandhi overthrew the British rule of India, and he did it with complete love and respect for all British people. Gandhi would say, "We will not submit to this injustice, not merely because it is destroying us, but because it is destroying you as well."

People living in Britain began to awaken to his soul-awareness. It all came to a head when Gandhi's American missionary friend, Stanley Jones, was asked by Lord Irwin if Gandhi should be invited to a roundtable conference on the subject of India's political freedom. Stanley Jones replied, "Gandhi is India. If you invite him, you invite India. If you do not, no matter who else you do invite, all India will be absent." Gandhi received his invitation in his jail cell.

While in England, Gandhi visited the textile mills. The people working in the mills were angry with Gandhi because thousands had lost their jobs due to Gandhi's civil disobedience movement that encouraged people to not buy British cloth. A great crowd of workers came to see Gandhi and this is what he said, as quoted in Eknath Easwaran's book: "Please listen to me for just a few minutes. Give me a chance to present our point of view, and then, if you like, condemn me and my people. You tell me that three million people are out of employment here, have been out of employment for several months. In my country, three hundred million people are unemployed at least six months in every year. You say there are days when you can get only bread and butter for your dinner. But these people often go for days on end without any food at all." At the end of his speech, even the people who had lost their jobs cheered the Mahatma.

Gandhi's views on love were quite explicit. "When another person's welfare means more to you than your own, when even his life means more to you than your own, only then can you say you love. Anything else is just business, give and take."

Another interesting thing about Gandhi was his love and respect for all religions. In his ashram they read the *Bhagavad-Gita*, the Bible, and the Koran. Because of this, he was hated by many fundamentalists.

Early in his life, while still in South Africa, Gandhi was stabbed by a radical protester. Luckily, the protester was only able to stab him in the leg. A week later Gandhi went to visit the man in jail and treated him like his long lost brother. The protester was so overwhelmed by Gandhi's love and forgiveness that when he got out of jail he became Gandhi's disciple.

On another occasion, during riots between the Hindus and Muslims in India, a violent sect member ran up to Gandhi and, in front of hundreds of people, began to choke him to death. Gandhi did not protest but just gave himself completely to love for that deluded soul. The man stopped and broke down sobbing at his feet.

One of the keys to Gandhi's success was his consistent repetition of the name of God. Maintaining such a practice was first suggested to him by his housekeeper when he was a young boy. She told him that if he would repeat the name Rama, it would provide him untold strength and confidence in life. Gandhi took her advice for a while but then forgot about it until his stay in South Africa when the idea came back to him. For the rest of his life he constantly chanted Rama, or God. (See the chapter on Rama.) He affirmed many times that it was one of the golden keys to his success.

One time Gandhi was asked if he had achieved the nonviolence of what he considered to be a brave man. He replied, "My death alone will show that. If someone killed me and I died with prayer for the assassin on my lips, and God's remembrance and the consciousness of His living presence in the sanctuary of my heart, then alone would I be said to have had the nonviolence of the brave." When Gandhi was assassinated, the last words he was heard to speak were "Rama, Rama, Rama." Bhagavan Krishna, in the *Bhagavad-Gita*, said that where you go when you die is determined by the last thought in your mind. Gandhi returned to Rama.

Gandhi's perspective on the *Bhagavad-Gita* can be summed up as follows: "The Gita has been a mother to me ever since I became first acquainted with it in 1889. I turn to it for guidance in every difficulty, and the desired guidance has always been forthcoming. But you must approach Mother Gita in all reverence if you would benefit by her ministrations. One who rests his head on her peace-giving lap never experiences disappointment but enjoys bliss in perfection. This spiritual mother gives her devotee fresh knowledge, hope, and power every moment of his life."

Gandhi considered that the Sermon on the Mount and the *Bhagavad-Gita* teach exactly the same thing. A principal tenet of Gandhi's philosophy was to do his duty and his work, but to renounce desire for reward for that work. That is one of the integral teachings of the *Bhagavad-Gita.*

## Verses from the *Bhagavad-Gita*

For Mahatma Gandhi it was the last eighteen verses of the second chapter of the Gita that contained the secret of living. About them he said, "Those verses of the second chapter have since been inscribed on the tablet of my heart. They contain, for me, all knowledge. The truths they teach me are the eternal verities. There is reasoning in them, but they represent realized knowledge. I have since read many translations and many commentaries, have argued and reasoned to my heart's content, but the impression that the first reading gave to me has never been effaced. Those verses are the key to the interpretation of the Gita."

He lives in wisdom who sees himself in all and all in him, whose love for the Lord of Love has consumed every selfish desire and sense craving tormenting the heart. Not agitated by grief, not hankering after pleasure, he lives free from lust and fear and anger. Fettered no more by selfish attachments, he is not elated by good fortune nor depressed by bad. Such is the seer.

When you keep thinking about sense objects attachment comes. Attachment breeds desire, the lust of possession which, when thwarted, turns to anger. Anger clouds the judgment and robs you of the power to learn from past mistakes. Lost is the discriminative faculty, and your life is utter waste.

But when you move amidst the world of sense, from both attachment and aversion freed, there comes the peace in which all sorrows end, and you live in the wisdom of the self.

The disunited mind is far from wise; how can it meditate? How be at peace? When you know no peace how can you know joy? When you let your mind follow the siren call of the senses, they carry away your better judgment as a cyclone drives a boat off the charted course to its doom.

He is forever free who has broken out of the ego cage of I and mine to be united with the Lord of Love. This is the supreme state. Attain thou this and pass from death to immortality.

When Gandhi was asked about his religion he replied, "You must watch my life, how I live, eat, sit, talk, behave in general. The sum total of all those in me is my religion." This is such a refreshingly enlightened understanding. Your religion is what you demonstrate.

Gandhi was perfectly punctual. In discussing the matter with a British minister, he said, "You may not waste a grain of rice or a scrap of paper and, similarly, a minute of time. It is not ours. It belongs to the nation and we are trustees for the use of it." Gandhi perceived his body as being not only his small physical body but, rather, all of India.

Gandhi didn't take credit for his philosophy, as evidenced by the following quotation: "I have nothing new to teach the world. Truth and nonviolence are as old as the hills. All I have done is to try experiments in both on as vast a scale as I could do. In doing so, I have sometimes erred and learned by my errors. Life and its problems have thus become to me so many experiments in the practice of truth and nonviolence."

## Summation

As I look at spirituality and politics, I see two diverse camps. Spiritual people very often tend to shy away from watching the news, reading the newspaper, and becoming politically active. The people who are involved with politics often have not integrated the soul aspect of themselves, which leads to psychic or physical violence.

Physical violence is obvious in the terrorist bombings, "pro-life" attacks, and the acts of other fanatical groups and individuals. Psychic violence is everywhere — between Democrats and Republicans, in the many demonstrations, in the nastiness between opponents on political talk shows, and it is cultivated by the political news reporters. That is why it has become a social courtesy not to talk about religion or politics: people don't know how to practice Satyagraha. Egos become attached to viewpoints, and self-righteousness results. People feel noble in their fight for their great cause when in reality they are losing their own souls because of the psychic violence they are perpetrating on their brothers and sisters.

It is easy for a person to be spiritual living in a cave by himself. Mahatma Gandhi demonstrated that it can be done in the marketplace while being married and fully integrated with Earth life. Worldly people must learn to be involved with politics without anger; spiritual people must leave their Himalayan-temple lifestyles and come back to Earth so Heaven can be created in this dimension of reality. No person in modern history has exemplified the unity of the two spheres better than the Mahatma Mohandas K. Gandhi.

# 14

## *Swami Nityananda,*
## *Guru of Muktananda*

*Go back and do your duty without desire for fruit
and without sacrificing efficiency. This is the
highest service that you can render.*

Swami Nityananda

Swami Nityananda, whose name means "eternal bliss," was already a Self-realized master when in his teens. Little is known about his early childhood years, because when asked about them he used to say that as long as his human form existed it did not matter where it came from; it was just idle curiosity to be interested in such limiting factors.

Strangely enough, he prescribed no special spiritual practices or course of study other than cultivating a pure mind and an intense desire for liberation and God-realization. Nityananda was a complete renunciate in the highest and most extreme sense of the term. He dressed in nothing but a loin cloth, and for a number of his early years didn't dress in any clothes at all. He ate only when fed and slept wherever spirit guided him to, with a complete disregard of the elements. He was an enormous powerhouse and transmitting center of spiritual energy.

He once said, as quoted from a book called *Nityananda, the Divine Presence*, by M.U. Hatengdi, "The ocean has plenty of water. It is the size of the container brought to collect it that determines the quantity taken." Nityananda never had a guru or performed any spiritual practices. Thus it might be said that he was an avatar (God-realized at birth). On the purpose of life, Nityananda said, "One must seek the shortest way and the fastest means to get back home, to turn the spark within into a blaze, to be merged in and to identify with the greater fire which ignited the spark."

When asked by one disciple what to read, he said, "Not necessary, not necessary. If you must read, read the *Bhagavad-Gita.*" I am sure Nityananda probably never read a book in his life; all his knowledge was directly from Source Itself. In his early years he was called Ram, which means God.

As Swami Nityananda grew into adulthood, he developed miraculous powers like those of Sai Baba and Jesus Christ during the last three years of his life. Thousands of people would line up to see him every day. On one occasion when a man came to see him for the first time, Nityananda asked, "Where is your brother?" It turned out his brother had been blind since birth, but a few weeks later he brought his brother to Nityananda who said to leave him at the ashram for three days. When the man returned in three days, his brother could see.

Early in his life as a renunciate, some boys decided to torment what they perceived of as merely a naked man. They tied a rag drenched with kerosene to Nityananda's left hand and set it aflame. His hand began to burn like a torch. The only problem was that the boy who had lit the fire was crying in agony from the pain, not Nityananda. The boy apologized and Nityananda stopped the pain.

Nityananda did not talk a lot or explain himself very well. He would often make very short statements and no one would understand what he had been talking about until much later. On one occasion he was standing in a tree, as he often did in his youth, when he was asked for help in healing a particular illness manifesting as a lump on the person's calf. All Nityananda said was, "This one knows and is there." Even though they had never met, he went on his own to the woman's home. He massaged the calf for a couple of minutes and left. The woman completely recovered.

A mother took her daughter to see Nityananda, asking him to heal her blindness. Nityananda said, "Let the child ask for what she wants, not you." The child said she just wanted to see her mother once. The next day the child ran to her mother, saying she could see. After that, her blindness returned. The child had received exactly what she had asked for.

Nityananda was perceived to be very eccentric by most worldly people, but not by those with eyes to see and ears to hear. On one occasion he was briskly walking past a woman he had never met and he squeezed her breasts as he walked by. The people in the community were greatly angered and wanted to put him in jail. When confronted, Nityananda told them not to get excited, for the child would not die. The woman confirmed that she was pregnant and that her three previous children had all died at their first breast feeding. She delivered in the next few days and her child survived. A delegation went to him and begged his forgiveness.

A lot of people thought that he just lay around a lot, doing nothing. To this Nityananda said, as quoted in Hatengdi's book, "One must live in the world like common men. Once one is established in infinite consciousness, one becomes silent and though knowing everything, goes about as if he does not know anything. Though he might be doing a lot of things in several places, to all outward appearances he will remain as if he does nothing. He will remain always as if he is a witness to everything that goes on, like a spectator at a cinema show, and is not affected by the pleasant or the unpleasant."

On another occasion, two men were hired to assassinate him by a father who didn't like his son's associating with a dirty renunciate who wore a loin cloth. When the assassins caught Nityananda one of the assassin's arms became frozen in midair and he was in extreme pain and agony. A great number of people tried to pull his arm down but couldn't. Finally, Nityananda touched his arm and it relaxed. The men were taken to jail, but Nityananda asked that the men be freed. He sat in vigil outside the jail and said he wouldn't move until they were set free. After much trouble they were finally released, and they became devotees of Nityananda.

Many of the things Nityananda did were very bizarre. On one occasion he walked into a house where a child had been born a number of hours earlier. He proceeded to swallow the dried remnants of the child's umbilical cord. Then he left. When asked by devotees why he had done it, he said that many children of the family had passed away in infancy, but this child would now live.

In another demonstration of his awesome powers, Nityananda was roughly thrown off a train because he had no ticket and no money to buy one. When it was time for the train to depart, it couldn't move. Passengers saw Nityananda and explained that he was no ordinary sanyasin (renunciate). He was allowed to get back on the train and it immediately started. Then the train passed the next station even though the engineer tried to stop it, and it continued a number of miles farther to the location of Nityananda's ashram and then stopped. When he left the train he was wearing a garland of ticket stubs given to him by the passengers, and he handed it to the train official who had tried to throw him off the train in the first place. The man profusely apologized, whereupon Nityananda slapped the engine with his hand and told it to move; it went backwards to the station that had been passed.

Once Swami Nityananda walked into a devotee's kitchen while she was cooking, pulled out a burning piece of firewood, and hit her head with it. Then he walked out. Her children were very angry and wanted revenge, but she refused. A year later when an expert astrologer was doing the family horoscope, he said that she was supposed to have died a year before.

It was only then that the family realized what Nityananda had done for her.

On an occasion when it was raining very hard and Nityananda was standing under the awning of one of the shops in a village, the owners ordered the dirty, nearly naked renunciate out of the shelter, making fun of him and teasing him in the process. Appearing very sad, Nityananda is quoted as having said, "It would appear that God has decided that only Mother Ganga [the Ganges River] shall wash the sins of this place." The river overflowed and the shops were wiped out.

On another occasion Nityananda was meditating with his devotees when there was a blinding flash of light behind him. When they all opened their eyes, he was in a yoga posture and he appeared dead. He had completely stopped breathing. Devotees started spreading the news that Nityananda had died. Thirty-six hours later he came back to life and said that the time was not yet and that the five divine personalities who had met him had persuaded him to return.

During the building of the ashram, the workers needed to be paid. The work foreman was told to collect the money from under a certain tree, where the exact amount miraculously appeared. On other occasions as the workers would file past him, the money would miraculously fall from his hand as he opened and closed his fist.

At one time, Nityananda was taken to jail because a medical doctor in the community said he was insane. He told the jailer he needed to urinate. He was given a receptacle which he filled up. He then asked for another. He kept asking for more receptacles and they finally brought a large clay pot which he completely filled with urine, asking for still more receptacles. The police sergeant finally got the message and went to the magistrate to ask that Nityananda be released, realizing that what he had just witnessed was not humanly possible. He was let go, and when the doctor who had falsely accused him went home to his wife, she was dancing around without any clothes on. He went to see Nityananda and begged for his forgiveness.

Sometimes he would emerge from his morning bath and not even be wet. This would occur when it rained, also. On one occasion he drank seven bottles of hard alcohol, enough to kill a normal person. When asked why, he said he hadn't drunk any of it; it was for the spirit that was haunting a particular rock and bothering people. The spirit was now satisfied and would not harm anyone in the future.

Another time Nityananda asked to be buried in the sand as though in a grave, saying that three hours later he would dig himself out. He had to travel to Delhi for some work so was just leaving his body there.

One devotee asked for the awakening of his kundalini. Nityananda touched his spine and the kundalini shot up his spine like a rocket. On another occasion, Nityananda offered some food to a devotee, but she wasn't eating it because there had been a drought and there was no drinking water. Nityananda told her not to worry for she could drink rain water. The sky was totally blue and it was a bright sunny day, but five minutes later it started to rain.

He once told a devotee to go to the temple and not look back under any circumstances. The devotee came upon a cobra but didn't look back. He heard a whispering right behind him. He still didn't look back. When he had nearly arrived at the temple, he finally looked back and saw a gigantic figure, like a genie with folded arms, standing in the middle of the river saying mantras. That was the whispering he had heard throughout his walk to the temple.

One day the work foreman was bitten by a cobra. Nityananda asked a devotee to get some balm and told him to rub it on his own leg, not on the foreman's leg. He was totally confused by this but did what Nityananda said. When he arose in the morning the foreman was completely healed. Another devotee had a severe heart attack and was very weak. Nityananda sprinkled some water on him and he was completely healed. Some devotees of Shirdi Sai Baba visited Nityananda one day, but before they could enter his room, he shouted at them, "Go to Shirdi. Is the old man sitting there different from the one sitting here?"

When asked by a disciple if he could see God, he said, "More clearly than you can be seen." When asked about the need for his physical presence, he said, "This one is here, there, and everywhere. There is not a pinhole where this one will not be found."

An interesting event occurred when a family came to him with their young child who was dying of pneumonia. The child had not opened his eyes in three days. Nityananda passed his hand over the child's eyes and they opened and then again they closed. Nityananda told the family to perform the last rites, for the child was dead. One of his devotees questioned him about what appeared to be a terrible occurrence. Nityananda rebuked him, saying, "What do you know or understand about these matters? This is the fourth time the same child has come out of the same mother's womb. It has been seeking liberation. It has been wanting freedom but karmic law has been dragging it down again and again for manifestation in the same family. Its intense desire has been fulfilled now and it won't have to come again." Three previous children had all died shortly after birth, he was later to find out.

Another couple took to him their child who had smallpox. Swami was not seen for ten days; he was then seen taking a bath and he had skin eruptions on his body.

A devotee asked to be cured of tuberculosis. Nityananda told him that he had to eat one small frog a day fried in cow's ghee (butter). Being a vegetarian, he was horrified, but he did as he was told and was healed.

Nityananda and his devotees were sitting outside in the evening when a wild tiger approached their campfire. No one moved. The tiger proceeded to rest its forepaws on Nityananda's shoulders. Nityananda petted the tiger and it jumped down and walked away.

Nityananda told a devotee to empty the donation box at the Krishna temple but to leave one quarter of the money in the box. The next day the money left in the box was stolen. Nityananda later said that the previous evening a poor man had prayed that he wanted to break into the box and steal the money because he was starving.

When Nityananda was asked why he was called a god, he replied, "Everyone is a god here, including yourself and all the ones who are seated here."

A famous singer once came to the ashram. A little too much false pride and ego made him decide not to sing because he felt he would be wasting his talents on these tribal people. Someone else ended up singing and the famous singer changed his mind. The next day when he was about to sing he could make no sound at all. The Master said, "Sing! Why not? God has given you the voice. Sing His praise. What do you care who listens and who does not?" Immediately, his voice was restored.

A devotee was having darshan at another temple in a distant part of India, under Nityananda's orders. When he returned from his trip the devotees asked him what time it had occurred. The devotees were amazed because at that exact time Nityananda had been sitting in the ashram and had said that the particular devotee was having darshan at that distant temple.

Nityananda taught his devotees to maintain mental equilibrium at all times. He said, "Go back and do your duty without desire for fruit, and without sacrificing efficiency. This is the highest service that you can render." As for spiritual progress, the essential thing is vairgya, an intense sense of renunciation and dispassion for worldliness. "Without vairgya there can be no progress whatsoever, and if you don't listen, you will fail in the end."

He also told his devotees that "Whenever devotees meet and talk about him, this one is there." He always spoke of himself as "this one," showing his complete identification with the atman, the Eternal Self, and his lack of body identification. When asked why his feet had become swollen he responded by saying, "All people come here for seva [selfless service]. They also deposit their desires and difficulties at the feet and while the Ocean of Divine Mercy washes away much of the effect, a little has to be accepted by the body, which has been assumed only for the sake of the devotees."

In 1961, near the end of his life, a devotee psychically picked up that

Nityananda was close to leaving his physical body. She began to cry and begged the master not to go away. He said, "Why are you crying? Don't cry. More work is possible in the subtle than in the gross."

On the morning of the day Nityananda attained mahasamadhi (conscious death), a young boy in a village in another part of India told his parents an extraordinary thing. As reported in Hatengdi's book, the boy said to his parents, "What are you doing here? Go to Ganeshpuri [Nityananda's ashram]. He will be going today. There is a call for him from the assembly of the sages for help he alone can render in connection with the forthcoming ashtagraha yoga which portends great evil to the world in general and to India in particular." The parents ignored and rebuked the boy. That night they received word that Nityananda had had mahasamadhi. The day was August 8, 1961.

The day before his death he is quoted as having said, "Everyone comes here for money and only money. The more they are given, the more they seek. There is no end to their greed. When they come, they are pedestrians, sometimes without a proper dwelling place; and when they get the necessities, then comforts and luxuries are demanded — a car, a bungalow, and so on. When earlier prayers are granted in the hope that contentment would follow, and that they would then seek higher values, another demand is placed in a never-ending series of wants and desires. Not much point in allowing the body to continue; hence, samadhi tomorrow."

I would like to close this chapter with a longer quote from Swami Nityananda concerning the nature of the mind and the spiritual path.

> "The mind should be like a lotus leaf which, though in water, with the stem in the mud and the flower above, is yet untouched by both. Similarly, the mind should be kept untainted by the mud of desires and the water of distractions, even though engaged in worldly activities. Then, just as the stalk, stem, and leaf, when properly cultivated and not disturbed, will culminate in the lotus blossom, similarly, if the detached mind and faith are firmly established in the lotus of the heart and never allowed to wax or wane with happiness and difficulties, His grace will be invoked.
>
> There are various tests to which a devotee is subjected: they could be of the mind, of the intellect, of the body, and so on. A number of such tests are there. In fact, God is conducting tests all the time. Every occurrence in life is a test. Every thought that crops up in the mind is in itself a test to see what one's reaction will be. Hence, one must be always alert and aloof, conducting oneself with a spirit of detachment, viewing everything as an opportunity afforded to gain experience, to improve oneself and go on to a higher stage.
>
> Desires are the only cause of sorrows in this world. Nothing is brought into this world and nothing can be taken. There are, for instance, so many things in this ashram. They are all meant for use by devotees

visiting the place. If this one goes elsewhere, none of these things would be taken. Whatever is needed there will come separately. This one is not flattered because some important persons have visited or depressed because someone that used to come has not turned up. Whether people who come here offer or do not offer anything, it is the same. There is no desire to go anywhere or see anything, nor is there any longing for any visitors to come.

Whatever one says must be reflected in one's thinking and actions. If one is advised to be like a lotus leaf, that is because of the practice prevailing here. There is not even the desire to do good to anyone. Everything that happens happens automatically, by the will of God. Nevertheless, if anyone is genuinely interested, some words come out of this one."

## Summation

If you would like to learn more about Swami Nityananda, I recommend reading M.U. Hatengdi's book, *Nityananda, the Divine Presence*, which is the source of most of the material in this chapter. I hope it has provided a small glimpse into what is available to you when you merge with the Eternal Self and Spirit.

# 15

## Baba Muktananda
## and the Path of Siddha Yoga

*Shiva, the Self of all,*
*has already been attained. These upayas*
*[spiritual techniques] exist not to make us attain*
*the Self but to remove our forgetfulness, our*
*errors, and our ignorance of that Self.*
*Everyone has already attained the Self,*
*but is unaware of it.*

Baba Muktananda

Disciples of Baba Muktananda follow the path of Siddha Yoga which requires surrender to a particular lineage of Siddha gurus. According to Baba Muktananda, receiving from a Siddha guru shaktipat, the transmission of spiritual power and particular mantras and meditations, is essential.

My personal path is much too universal and eclectic for me to be comfortable following this path. Rather than having a guru, I choose to listen to spiritual teachers and to God, my monad, and my soul. In saying this, I do not in any way mean to criticize the Siddha path. It is actually one of the most popular Eastern paths in America. Baba Muktananda was an extraordinary spiritual master, and his teachings and meditation experiences are universalistic.

Baba Muktananda was born in 1908 near Mangalore in southern India. At the age of fifteen he left home to begin his life of seeking God. He immediately took his initiation as a sanyasin (renunciate) from a Siddha master named Siddharudha Swami. He was given the name Muktananda which means Bliss of Liberation. He traveled throughout India for the next thirty years, searching for God-realization. During that time, he met more than sixty great spiritual masters but it wasn't until he met Bhagawan Nityananda that he recognized his true guru and teacher. Nityananda gave him the shaktipat initiation to awaken his latent kundalini which initiated a nine-year period of intense meditation, culminating in his attaining Self-realization in 1956.

During that same year, Bhagawan Nityananda took mahasamadhi (conscious death) and transmitted the power of the Siddha lineage to Swami Muktananda. During the following years, many people traveled to India to see Baba Muktananda and eventually, in 1970, he was invited to the West. He went on to make three successive tours of the West, teaching meditation and giving the shaktipat initiation into the Siddha Yoga lineage to hundreds of thousands of people. Before Baba's passing in 1982, he transferred his full spiritual power to his disciple Gurumayi Chidvila-sananda.

## The Teachings of Baba Muktananda

The term Siddha means, in essence, that one has realized the Self. The path of Siddha Yoga does not exclude any religion, sect, or code of ethics a person may be involved with, so it has universal appeal. The essence of the teachings is that everyone is already the Self and is here just to remember that great truth. It is a path of love that recognizes that the Self is embodied in all aspects of creation, not just in puny little physical human bodies. The Siddha path culminates in the experience of "I Am That," identity with God. The Siddha path eradicates all differences and leads to transcendence of duality. That results in unchanging joy, bliss, and the release of all negative emotions and qualities.

The Siddha path leads to the full awakening of the kundalini which begins when the disciple receives the shaktipat initiation which is given through touch, word (mantra), look, or thought. Any of these can be very powerful if the Siddha Yoga master has fully raised his or her own kundalini. That starts the process, and it is then increased by devotion to God, pure and regular life, repetition of a mantra, meditation, study of scripture, chanting, faith in and love for guru, darshan with the Siddha master, satsang (keeping company with truth-seekers), and asanas (yoga postures).

The chant used is "Om Namah Shivaya" which means, "I bow to the Lord, who is the inner Self." The chant is to be done at the speed of normal conversation with great love and with the understanding that you, yourself, are the deity of the mantra. The other recommended mantra is "So Ham" which means "I am He" – I am God, I am Shiva, I am the Self. Interestingly enough, this is the same mantra that Sai Baba recommends.

The idea is to say this mantra in accordance with the breath: on the in-breath say, "So," and on the out-breath say, "Ham."

Often, after receiving the shaktipat initiation and performing the Siddha Yoga spiritual practices, the devotee experiences involuntary bodily movements called kriyas which are the result of spontaneous movements of the kundalini, or shakti, rising, and which bring purification. When the kundalini rises through the central canal, it pierces the six chakras and finally enters the crown where samadhi is experienced. During meditation experiences can include inner sounds, tastes, smells, and visions in the form of colored lights, gods and goddesses, saints, or holy rivers and mountains.

Baba Muktananda speaks of four bodies: the gross physical body, the subtle body in which dreaming occurs, the causal body, which is the body of deep sleep, and the supracausal body, which is the body of the superconscious. As it rises, the kundalini purifies and cleanses all four bodies. Baba Muktananda gives a fascinating account in his autobiography, *Play of Consciousness*, of his experiences in meditation with these four bodies.

He perceived them as four Lights, the physical body as red Light, the subtle body as white Light, the causal body as black Light, and the supracausal body as blue Light. Every time he meditated, he perceived these colors one within the other. The red Light was the size of the physical body; the white Light was thumb-sized; the black Light the size of a fingertip; and the blue Light the size of a sesame seed. As the kundalini rose, it would slowly but surely purify the bodies, the sense organs, and the chakras themselves, and he would experience deep levels of meditation. When the kundalini finally reached the crown he saw a triangle. In the center of the triangle resided Shiva, or God, the ultimate goal of the raising of the kundalini. At that point, he saw a brilliant Light like that of a thousand suns. In the center of the Light, as it quieted down, he saw the Blue Pearl, the divine Light of consciousness that dwells within every person. It is the actual form of the Self. It is the size of a sesame seed; the infinite universe is contained within it.

The goal of meditation in the Siddha practice is to see this Blue Pearl and ultimately to go inside it and to merge with it. Within the Blue Pearl you will see the deity you feel personal devotion to, be he Jesus, Buddha, Sai Baba, Krishna, or Rama. At one time, Baba had the experience of watching the Blue Pearl expand until it became the size of a human being. He saw a magnificent being made of shimmering blue Light. This blue being gave Baba some advice and blessed him. Then he returned to being the size of the Blue Pearl and entered into Baba Muktananda. (It is interesting that Krishna was often seen as a blue being.)

As meditation is continued, Baba says, the Blue Pearl will eventually explode, its Light will fill the universe, and you will have a direct experience of yourself as omnipresence, as the Eternal Self. You will no longer identify yourself with the physical body's consciousness.

Baba also had an experience in which he saw himself as the blue being inside the pearl. The blue person in Hindu scripture is seen as the one who grants the realization of God within form; Shiva is seen as the Blue Lord. This is the goal of the Siddha path. The blue person is also known as the sphere of unmanifest Light. Experiencing that causes the feeling of Shivo' Ham (I am Shiva). When vision has been completely purified, a person can see himself as a blue color in the crown chakra.

Baba also heard divine music, something that Paramahansa Yogananda has spoken of in his writings, as well. Just as each body and dimension has a certain Light frequency, so each dimension, chakra, and body has a certain divine sound. Some of the divine sounds Baba heard in meditation were the breaking of waves, the roll of thunder, the rippling of a stream, the clack of a speeding train, the sound of an airplane in the distance, the crackle of a funeral pyre, the banging of a kettle drum, the sacred sound of a conch shell, honey bees, the calling of a peacock, the cries of the cuckoo and other birds, cymbals, and the flute. In yogic teachings it is said there are ten divine sounds that can be heard one after another as meditation deepens.

Some other experiences Baba had in meditation included seeing future events, smelling divine scents, soul traveling to spiritual cities on the inner plane, and visitations by divine saints and past Siddha Yoga masters. Once he went to Siddhaloka, the spiritual world of the siddhas, great saints, and yogis of the Siddha path who have achieved soul liberation. On other occasions he had visions of the inner workings of his physical body.

It is worth noting that many of these experiences are available to people even if they are not disciples of the Siddha path, and most of them are quite universal and are spoken of by many of the great spiritual masters of all paths who have achieved Self-realization.

## The Philosophy of Siddha Yoga

Siddha Yoga sees the individual soul as being no different from God. It is attachment to the body and identification with ego and desire that result in being bound to the cycle of rebirth. Siddha Yoga makes no distinctions in caste, creed, sex, color, or religion. It advocates the avoidance of drugs and the consumption of a purified diet on all levels.

It teaches its followers to love and bless those who hate them and to pray for those who hurt them. Most of all, it teaches them to see their own loving selves in all. True renunciation does not mean renouncing involvement with life but, rather, means renouncing all ego, fear, selfishness, material desire, attachment, and negative thoughts and emotions. All suffering is caused by lack of understanding, or ignorance. All beings are seen as equals because the Self lives in all beings. Since reality is created by perceptions, interpretations, and thoughts, equal vision is the means of attaining Siddhahood, which sees the entire universe as the Self. The Siddha forgets the dream of bondage and sees himself or herself as everything, both visible and invisible, realizing that the dream of bondage never truly existed in the first place. The Siddha renounces all enmity, delusion, fear, jealousy, criticism, anger, duality, suffering, ego, desire, greed, pride, arrogance, hatred, self-praise, differences, harsh words, expectations, fame, hunger for power, and hedonism, for all these qualities are the progeny of ignorance or nonunderstanding.

The entire world is seen as the play of the consciousness of Shiva. Forgetfulness of his own true nature is the cause of all human suffering. Constant joy, happiness, and contentment are a sign that a person has achieved realization of the Self. A guru is considered essential to Self-realization, for he or she leads the seeker to the discovery of that which was never lost.

Shiva is the ultimate goal. A Siddha is involved with the outer world but is always remembering God. The previous belief in an illusionary, separative ego identity merges into the divine "I" that is the Eternal Self.

Siddha Yoga sees only one Self in all human beings, but many paths to realizing it. The true Siddha rejects any infatuation with the supernatural powers that come from the process of realizing the Self. The Siddha is the physician that cures the disease of worldliness.

Baba Muktananda sums up the Siddha path in *Secret of the Siddhas* when he says, "Shiva, the Self of all, has already been attained. These upayas [spiritual techniques] exist not to make us attain the Self, but to remove our forgetfulness, our errors, and our ignorance of that Self. Everyone has already attained the Self but is unaware of it. The way to Self-realization is to recognize your own Self as Shiva, and this occurs through the upayas. You are perfect, you have come from perfection, you live in perfection, and this perfection is the supreme truth."

The Siddha rejects all such thoughts as "I and mine," "his and theirs," "I am different from others." These are the great illusions of ego and duality. Ordinary people become great by spending time with great people. All actions are seen to be service to God; the fruit of all actions should be renounced. As a seeker who is truly spiritually ripe, you do not need any spiritual techniques to realize that you are Shiva, just as you do not need any special spiritual technique to recognize that you are the son or daughter of your parents..

Another of Baba Muktananda's mantras from the ancient scriptures is

"I am Shiva and Shiva is me. You are also Shiva. Everything is Shiva. Everything is Brahman. Everything is consciousness. There is nothing different from Shiva." This leads to the firm conviction that all the people of the world are God, and each shares the same identity as Shiva, or the Eternal Self. The infinite physical universe is, hence, your true physical body. The Siddha sees equality and the Eternal Self in all beings, including insects, plants, animals, and the mineral kingdom. The Siddha has mastery over the body, emotions, mind, intellect, desire, ego, and the subtle bodies.

The world of thoughts is the source of all pain. The ignorance that is destroyed in Self-realization never really existed except in the illusionary consciousness of body-identification (ego). So, in essence, bondage is not real. You can let go of it any time you choose to. Although thousands of lamps may be blazing, the light in all of them is the same.

Baba Muktananda says, "If a person leads his life seeing God and all beings as identical, he becomes liberated in this lifetime." Meditation is the power that lets a human being become the Lord, an individual become Shiva, and the soul become God. To the Siddhas there is no spiritual practice more important than meditation. Chanting "Om" is also a method of reaching Brahman.

When Self-realization is achieved, the person realizes in his thoughts, feelings, and body that he is one with the infinite universe. (It had always been so, even though he did not realize it.)

The spiritual path is thought to be a step-by-step process until the yogi has finally achieved the highest stage of oneness with Shiva. When he sees the world as a playground on which to practice joy, bliss, unconditional love, and being God with his brothers and sisters in all kingdoms who are God also, duality disappears.

The key to the Siddha path is to attain God's viewpoint at all times instead of operating from the delusionary ego's viewpoint. When you always interpret life from God's viewpoint, you remain in joy, bliss, love, and inner peace at all times, for the world of pain and pleasure, of duality, is a product of a human's interpretation of life. It all exists within his own mind, not within God's mind. Whether a person is enlightened or ignorant, it is the same Self in all people. Whoever loves himself and other people loves God. Whoever loves the world loves God. By perceiving people as other than himself, a person falls into bondage.

A person becomes like the object upon which he meditates, so all meditation is best focused on a guru or on the Eternal Self. The guru and the Eternal Self are seen as being one and the same. In truth, all people are present everywhere and in everything. Hence, Siddha Yoga teaches its followers not to think of themselves in terms of statements like "I am here" or "I am not there." The affirmation Baba recommends is "I am everywhere; I am the Self in all." Nothing else exists in the world.

When a seeker of God sees the world as empty and sees the Self as pervading all beings and all objects, then he or she becomes filled with love. The Siddha path is appropriate for the householder as well as for the ascetic monk.

I would like to finish this chapter with a final statement by Baba Muktananda, quoted from his book, *Kundalini: the Secret of Life*: "And this is why I always tell everyone, 'Meditate on your Self, honor your Self, worship your Self, for God dwells within you as you.' "

# 16

## *The Life and Teachings of Buddha*

*Immortality can be reached only by continual
acts of kindliness; and perfection is accomplished
by compassion and charity.*

Buddha

Siddhartha Gautama was born in about 563 B.C. At his birth, a holy man prophesied that he would become either an emperor or a renunciate who gave up the material world in favor of a great spiritual destiny. His parents gave him the name Siddhartha, which means "he whose purpose in life has been attained."

Siddhartha tried to live the life in which he was being trained to become the emperor; however, his compassion for the suffering of others directed him to the spiritual path. Having led the pampered life of an emperor's son, he then chose the life of the ascetic. It was these experiences that molded his philosophy of following the Middle Way, a life of moderation rather than of extremes.

One day when he was about forty years old, he found himself near the city of Gaya. He discovered a tranquil spot under a sacred fig tree, folded his legs, and prepared himself for meditation. It was at that moment that he took a solemn vow: "Come what may – let my body rot, let my bones be reduced to ashes – I will not get up from here until I have found the way beyond decay and death." Thus determined and filled with peace, Siddhartha passed into deep meditation. At the time of the full moon of May in 544 B.C. (now known as the festival of Wesak), he no longer was Siddhartha, the finite personality; he was Buddha – He Who is Awake.

The tree under which he sat burst forth into blossom and a fragrant spring breeze showered him with flowers. He had achieved nirvana. Djwhal

Khul has told me that he achieved the fourth initiation at that time. That is the first state of nirvana, liberation from the wheel of rebirth and complete soul-realization.

Buddha remained at that place, as the story is told, for four weeks or more, immersing himself in the experience of illumination. It was during that time that his future teaching was worked out. Buddha's decision to return to the world and serve is much like that of Moses' return from Mount Sanai and of Jesus' leaving the River Jordan after being baptized by John.

When he was greeted by the initial group of people on his return to the world, they saw his dazzling radiance and said, "Are you God or an angel?" He said, "No, I am awake." With his first five disciples, Buddha began the next stage of his life: teaching the dharma, the path that leads to liberation and the end of sorrow. It was at that time that Buddha elucidated the Four Noble Truths.

## The Four Noble Truths

The first Noble Truth states that suffering and frustration are the result of the difficulty of facing the basic fact of life that everything is impermanent and transitory. "All things arise and pass away."

The second Noble Truth states that the cause of suffering is the clinging to wrong points of view. Out of ignorance, humans divide the perceived world into individual and separate things, attempting to confine the fluid forms of reality into fixed categories created by the mind.

The third Noble Truth states that suffering and frustration can be ended. It is possible to be free from bondage and to reach the state of total liberation.

The fourth Noble Truth states that it is possible to end all suffering through self-development, which leads to enlightenment; enlightenment is achieved through right seeing, right knowing, right action, right awareness, and right meditation.

The following quotation from Buddha describes his experience while meditating under the fig tree where he obtained his illumination.

> I roused unflinching determination, focused my attention, made my body calm and motionless and my mind concentrated and one-pointed.
>
> Standing apart from all selfish urges and all states of mind harmful to spiritual progress, I entered the first meditative state, in which the mind, though not quite free from divided and diffuse thought, experiences lasting joy.
>
> By putting an end to divided and diffuse thought, with my mind stilled in one-pointed absorption, I entered the second meditative state quite free from any wave of thought and experienced the lasting joy of the unitive state.

As the joy became more intense and pure, I entered the third meditative state, becoming conscious in the very depths of the unconscious. Even my body was flooded with that joy of which the noble ones say, "They live in abiding joy who have stilled the mind and are fully awake."

Then, going beyond the duality of pleasure and pain and the whole field of memory-making forces in the mind, I dwelt, at last, in the fourth meditative state, utterly beyond the reach of thought, in that realm of complete purity which can be reached only through detachment and contemplation. This was my first successful breaking forth, like a chick breaking out of its shell.

## Buddha

Buddha embodied the divine quality of wisdom. He was the manifestation of Light and the teacher of the way of enlightenment.

Christ, the next great divine teacher, who lived five hundred years later, embodied even a greater divine principle – love. Christ embraced within himself all that Buddha had brought forth of Light, and he added divine love. Buddha predicted the coming of his brother the Lord Maitreya and called him the future Buddha Maitreya. Buddha has now left the planetary hierarchy and has moved on to the council levels of evolution, although he still works with Planet Earth. Buddha's lifetime on Earth as Lord Gautama was his last. In that lifetime he completed his series of lives as a bodhisattva. (Bodhisattvas are enlightened beings who have already arrived at the state of Buddhahood but who have voluntarily postponed their own nirvana in order to help all forms of sentient life attain the supreme release. They are beings who have forever freed themselves from all ideas of "I," "mine," and "yours" – in other words, they no longer have any sense of separateness.)

## The Wesak Festival

The Wesak Festival, or the Festival of the Buddha, has been held every year down through the centuries in a valley in the Himalayas at the time of the full moon in May. At that time the Christ, the manu, and the mahachohan stand in triangular formation in front of an enormous flat stone on which there is a large crystal bowl filled with water. The moon rises above the horizon, and then at the moment of the full moon in Taurus, Buddha appears. Gautama Buddha comes from Shamballa and hovers over the crystal bowl on the stone, transmitting to the Christ the energy that is called the Shamballa force.

The force is the great first ray of will, or power. This force is circulated by the Christ through himself and then through the manu and the mahachohan; then it is gradually released to the world.

Although most people are not aware of it, the Wesak Festival might be considered one of the holiest days of the year. Part of the purpose of the festival is to prove the factual solidarity of the Eastern and Western approaches to God, for both Christ and Buddha are present. It also serves as a rallying point and annual meeting place for all those who serve the kingdom of God and humanity.

## Buddha's Teachings

The teachings of Buddha are beautiful, and they demonstrate the universality of all religions, for within them can also be found the teachings of Sai Baba, Jesus and Lord Maitreya, Djwhal Khul, and all the other great masters.

A fundamental aspect of Buddhism is a simple three-part statement which Buddhists all over the world recite:

I take my refuge in the Buddha.

I take my refuge in the dharma [teaching].

I take my refuge in the sangha [spiritual community].

A basic precept of Buddha's teaching was the need to let go of all attachments. All suffering comes from wrong points of view and from clinging to ego-oriented attitudes. In Buddhism the idea of a separate self and ego is considered a mere intellectual invention that has no basis in reality.

Buddha stressed the importance of living according to what you have discovered to be true. In the *Dhammapada*, a chapter in the bible of Buddhist literature, Buddha states, "A man who talks much of his teaching but does not practice it himself is like a cattleman counting another man's cattle." Buddha also states in the *Dhammapada*, "All that we are is the result of our thoughts." One of his famous aphorisms was "Look within; thou art the Buddha."

Integral to all forms of Buddhism is the ideal of helping your fellow human. Buddhism teaches you to free yourself from the distortions of self-centeredness through the development of mindfulness. In Buddhism it is ignorance, not sin, that creates difficulties for a human being, and ignorance can be modified and overcome by means of specific, teachable techniques. Self-knowledge is one sure, indisputable path by which you can extricate yourself from the suffering of human life. The Four Noble Truths, the Eightfold Path, and the Middle Way serve all Buddhists.

Buddha is not considered to be supernatural or divine. This belief is held to strengthen followers' faith in personal effort and to intensify the belief that the goal of heightened consciousness can be reached.

Another significant facet of Buddhist thought is the goal of achieving a state of desirelessness.

A significant key to Buddhism is the development of character which results from strengthening the mind and controlling the emotions. It is only then that the disciple can demonstrate loving kindness to all sentient beings.

## The Three Major Divisions of Buddhism

There are three major divisions of Buddhism in the world today: the Hinayana Path, the Mahayana Path, and the Tantrayana, or Vajrayaba, Path which is Tibetan Buddhism.

### The Hinayana Path

The Hinayana ideal is embodied in the term "arhat." An arhat is a Buddhist who, by his own strenuous effort, has reached the stage of enlightenment and has attained nirvana. An arhat has extinguished greed, anger, and delusion. The arhat's heart and mind, hence, dwell in peace and love. The Hinayana conception of nirvana is merely the extinction of false ideas, in particular, the false belief in a separate ego.

### The Mahayana Path

The Mahayana school of Buddhism teaches the possibility of universal salvation and places great importance on service to all beings.

### Tibetan Buddhism

The seeds of Tibetan Buddhism can be seen clearly in Djwhal Khul's teachings, for in his last life as Djwhal Khul, he was a Tibetan Buddhist master. One of the basic tenets of Tibetan Buddhism is that each seeker must work out his own salvation by his own efforts. The most famous chant of Tibetan Buddhism is "Om Mani Padme Hum" which has been translated as "Hail to the Jewel [of compassion] in the Lotus [of the heart]." It is probably the most universal of all mantras after the Aum mantra; I feel it is one of the most powerful mantras I have found.

Integral to Tibetan Buddhism is the belief in reincarnation. One aspect of that belief is the recognition of tulkus, children who are identified when still quite young, usually between the ages of two and five, as reincarnations of specific well-known religious figures of the past.

The Dalai Lama is the most famous of the tulkus. At the death of the Dalai Lama, the state oracle, a channel, is consulted for a preliminary reading on the geographic region in which the Dalai Lama's successor should be sought. The present Dalai Lama, when he was found by the search party, immediately ran to greet the visitors with open arms. Traditional tests were then put to the child. From among the rosaries shown him, he chose, without hesitation, the one that had belonged to his predecessor – in actuality, to himself. He also selected unerringly from among a number of predominantly counterfeit personal walking staffs and drums. Further, to every one's amazement, he was able to recite a certain six- syllable mantra sacred to the Bodhisattva of Compassion, Avalokitesvara, also known as Quan Yin. The child passed every test, which offered impressive proof of his identity.

Well-known among Tibetan Buddhist teachings is *The Tibetan Book of the Dead,* a complete description of the death process, including rituals of dying and the science of the bardo.

The Dalai Lama heads the Gelugpa, or yellow-hats, school of thought which is the youngest of four branches and dates back to the fourteenth century.

Followers of the Tibetan form of Buddhism do not necessarily confine their homage to their own familiar forms but will bow as naturally before a crucifix as they would at the feet of the Buddha.

On the prime importance of meditation as a means of comprehending reality, all Buddhists agree. The meditation tools of the Tibetan Buddhist include the mandala, the mantra, and a great deal of elaborate visualization.

An important aspect of Tibetan Buddhism teaches followers to see all beings as Buddha. This practice leads the practitioner to act with loving kindness, compassion, and respect for every person and thing that crosses his path. A parallel practice admonishes followers to hear all sounds as mantra.

Tibetan Buddhism places great importance on finding a responsible guru or spiritual teacher. In fact, it was determined to be of such import that it was added to the official formula of finding refuge in the Buddha, the teachings, and the spiritual community.

# 17

## *Quan Yin, Bodhisattva of Compassion and Mercy*

*The mysterious sound
of Quan Yin's name is holy like
the ocean's thunder. There is no other
like it in the world!*

Lotus Sutra

No discussion of Buddhism would be complete without mentioning Quan Yin who carries the Goddess and Divine Mother aspect of Buddhism. The same Goddess and Divine Mother energy is carried by the Virgin Mary in Christianity. In the Egyptian mysteries it is carried by Isis. In Hinduism it is carried by Shakti, by Lakshmi, wife of Vishnu, by Parvati, wife of Shiva, by Radha, wife of Krishna, and by Sita, wife of Rama.

Quan Yin's name is a translation of the Sanskrit name of her chief progenitor which is Avalokitesvara, also known as Avalokita. In its proper form it is Kuanshih Yin, which means "She who harkens to the cries of the world."

In Korea, Japan, and China, however, she is called Quan Yin. She is a celestial bodhisattva and an ascended master. One of her jobs in the celestial spheres is to sit on the board of the Lords of Karma.

My interest in Quan Yin began when I became involved with Johrei, a Buddhist religion based on the teachings of a Japanese master, Meishu-Sama, who had an experience of being overshadowed by Avalokitesvara in much the same way Lord Maitreya overshadowed Jesus Christ; they seemed to share the same body.

Avalokitesvara taught Meishu-Sama to channel divine Light through his hands with his help. (I say "his" because in the Avalokitesvara form, Quan Yin is considered male.) Meishu-Sama started to heal people miraculously with the help of Avalokitesvara. He was guided to teach all his followers to channel the divine Light as part of their church service.

They usually have a booth at the Whole Life Expos. There is a six-week course that is inexpensive in which the Buddhist principles are taught. Then the student is initiated and given what looks like a thick golden coin with a sacred piece of paper inside it. Keeping this locket in a pocket or wearing it as a necklace is supposed to activate the flow of divine Light from Avalokitesvara and that particular line of energy. The teachings are very beautiful and the people in the church are loving.

I became interested in Avalokitesvara and the amazing story of Meishu-Sama, so I did some research. The Tibetans and Mongols worshiped a female form of Avalokitesvara called Tara. In ancient paintings, Quan Yin and Tara look almost identical. The Chinese seem to have combined Avalokitesvara and Tara and called her Quan Yin. Quan Yin is often depicted as a member of a trinity with the Celestial Buddha, Amitabha, in the center and Quan Yin and Tashih-Chih, a bodhisattva master, standing on either side, but Quan Yin is also worshiped independently by millions of people.

Buddhist mythology tells of Avalokitesvara's being born from a ray of light that sprang from Amitabha Buddha's right eye. He immediately said, "Om Mani Padme Hum." This is one of the mantras by which he can be invoked, in Buddhist tradition.

Avalokitesvara came to be recognized by most Tibetans as Buddha's Earthly representative and as chief guardian of the dharma (doctrine) until the advent of Maitreya Buddha. (This is interesting, as Maitreya Buddha is now living in England; Buddha's prophecy of his coming has come true.)

Both Avalokitesvara and Quan Yin are embodiments of compassion. In Tibetan Buddhism, Quan Yin is seen in her male form as Avalokitesvara. As a matter of fact, the current Dalai Lama is thought to be an incarnation of Avalokitesvara. It is thought that the female form of Avalokitesvara, Quan Yin, originated in the twelfth or thirteenth century in both China and Japan. The Saddharma Pundarika Sutra affirms that Avalokitesvara had three hundred thirty-seven incarnations.

Tara, the female aspect worshiped in Tibet but not in China or Japan, is said to have been born of a tear shed by Avalokitesvara in sorrow for the world.

Like Amitabha Buddha, Avalokitesvara is cherished for his vow to renounce nirvana as long as there are sentient beings still lost amidst worldly bondage. This is just one of the reasons Quan Yin is adored by millions.

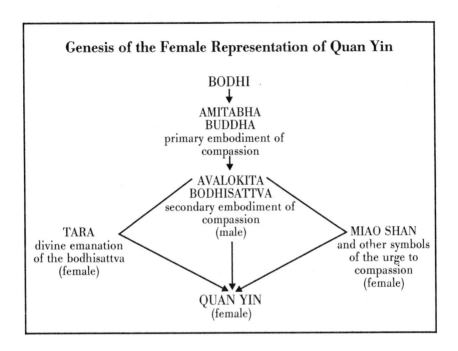

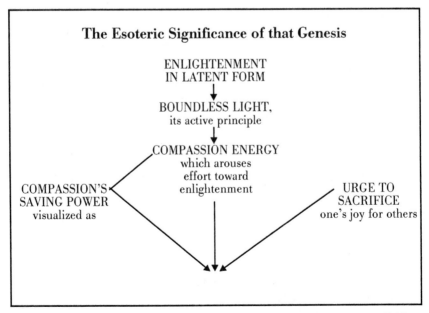

The source of these charts is *Bodhisattva of Compassion: the Mystical Tradition of Quan Yin* by John Blofeld.

In the Lotus Sutra it is said about Quan Yin, "The mysterious sound of Quan Yin's name is holy like the ocean's thunder — no other like it in the world! . . . Therefore should the mind be constantly fixed on her. . . . She is imbued with supernatural power and is wise in using skillful means. In every corner of the world she manifests her countless forms."

The supreme compliment to Avalokitesvara and Quan Yin is given in the book *Sutra of the Lotus Flower: The All-Sidedness of the Bodhisattva Regarder of the Cries of the World,* which is revered by millions of Buddhists because contains the core and culmination of the Buddha's teaching. In *The Threefold Lotus Sutra* by Kosei, Buddha has included a whole chapter on Avalokitesvara/Quan Yin. I would like to quote from the chapter concerning Buddha's opinion of Avalokitesvara, Regarder of the Cries of the World:

> "World-honored one! For what reason is the bodhisattva Avalokitesvara named Regarder of the Cries of the World?"

> "Good son! If there be countless hundred thousand myriad kotis of living beings suffering from pain and distress who hear of this Bodhisattva Regarder of the Cries of the World, and with all their mind call upon his name, the bodhisattva will instantly regard their cries, and all of them will be delivered.

> "If there be any who keep the name of that Bodhisattva Regarder of the Cries of the World, though they fall into a great fire, the fire will not be able to burn them, by virtue of the supernatural power of that bodhisattva's majesty. If any carried away by a flood call upon his name they will immediately reach the shallows.

> "If, again, there be any man on the verge of deadly harm who calls upon the name of the Bodhisattva Regarder of the Cries of the World, the word of the attacker will instantly snap asunder and he will be set free.

> "If any living beings much given to carnal passion keep in mind and revere the Bodhisattva Regarder of the Cries of the World, they will be set free from their passion. If any much given to anger keep in mind and revere the Bodhisattva Regarder of the Cries of the World, they will be set from their anger."

> "If any woman desiring a son worships and pays homage to the bodhisattva Regarder of the Cries of the World, she will bear a son happy, virtuous, and wise.

> "If the living in any realm must be saved in the body of a Buddha, the Bodhisattva Regarder of the Cries of the World appears as a Buddha and preaches to them the law.

> "He who bears him unremittingly in mind will be able to end the sorrows of existence."

## Summation

I highly recommend, if you desire help, that you call to beloved Quan Yin, Bodhisattva of Compassion and Mercy and Regarder of the Cries of the World. She cannot fail you, as Buddha has stated quite clearly.

# 18

## *Tibetan Buddhism and the Dalai Lama*

*Happy is he who has overcome all selfishness;*
*happy is he who has attained peace; and happy*
*is he who has found the truth.*

Buddha

The great Indian spiritual master Padmasambhava, also called "the Lotus-Born," is known in Tibet as Guru Rinpoche, "the Precious Teacher." He overcame all opposition and established Buddhism in Tibet in 747 A.D.

The current Dalai Lama is the Buddhist monk Tenzen Gyatso. He is the absolute spiritual and temporal head of his people. He is the fourteenth Dalai Lama in a chain of beings Tibetan Buddhists believe to be reincarnations of the same soul. The Dalai Lama is thought to be an extension of the deity known as Chenrezi, the embodiment of compassion who is also known as Avalokitesvara, or Quan Yin.

The Dalai Lama's home is really the whole world since he was forced to flee Tibet in 1959 because of the Communist Chinese invasion. India has provided a base of operations for him in Dharamsala and in recent years he has done an enormous amount of traveling. In 1989 he was the winner of the Nobel Peace Prize. He describes his work as being first for the Tibetan people and then for the good of all sentient beings. The Dalai Lama is a bodhisattva, a being who has voluntarily remained on Earth after achieving enlightenment in order to help and serve humanity.

After the death of the thirteenth Dalai Lama, a regent was appointed to search for the fourteenth Dalai Lama who, of course, was the thirteenth Dalai Lama in his next incarnation. The regent gathered all the signs that had already been obtained and then went to Lake Lhamo. In the waters of this lake adepts can see visions of the future; the lake functions as a crystal ball. The regent saw in the lake the letters "ah," "ka," and "ma." He saw a vision of a monastery with roofs of gold and copper and a twisting road leading to a nearby mountain. He saw a distinctive house with a peach tree in bloom, and he saw a woman with a baby in her arms. The regent had a clear knowingness that the baby was the fourteenth Dalai Lama.

The regent then went to Samye and consulted the local oracles who were able to see the future in a mirror. The regent got further confirmation, so a search party was formed and possessions of the thirteenth Dalai Lama were carefully packed. The search party disguised themselves so no one would know who they were or what their mission was.

They finally came to the house in the vision and everything looked exactly as the regent had seen it in the lake. The disguised lama, Tsedrung Lobang Tsewant, walked into the kitchen where the boy was playing and the boy ran to him shouting, "Lama, lama," even though he was disguised. He sat in the lama's lap and grabbed the rosary that had belonged to him in his past incarnation, saying, "This is mine. Please may I have it?" The lama told him he could have it if he could guess who he was. The child said "Sera-aga." Sera was the monastery from which the lama had come.

As a young child the boy had told his parents he would be going to Lhasa at an early age. The parents suspected he might be an incarnate lama, but they never dreamed he was the Dalai Lama.

They began giving the child tests in which he had to choose objects that had been his in his past life from among many that had not. He chose correctly on all accounts. On being given a physical exam he was discovered to have a birthmark in the shape of a conch shell which is a traditional sign  associated with the Dalai Lama. He was also able to speak and understand the Lhasa dialect even though he did not speak it at home. The child was only two years old.

On a later occasion, after being taken to Lhasa, the child insisted that a certain box that had not been opened contained his teeth. Sure enough, when the box was opened it was found to contain the false teeth of the thirteenth Dalai Lama.

This being's first incarnation as Dalai Lama occurred 1391.

When China attacked Tibet in 1950, the Dalai Lama was only fifteen years old, yet it was then that he was given the temporal leadership of Tibet. Tibetans appealed for help from the entire world, including the United Nations, but no one went to their aid. During the nine-year period before the Dalai Lama's exodus from Tibet he had an opportunity to have a personal meeting with Mao Tse Tung, the leader of Communist China at the time. At one point during the meeting, Mao described religion in the following manner, as quoted from a book called *Great Ocean: the Dalai*

*Lama* by Roger Hicks and Hgakpa Chogyam: "I understand you very well, but of course, religion is poison. It has two great defects. It undermines the race and, secondly, it retards the progress of the country. Tibet and Mongolia have both been poisoned by it." (I think this statement shows why Communism is destined to fail.)

By 1959 Communist China had dissolved the Tibetan government, thus completely violating the Seventeen Point Agreement the political leaders had set in place. China was interested only in a complete military takeover. The Dalai Lama had to flee and set up a Tibetan colony in exile in Dharamsala, India. It has come to be known as "Little Lhasa."

It was in 1967 that the Dalai Lama began to travel. His first trip was to Japan for four weeks and then to Thailand. Later he made a tour of Europe which included an audience with Pope John Paul II, and in the late 1970s he traveled extensively in the United States. He was extremely well received by the American people. He was not officially received by the United States government at that time, but he did meet with the Senate Foreign Relations Committee. The Republican senator from New York, Jacob Javits, said, "His Holiness is a fabulous man, a devoted patriot, and he gave us all the impression that he was the symbol of freedom." He lectured all over the country.

While in Los Angeles, he met with a party of Hopi elders. The elders had driven all night to see him. They told him that his arrival had fulfilled an ancient Hopi prophecy, as well as a Tibetan prophecy: The Hopi prophecy states that the world's axis passes through both the Hopi land and that of Tibet. At the end of one thousand years of Hopi religious practice, a great spiritual leader would arrive from the East. He would be the Sun Clan Brother, and his name would be linked with salt water. (Gyatso means ocean in the Tibetan language.) An ancient Tibetan prophecy states, "When the iron bird flies, and the horse runs upon rails, the Dharma will travel West to the Land of the Red Man."

By the end of his trip he had visited twenty-five American cities. His next trip to the United States was even more significant because on that trip he gave the Kalachakra initiation; never before in all of history had it been given outside of Tibet and India.

The Dalai Lama firmly believes that one day he and his people will return to Tibet. His Holiness has said, "China may have swallowed Tibet, but they have completely failed to digest it. Sooner or later they must realize that they will never do so."

## The Teachings of Tibetan Buddhism

I have always had a special interest in Tibetan Buddhism because Djwhal Khul (who wrote the Alice A. Bailey books and ascended as a

Tibetan Buddhist), Kuthumi, and El Morya were all Tibetan Buddhists in the later sequences of their past lives.

Tibetan Buddhism is based upon the understanding that you are your own master and you cause your own reality. The goal of life is enlightenment and becoming a bodhisattva and a perfect Buddha.

Djwhal Khul has told me that a perfect Buddha is someone who has achieved the sixth initiation, or ascension. A bodhisattva is a being who has achieved enlightenment yet returns to Earth to help all sentient beings.

Tibetan Buddhism, like other forms of Buddhism, is based on the Three Jewels: Buddha, the doctrine, and spiritual practice. To be a good Buddhist you must practice altruism, compassion, honesty, kindness, and selflessness, and you must hold a deep and abiding concern for the welfare of others. These are developed through meditation and the cultivation of wisdom. Buddha emphasized the perfect balance of a good brain and a good heart.

Tibetan Buddhism emphasizes the letting go of material desire and the letting go of all afflictive, or negative, emotions. The basic nature of the mind is seen as being made up of the clear Light. It is the same clear Light the Tibetan Buddhist merges with in the bardo (after-death) experience.

Defilements, or negativity, do not reside in the enlightened mind. It is the job of the Buddhist to clear all delusion and ignorance from the mind. The complete removal of this psychic debris is called liberation; a person who achieves such liberation is called a foe destroyer, or arhat. Interestingly, in Theosophy and in Djwhal Khul's writings, arhat is the term that indicates achievement of the fourth initiation.

When this important altruistic attitude is achieved, it is put into action by practicing the Six Perfections:

> Giving,
> Ethics,
> Patience,
> Effort,
> Concentration,
> Wisdom.

Tibetan Buddhism sees all religions as having more or less the same viewpoint and goal; no one religion is seen as being better than another. Each person must decide which religion is right for himself. According to the Dalai Lama, the practice of Tibetan Buddhism includes the complete forms of practice of all systems of Buddhism — the low vehicle, the sutra great vehicle, and the mantra great vehicle. A guru or teacher is selected according to a person's interest and disposition, and careful discernment is used to make sure the teacher is qualified.

Crucial to being a Buddhist is the commitment to help others and to avoid harming others. The focus on altruism, unconditional love, compassion, and kindness is the crux of Buddhism. Remaining within society rather than withdrawing is considered important. Great emphasis is placed on doing bodhisattvic deeds; if you read and talk about the doctrine but don't practice it, you are not a true Buddhist. The path is seen as a step-by-step process that does not occur overnight. It is important to develop will power and the recognition that you are limitless and can do anything with the power of your attention and thoughts. Suffering is caused by ignorance and attachment; they must be renounced.

Buddhists do not believe in God in the way members of Western religions do. However, they do believe in Buddha and in deities of a mundane and a supramundane variety. The mundane deities are the Hell beings – hungry ghosts of animals and humans, demigods, and bad spirits. The supramundane deities are the bodhisattvas and the perfected Buddhas. These are the only ones that appear in the Tibetan Buddhist paintings and mandalas. Although not believing in a supreme being, they do practice Deity Yoga which I will explain later in the discussion of meditation practices. A Buddhist practitioner is seen as a soldier in spiritual combat who is fighting ignorance, anger, attachment, pride, ego, negative emotions, negative thoughts, fear, and jealousy. Enemies are not outside but within. As soon as afflictive, or negative, emotions or qualities arise, the Tibetan Buddhist is guided to shift his or her attention and cultivate the opposite quality, using the rational mind. If a person isn't successful at this, then he is guided at least to distract his mind and go for a walk, practice deep breathing, or do anything that will help him to avoid feeding energy to the negative quality.

Buddhists are taught to love their enemies, surrender their negative egos, and give up all desire of trying to win. This is beautifully stated in a Buddhist sutra that says, "When others, out of jealousy, treat me badly with abuse, slander, and so on, I will learn to take all loss and offer the victory to them." Holding this consciousness means looking at those who attack you or are your enemies as spiritual guides and teachers; it is obvious that even greater kindness and altruism should be generated toward such people.

Tibetan Buddhism emphasizes the use of mantras. The most well-known mantra is "Om Mani Padme Hum" which means "Hail to the jewel in the lotus."

Other essential teachings include the necessity of generating the intention and desire to achieve liberation from the wheel of rebirth; holding the correct view of emptiness; and cultivating an altruistic mind.

To achieve an attitude of refuge and a mind of enlightenment, the following verse is often chanted and meditated upon: "Until enlightenment, I go for refuge to the Buddha, the doctrine, and the spiritual community. Through the merit of listening to the doctrine may I achieve Buddhahood in order to help transmigrating beings." (This verse is from Nagarjuna's treatise on the Middle Way.)

Suffering and afflictive emotions are caused by lack of control over the mind and by the actions that stem from this lack of discipline. The Tibetan Buddhist is taught to develop what is called bodhichitta – the intention of obtaining the "omniscience of a Buddha" in order to be of service to others, the all-consuming fire to achieve liberation and Self-realization. This is the mind of enlightenment. Maintaining this state of consciousness at all times will lead to the achievement of the goal. It is this state of mind that keeps the seeker focused on the path and vigilant at all times. Through this practice nirvana will gradually be attained. Among the three jewels, the doctrine is most important.

The overcoming of negative and afflictive emotions is seen as the overcoming of death because birth and death both cease when it is achieved. In Buddhism, a good mind, a good heart, and warm feelings are the most important things. All humans are seen as brothers and sisters, regardless of race, creed, or color. The essence of all spiritual life is the Buddhist's attitudes and feelings toward others. To maintain wisdom, however, it is necessary to have inner strength as well as loving kindness. It is only by mastering the mind that happiness, unchanging equanimity, and inner peace can be attained.

According to the Dalai Lama, anger is the most serious problem facing the world today. When enlightenment and liberation have been achieved no external circumstance can create a negative emotion; all hatred, lust, self-centeredness, harmful intentions, and ego will have been removed.

The generation of bodhichitta, the mind of enlightenment, leads to the practice of the "four immeasurables": love, compassion, joy, and equanimity. This leads to the development of what is called "exceptional bodhichitta," the state of mind of working to achieve complete enlightenment within this lifetime. The cultivation of this attitude is of the highest importance. It is the all-consuming spiritual fire that keeps the Buddhist from giving in to the temptation of the lower self.

Tibetan Buddhists are taught to keep constantly in mind the impermanence of the material world, the precious nature of human life due to the rarity of human birth, and the ease with which death or disease can strike. Thus, it is important not to waste a single moment or bit of energy.

Sensual gluttony is seen as the gate to suffering. For this reason, mindfulness and vigilance are of the highest importance, as are the maintaining of the bodhi mind (the bodhisattva mind) and the Buddha mind. Great determination, courage, and perseverance are needed.

When a mistake is made, regret should be cultivated with firm resolve and a vow never to let it happen again. Tibetan Buddhists are guided to go to sleep thinking a virtuous thought, because that can guide them into the spiritual world where they can perform practices in the dream state. The Dalai Lama has referred to the dream state as a dream within a dream.

A motivational technique to inspire the Buddhist to stay on the path is meditation upon the sufferings of the lower realms. A Tibetan Buddhist is also taught to reflect on what his fate is going to be at the end of his present incarnation. How he lives in this life will determine where he goes in his next life.

All states of consciousness are said to have come from the Clear Light, so the Clear Light mind is the fundamental and innate consciousness of all beings. The Clear Light mind is the true being. It need not be achieved; it is what exists when the illusionary obstructions of ego are removed.

Tibetan Buddhism conceives of two realms of existence after death: favorable or unfavorable, or higher or lower rebirths. A favorable transmigration would include being reborn as a celestial being, a demigod, or a human being; an unfavorable transmigration would include being reborn as an animal, a wandering spirit, or a Hell being. (I personally don't believe that human beings become animals; I do believe, however, an animal can eventually evolve into the human kingdom.)

Once liberation is attained there is no possibility of suffering. Following your dharma is the path that leads to the state of liberation. If you don't have a guru or teacher then you should rely on the Buddha – the word "Buddha" means "fully enlightened."

The Dalai Lama, in his book *The Path of Bliss*, has recommended saying the following statement to yourself when you are about to commit a negative action: "I should not do that as it is against the ideals of the Buddha and his doctrine, and I am a spiritual person, a bhikshu, so I should refrain from such actions." This restraint eventually extends to your dreams as well.

The teachings of compassion and non-harmfulness also apply to animals and nature. Tibetan Buddhists are guided to take refuge in their spiritual communities and not spend time with people who are not dharma practitioners. Some of the methods and techniques of purification in Tibetan Buddhism are reciting mantras, meditating on emptiness, doing prostrations, engaging in Deity Yoga, making offerings, taking religious vows, and reading religious texts.

There are ten negative actions that all Buddhists are guided to renounce: killing, stealing, sexual misconduct, lying, divisive speech, harsh words, senseless gossip, covetousness, harmful intent, and the holding of perverted views.

The root of all suffering is the mind. Practice involves recognizing the negative states and putting an end to them, then identifying the positive states and cultivating those virtues. Negative emotions such as hatred, anger, and desire are the real enemies and should be eliminated. The path to liberation is paved with the releasing of these delusions. There are three higher traits in Tibetan Buddhism: the training of morality, the training of meditative stabilization, and the training of wisdom.

The motivation of the practitioner should be to attain liberation not only for self but for all sentient beings. This requires the rooting out of all self-centered attitudes.

Buddhists are taught not to react emotionally to people who are negative or who are enemies. This attitude is cultivated by seeing all sentient beings as having been friends and relatives in past lives. Such a viewpoint results in feelings of affection and kindness for all people. (In Hinduism or Christianity, this concept is expressed by seeing each person as the Christ, Atma, or Eternal Self.) Buddhists are taught to think of the kindnesses these people have shown them in past lives. That cultivates the desire to repay those kindnesses by helping those people to be free of suffering and to achieve happiness.

The Buddhist begins to see all sentient beings as being the same as himself in desiring to avoid suffering and achieve happiness, thus recognizing the oneness of all humanity. That leads to a feeling of responsibility and a genuine desire to take physical action to help humanity alleviate its suffering. The final step is bodhicitta, the desire to achieve enlightenment in this lifetime so as to be able to help all one's brothers and sisters as much as possible.

When dealing with enemies it is important for the Buddhist to ask himself if the person will always remain that way or if he is capable of change. The recognition that the present state of consciousness is not necessarily permanent serves as a motivation to be concerned with the person's spiritual welfare.

Tibetan Buddhists are taught, in a sense, to exchange themselves for others in terms of their priorities. They are expected to feel indifferent toward themselves and to hold the welfare of others in the position of primary importance. (In Christian and Hindu terms could be equated to the concept that in truth, there is only one being incarnated in all people, animals, plants, and minerals, and that being is God.)

It is highly recommended that the practitioner, when ready, take the vow of the bodhisattva. This is usually done with a guru or spiritual teacher, but if you are not on the Buddhist path yet feel inclined to take this vow, you can do it alone by performing some form of ritual at your own personal altar.

One of the bodhisattva pledges given in the Dalai Lama's book *The Path of Bliss*, is as follows: "Just as the great bodhisattvas of the past first generated bodhicitta [mind of enlightenment], took the vows and dedicated themselves to the bodhisattva deeds, I, too, will take the vows and observe them by engaging in the bodisattva deeds."

Tibetan Buddhists are also taught to practice the Four Ripening Factors which attract disciples and enhance their spiritual potentials:

1. Giving material aid;.
2. Speaking eloquently;
3. Always giving the right counsel;
4. Setting an example by living the principles taught.

Other ideals of the Tibetan Buddhist are:

To not speak of the faults of others;

To not break the spiritual vows you have made;

To not think of the failings of others, even when you see them;

To not respond in kind when scolded by others;

To not retaliate when harmed by others;

To not blame others for one's own shortcomings;

To not become inflated or arrogant on account of one's spiritual practices;

To undertake all activities with the single thought of benefiting others.

## Tibetan Buddhist Meditation

The first precept in understanding Tibetan Buddhist meditation is having an object upon which to meditate. Tibetan Buddhists usually use the visualization of Buddha Shakyamuni. Also used are Avalokitesvara (Quan Yin), the bodhisattva of compassion and mercy, and Manjushri, the deity of wisdom.

After clearing and organizing your meditation area and finding a comfortable place to sit, face the east. Rejoice in the fortunate opportunity you have been given to practice the dharma which will lead to enlightenment for yourself and all sentient beings.

Begin the meditation by visualizing your object of refuge in front of you in space, seated on a small throne. This is your own spiritual master or teacher in the form of Buddha Shakyamuni. His or her left hand is holding a bowl of nectar symbolizing victory over death and all negative obstructions. Behind him or her, Buddha is seated on a vast throne. Surrounding him are all the gurus from whom you have received teachings. On Shakyamuni's left, imagine Manjushri (the deity of wisdom) and on the right, Maitreya Buddha. All of them are surrounded by meditational deities called bodhisattvas, arhats, heroes, heroines, and protectors. Imagine, in front of these great Buddhas, their holy scriptures which are created of Light. This entire scene is called the merit field. See everyone in your merit field looking at you pleasantly. Then repeat the refuge formula:

I go for refuge to the guru.

I go for refuge to the Buddha.

I go for refuge to the dharma (the doctrine).

I go for refuge to the sangha (the spiritual community).

Imagine that surrounding you are all the sentient beings of humanity. When you recite the refuge formula, imagine that all sentient beings are reciting it in unison with you.

Visualize the nectars from the bowls of the Buddhas descending in different colors and purifying your mind, body, and emotions in relation to the Three Jewels (Buddha, the dharma, and spiritual practice). Imagine that you are personally being placed under the care of all the Buddhas. This can also be visualized as Light rays extending from the Buddha's heart and entering you and all other sentient beings. Spiritual nectar flows through these Light beams. Then recite the formula to create the bodhicitta, the mind of enlightenment:

I go for refuge, until I am enlightened, to the Buddha, the dharma, and the highest assembly. From the virtuous merit that I collect by practicing giving and other perfections, may I attain Buddhahood to be able to benefit all beings.

Recite this verse three to seven times. Visualize the Buddha Shakyamuni floating above your crown chakra and then moving down into your body and dissolving and merging into you. See your body, speech, and mind becoming one with the Buddha. Then dissolve into emptiness.

Imagine yourself arising into Buddha Shakyamuni sitting on a throne upraised by lions. Imagine that you have achieved perfect Buddhahood using thought, feeling, and visualizations. Then send infinite numbers of Light rays from your heart to all sentient beings, transforming all of them into Shakyamuni Buddhas also.

Rejoice at being able to be of service to all sentient beings. See all the other deities as being pleased and see them all dissolve into you through your crown chakra. See yourself merge with your own spiritual teacher and guru. See yourself dissolve and become the Clear Light of emptiness.

At the very end of the meditation, if you like, you can chant the Aum mantra, or Om Mani Padme Hum, or any other mantra or name of God you desire to attune to.

# 19

## *Lao-tzu and the Taoist Religion*

*Vast, indeed, is the ultimate Tao,
spontaneously itself, apparently without acting,
end of all ages and beginning of all ages,existing
before Earth and existing before Heaven, silently
embracing the whole of time.*

Tao Te Ching

Taoism is one of the three main religions of China, along with Confucianism and Buddhism. It was created by Lao-tzu in the sixth century B.C. It was he who wrote the book that is considered the bible of the Taoist religion, the *Tao Te Ching*.

The first section of the book tells the why of the universe, and the second section tells the how of life. The word Tao is very difficult to translate and that is how Lao-tzu wanted it. The closest approximation is "nature," or "the way of the universe."

Lao-tzu attempted to describe the Tao when he said, "There is something undifferentiated and yet perfect which existed before Heaven and Earth ever came into being. I know not its name, and if I must designate it, I can call it only Tao." It is this Way, or Tao, that sets the standard for the proper life of every human being.

Lao-tzu said that there was but one virtue – to stay in harmony with the Tao. He said that to do so was the only way to know well-being, harmony, health, and abundance. If a person, city, state, or country rebelled against the Tao, disaster and suffering would surely follow. Taoists are taught to see the Tao in all beings and all things.

Part of understanding the Tao is understanding the Taoist concept of wu-wei, or non-action. It does not mean no action but, rather, no going beyond spontaneous action. When a person is in tune with the Tao, he acts spontaneously, effortlessly, and efficiently, hardly giving the matter a thought, just as branches naturally bend toward the sun. Being in the Tao is an attempt to stay in harmony with nature.

Taoist literature has defined the Tao in the following manner:

> The eternal may best be described as the Tao, or Way, signifying these three and more: the moral and physical order of the universe, the path of perfect virtue which Heaven itself follows, and the absolute; yet so great it is that the Tao that can be described is not the eternal Tao.

> I believe that the goal and the path of life are essentially the same, and that man's highest ideal is to follow the Tao which can be known only to those exalted beings who have realized it for themselves. Reflections of the beyond are of no avail; better to live in perfect harmony now by seeking the depth of things.

I have always related to the concept of the Tao, even though it is difficult to explain. To me, it clearly is about the concept of yin and yang. The Tao is like surfing a wave: if you go too fast and get ahead of the wave, it will crash behind you and you will get dumped; if you go too slowly, you will miss the wave. The Tao means finding perfect harmony, the balance that lies right in the center of the wave of yin and yang. Tao is the still point at which you are in attunement with your soul, your spirit, and God.

Everything has a Tao. When you are dating, for example, there is a certain Tao of divine timing for moving the relationship along. There is a Tao of working and even a Tao of sleeping for a given day. There are infinite polarities and balances, all of which have a Tao. That does not mean you have to think about them necessarily, it is just a matter of staying in harmony with them. To my way of thinking, if you always listen to your higher self, soul, or God rather than to your negative ego and lower self, then you stay in the Tao.

The Tao also represents universal law. If you are out of harmony with universal law, then you suffer. When you are in the Tao, you are guided by your intuition, and your three minds and four bodies are in harmony.

There is a Tao of working and playing, of talking and being silent, of when and how long to exercise; the list of examples could be infinite. There is a subtle intelligence within you which the Chinese call the Tao and which Westerners might call God that gives you guidance, moment to moment, if you tune into it. When you live in the Tao you are living in grace instead of under the strictures of karma. You are learning the easy way instead of in the school of hard knocks.

The *Tao Te Ching* treats the Tao as the great, all-controlling principle of the universe. The purpose of life is to realize the Tao on a daily basis and, hence, achieve inner peace and enlightenment. Lao-tzu believed that if every person stayed in harmony with the Tao, spiritual fellowship and brotherly love would be manifest among all people, and war would be an impossibility. Even though he lived six hundred years before Jesus Christ, he said, "Repay evil with good." Taoist philosophy teaches the virtues of a simple life, denial of selfishness, and mystical union with the Ultimate.

Taoism and Confucianism were a good balance for each other, and it is interesting to note that the founders of both paths lived in the same century. To apply Djwhal Khul's terminology, the two seemed to embody the paths of the mystic and the occultist, with Confucianism being practical and down to Earth in its ethical and moral concerns for society, and Taoism having a certain mystical and free-flowing quality, such as that which is indicated in the following quote from the Taoist scripture: "I believe the omniscient and impersonal Supreme is implacable, beyond concern for human woe, but that there exist lesser divinities, from the high gods who endure for eons to the nature spirits and demons, and that the lives of these angelic and satanic beings are interwoven with our own."

Clearly, a belief in God is indicated here and a belief in a certain hierarchy of spiritual beings. Taoist thought also carried a belief in resurrection of the soul as can be clearly seen in the following passage in the *Tao Te Ching*: "He who contains within himself the richness of Tao's virtue is like a babe; no poisonous insects sting him nor fierce beasts attack him. He who attains the Tao is everlasting. Though his body may decay, he never perishes." In time, the hope of attaining the Tao became the hope of attaining immortality on this Earth. Clearly, realizing the Tao is, to the Taoist, equivalent to the realizing of the Christ by the Christian; the words are different, but the ideal is the same.

The cosmology of Taoism speaks of a variety of different heavens where spiritually minded people go after death. These heavens have served as powerful sources of inspiration for many paintings.

The Chinese family includes ancestors who have passed on to the spirit world. Property and possessions belong to the ancestors as well as to those who are living. When a person dies, it is his or her hope to become a good spirit who is helpful and beneficent to his heirs. The dying pilgrim's fate is determined by his own past actions in the lifetime he has just lived.

Next to the quality of wu-wei (inactivity, or unforced action), the most precious jewel is the quality of humility. The third most important jewel is frugality. Lao-tzu said, "The wise man doth not accumulate. The more he expends for others, the more doth he possess of his own. The more he giveth to others, the more hath he for himself." Generosity might be a better term to describe this jewel.

Lao-tzu's teachings remind me of Buddhism in their minimizing of the concept of a Supreme Being, or God. Buddhism asserts belief in Buddha;

Taoism is similar, although God is mentioned. His name is Shang-ti. It is quite a curious phenomenon that both these religions accept immortality, other dimensions of reality, and hierarchies of spiritual beings, despite their nonacceptance of the Western concept of God; at the same time, the ideals of all are almost exactly in harmony with each other.

# 20

## Confucius and Confucianism

*I believe that man is master
of his own life and fate, free to conduct himself
as he wills, and that he should cultivate qualities
of benevolence, righteousness, propriety,
wisdom and sincerity.*

Confucius

Confucius, or K'ung Fu-Tse as he was called in Chinese, was an early incarnation of Ascended Master Djwhal Khul. Born in 551 B.C., Confucius supported his mother after his father died at an early age. She, in turn, saw to it that he was properly educated in music, history, poetry, and sports. Confucius was both a gentleman and scholar. He had one unsuccessful marriage and was graced with a son. After his mother's death, he went into mourning and at the end of that period he became a teacher of the six disciplines – poetry, music, history, government, etiquette, and divination.

Confucius aspired to a high office in the government. He proceeded through the ministries and became the chief justice in his state. Upon leaving that position, he spent a long time wandering with several disciples. After that period, he received an appointment by the duke to a prestigious post which enabled him to spend the rest of his life compiling his writings, which are known as the Confucian classics. They are *The Book of History, Shu-Ching; The Book of Poetry, Shih-Ching; The Book of Rites, Li-Chi; The Book of Changes, I-Ching; The Annals of Spring and Autumn, Ch'um Ch'iu;* and *The Book of Music, Ueh-Ching.* Some of these books were compilations of material from ancient Chinese history.

The basic ideal of Confucius was that of Jen which means benevo-

lence, true manhood, altruism, character, human-heartedness, steadfast-
ness, humanity. It is this quality that makes a human different from an
animal. When Jen is applied to human relations it becomes Te, which is
translated as "virtue."

A secondary significant ideal was to live by Li, which means living with
reverence, or propriety. To Confucius this meant living according to
appropriate form, social ceremonies, and the proper manner of public
conduct. It meant to have courtesy in all social and religious behavior. It
meant living a moral and religious life. Living that way meant that people
would give proper reverence and sanctification to the spirit of the universe.
Li establishes harmony in the individual, the home, the village, and the
country.

Confucian philosophy emphasized the formal and accepted patterns of
politeness and good manners of his time. Five hundred years before Christ,
Confucius said, "What you do not want done to yourself, do not do to
others." This golden rule was referred to as Shu, or reciprocity.

Confucius' ideal was the Chun-Tzu, also known as the superior man.
The superior man followed the five constant virtues — self-respect, magnanimity, sincerity, earnestness, and benevolence. To Confucius, life's central purpose was to serve humankind; his focus was on right human
relationships. God's will was fulfilled when man practiced right moral law.
Chinese people, even to this day, have concerned themselves less with the
hereafter than with the proper conduct of affairs and the attainment of
happiness on Earth, very much a Confucian goal..

When asked by a disciple about life after death, Confucius replied,
"We have not yet learned to know life. How can we know death?" His focus
was on ethical teaching rather than on a revealed religion.

Confucius' teachings have dominated every aspect of China's thought
and culture for twenty-five centuries which is quite amazing, for Confucius
was not really a founder of a religion but more of a reformer and conserver
of it. When it was starting to decay, he revived it. Confucius, himself, said
that he was "not a maker, but a transmitter, believing in the ancients."

The century during which Confucius lived was one of the most
extraordinary in the history of this planet. The sixth century B.C. saw not
only Confucius but also Buddha in India, Zoroaster in Persia, Jeremiah
and Ezekial in Israel, Mahavira in India, Pythagoras in Greece, and
Lao-tsu, also in China, a contemporary of Confucius. Five different major
religions arose during that century, including the three main religions of
China to this day — Confucianism, Taoism, and Buddhism.

By the time Confucius was twenty-two years of age, he was already
considered a great teacher. He was a man who loved the ancients, and he
devoted his life to the study of their teachings. For many years Confucius

spent all of his time collecting and editing the old writings. Confucius did not seek to break with the past but rather to heal the breach that had already occurred, infusing life into China's decaying religion. By editing and compiling the sacred writings, he established their supreme authority. His most important contribution was in the field of ethics and his proverbs are quoted to this day. A century after Confucius died, the great sage Mencius arose to spread the Confucian doctrine.

The essence of the teaching is to strive for perfect virtue in every thought, word, and deed. In Confucianism there are five great relationships that, if virtuous, make society work in perfect order and harmony. These five relationships are those between father and son, elder brother and younger brother, husband and wife, elder and junior, and, lastly, between a ruler and his subjects. Many of Confucius' teachings deal with the standards and moral codes of behavior that should be met in these five areas.

Confucius perceived that all people were inherently good at heart, and that salvation could be achieved through the realization of this essential nature. Charity, righteousness, propriety, and moral consciousness were not qualities that had to be drilled into humans; they were innate. Confucius considered character to be the root of all civilization.

Confucianism is rational, orderly, practical, and humanistic. Taoism, on the other hand, is romantic, intuitive, mystical, and vague. To my way of thinking, together they make up a whole, the balance of yin and yang. Confucius was not seen as a god but rather as a sage or an ideal.

## Proverbs and Teachings of Confucius

I believe in the presence of the Supreme Ruler in all things and in Heaven as the ethical principle whose only law is order, impersonal and yet interested in the affairs of mankind.

I believe that man is master of his own life and fate, free to conduct himself as he wills, and that he should cultivate qualities of benevolence, righteousness, propriety, wisdom, and sincerity.

I believe that the family is the most essential institution among men and that religion should lend its potency to the family as well as to the state.

I believe that the purpose of life is to pursue an orderly and reverent existence in accord with the principle of Li [propriety and virtue] so as to become the superior man or woman.

# 21

## *Hermes-Thoth and the Seven Great Universal Laws*

*Everything is dual;
everything has poles; everything has
its pair of opposites; like and unlike are the same;
opposites are identical in nature, but different in
degree; extremes meet. All truths are but
half-truths; all paradoxes may
be reconciled.*

Hermes-Thoth

Hermes Trismegistus, also known as the Egyptian god Thoth, lived in Atlantis and Egypt for over two thousand years, according to the channelings of Djwhal Khul and Vywamus. While alive, he was known throughout the world as the Master of the Masters.

Egypt was one of the highest spiritual civilizations that has ever existed on Planet Earth, and Hermes played a key role in its flourishing. He was the father of occult wisdom and one of the founders on Earth of astrology and alchemy. The Egyptians were so amazed by the profundity of the man and his teachings that they deified him under the name Thoth, and he became one of their gods. In later times, the civilization of Greece made him one of their gods also, calling him Hermes, God of Wisdom. He was considered the messenger of the gods.

The term "trimegistus" means thrice great. Hermes' name became synonymous with "the Fount of Wisdom." In his later incarnation as Buddha, he would be known in a similar way, for Buddha embodied wisdom. (Christ embodied wisdom and love, while the Lord Maitreya currently embodies wisdom, love, and power.) Hermes was also called the scribe of the gods.

The Hermetic teachings are found in all lands and all religions because of the universality of their appeal. In early days a compilation of certain basic Hermetic maxims, axioms, and precepts was made and passed from teacher to student; it is called *The Kybalion*. The other important collection of Hermetic writing is *The Divine Pymander* which sets forth a complete system of metaphysical theology and philosophy.

Later, during the civilization of Rome, he was again deified. His name then was Mercury, and he was usually imaged with a winged cap and sandals.

Below are several quotations from the writings of Hermes.

> O people of the Earth, men born and made of the elements but with the spirit of the divine man within you, rise from your sleep of ignorance! Be sober and thoughtful. Realize that your home is not in the Earth but in the Light. Why have you delivered yourselves over unto death, having power to partake of immortality? Repent, and change your minds. Depart from the dark night and forsake corruption forever. Prepare yourselves to climb through the seven rings to blend your souls with the eternal Light.

> Where fall the footsteps of the master, the ears of those ready for his teaching open wide.

> When the ears of the students are ready to hear, then cometh the lips to fill them with wisdom.

## The Seven Great Hermetic Principles

"The principles of truth are seven; he who knows these, understandingly, possesses the magic key before whose touch all the doors of the temple fly open." — *The Kybalion*

    I.   The principle of mentalism
   II.   The principle of correspondence
  III.   The principle of vibration
  IV.   The principle of polarity
   V.   The principle of rhythm
  VI.   The principle of cause and effect
 VII.   The principle of gender

These seven Hermetic principles are the basis for the entire body of Hermetic philosophy. Below is an in-depth explanation of them.

### I. The Principle of Mentalism
"The all is mind; the universe is mental."

This principle embodies the understanding that everything in the universe is created by thought. There is nothing that exists in the material universe in which this is not the case.

Edgar Cayce, in his channelings of the Universal Mind, said over and over again, "Thoughts are things." The entire universe was created by the thought of God. As God's sons and daughters, humans create reality both metaphysically and physically by the power of mind. The great law of spiritual psychology is that thought creates reality. Everything that exists is spirit: matter is just densified spirit; spirit is just refined matter. All is simply energy.

### II. The Principle of Correspondence
"As above, so below; as below, so above."

This famous aphorism was created by Hermes. I have mentioned it many times in my books because it has such wide application. What this law means is that the thoughts and images you hold in your conscious and subconscious minds will manifest their mirror likenesses in your external circumstances. The outer world is a mirror of your inner world. If you hold thoughts of poverty, you will have no money. If you hold images of ill health, that will manifest in your physical body. This law works unceasingly for the good or the bad. By understanding the law, you can use it for your benefit instead of your detriment.

The most profound application of this law is seen in the life of Sathya Sai Baba. Whatever he thinks instantly manifests on a material level. He creates physical objects with a wave of his hand, and he says he does it by just thinking and imaging what he wants to create. This is the same law but here it is speeded up. Earth is a school for practicing these laws of mind control.

Imagine what would happen if the average person on the street were manifesting his thoughts instantly, as Sai Baba does. If he had a negative thought about someone at this level of vibration it might actually physically kill the person. Imagine what all your negative thoughts and emotions would instantly do to your health. For most people, it is a good thing that thoughts don't manifest that quickly yet, or they would be in a lot of trouble. The higher the level of your initiation and the higher your vibration, the more quickly your thoughts will manifest. That is why the spiritual path at the higher levels has been called the straight and narrow path and why it is visualized as a pyramid that gets narrower as you move toward the apex.

### III. The Principle of Vibration
"Nothing rests; everything moves; everything vibrates."

This principle explains the difference among the various manifestations of matter and spirit. From pure spirit all the way down to the grossest level of matter, there is a continuum of vibrations. Every atom and molecule is vibrating with a certain motion, speed, and frequency. It is the combination of these factors that determines the form of any given object, be it of a physical or metaphysical nature.

Everything is in motion and is vibrating, and nothing is at rest. Even a physical object, a chair, for example, is actually in a state of motion. The atoms and molecules are vibrating, and there is space between the atoms and molecules. This is true of the atom as it is true of the solar system, galaxy, universe, and omniverse, for the omniverse is nothing more than a large atom. The microcosm is like the macrocosm. Sai Baba can take a physical object and transform it into a new object just by changing that motion. You do the same thing using your thoughts.

The entire universe is in a state of motion revolving about the Great Central Sun. Every atom is a mini-universe within every molecule of your physical body. How you think manifests in your emotions, actions, health, and what you attract to yourself because energy follows thought. The ideal is to create a motion that is determined by your higher self, rather than by your lower self, or negative ego. Each of the seven initiations is a higher level of vibration and motion. God is the highest pinnacle of vibrational frequency. That must be your goal.

### IV. The Principle of Polarity
"Everything is dual; everything has poles; everything has its pair of opposites; like and unlike are the same; opposites are identical in nature, but different in degree; extremes meet; all truths are but half-truths; all paradoxes may be reconciled."

This is a fascinating principle. Take, for example, heat and cold. Although they are opposites, they are really the same thing; it is merely a matter of different degrees. The same could be said of spirit and matter. They could be likened to water: freeze water and it becomes ice, or matter; boil water and it evaporates and becomes a gas, or spirit. They are identical in nature but different in degree.

If you look at a thermometer, where does heat terminate and cold begin? In actuality, it is totally relative to body type and individual preference. The same principle applies to all pairs of opposites — light and dark, large and small, hard and soft, positive and negative.

The principle also applies to the mental plane. Take, for example, love and hate. They are the same but different in degree. The importance of this law lies in understanding your ability to transmute vibrations from one extreme to the other. This, in reality, is the study of alchemy.

The alchemists of the Middle Ages were preoccupied with changing base metals into gold. This is possible, as Sai Baba demonstrates so clearly and instantly. However, the real meaning of alchemy is that you can change your base thoughts and emotions into spiritual gold, or soul-realized energies.

Hate can be transformed by the power of your mind into love. Your lower self can be transformed into your higher self. Your physical body can be transformed into your Lightbody (ascension). Separation can be turned into oneness. Guidance by your negative ego can be turned into guidance by your soul. An empty bank account can be transformed in a full bank account. All this can be achieved by using the art of polarization.

To accomplish all that, you simply need to polarize your consciousness differently. If you are run by your emotional body, you need to become polarized in your mental body. If you are identified with your mental body or intellectual self, you might need to become polarized in your soul. If you are merged with your soul, you will need to become polarized in your monad. If you are merged with your monad, you need to become polarized in God. All are degrees of the same thing.

The science of attitudinal healing involves working with this art of polarization. That is why psychics were predicting a shift of the physical poles of Earth – the poles of humanity's consciousness were not shifting from fear to love.

### V. The Principle of Rhythm
"Everything flows, out and in; everything has its tides; all things rise and fall; the pendulum-swing manifests in everything; the measure of the swing to the right is the measure of the swing to the left; rhythm compensates."

You can see this law manifesting in every aspect of life: in the tides of the oceans, in your need for sleep after a day of work, in the creation of a star and its eventual collapse, in the rise and fall of nations, and even in the operation of the omniverse. For every action there is an equal and opposite reaction.

You see it in your breathing; you see it in God's breath as He breathes creation out and then breathes creation in. You see it in the movement of stars and in the science of astrology as the Earth moves through the signs of the zodiac.

You can also see the law of rhythm operating in human mental states, where the Hermetic practitioner finds its greatest and most useful application. Hermetists cannot annul this principle or cause it to cease operating; however, they have learned to escape its effects upon themselves to a certain degree by applying the mental law of neutralization. The degree to which they are able to do so is determined by their application of this law and their level of initiation. Hermetists have learned how to use the law instead of being used by it.

The Hermetist's understanding the law of polarity polarizes him at the point at which he desires to rest and then neutralizes the rhythmic swing of the pendulum which would tend to carry him to the opposite mental and emotional pole. The master does this by using will and detachment to create a state of consciousness that is not swung back and forth like a pendulum. Whereas the masses of humanity live on mental and emotional roller coasters, the ideal is to attain a state of consciousness of divine indifference, evenmindedness, equanimity, inner peace, joy, unceasing happiness, and bliss.

Krishna explains the very same teaching in the *Bhagavad-Gita* when he says that the goal is to remain evenminded in the face of profit or loss, pleasure or pain, sickness or health, victory or defeat, rejection or praise. There is a point of neutrality or objectivity or divine detachment that is not caught up in the pendulum-swing between polarities. There is a state called God-consciousness in which you don't have to have a bad day. In the highest application of this principle of neutrality, it is even applied to the physical body; for example, Sai Baba never sleeps, never needs food, never gets tired. He can bilocate and be in two places at the same time. This is the ascended state of consciousness in which the monad, or spirit, merges completely with the physical vehicle, and the physical body is turned into Light. Duality is transcended.

Whether you are on an emotional roller coaster or are evenminded and have unceasing equanimity and joy is determined by the polarization of your mind. That is why the understanding of these principles is so important.

In his later life as Buddha, Hermes expounded on this point further when he said, "All suffering comes from one's attachments and wrong points of view." Part of the purpose of writing this book is to show how the principles are the same in all religions — whether you study the Egyptian teachings, Hawaiian Huna, Buddhism, Christianity, Hinduism, Taoism, the Koran, or another — even though they might be expressed in slightly different ways. The other interesting thing, of course, is to see how it is often the same being who started two or three different religious movements in the course of several incarnations.

### VI. The Principle of Cause and Effect
"Every cause has its effect; every effect has its cause; everything happens according to law; chance is but a name for law not recognized; there are many planes of causation, but nothing escapes the law."

There are no accidents. Everything in the universe is governed by laws: there are physical laws, emotional laws, mental laws, and spiritual laws. By understanding these laws you can learn to operate in grace instead of accumulating karma.

Many times it is difficult to know why things happen. That is because there are seven dimensions of reality in which causations can occur. As Edgar Cayce said over and over again in his readings from the Universal Mind, "Every jot and tittle of the law is fulfilled." No one escapes anything, even though it might sometimes appear that some people are going unpunished. In truth, they are not.

The Hermetists understand the art of rising above the ordinary plane of cause and effect by moving onto a high plane of consciousness and, hence, becoming masters instead of victims, and causes instead of effects.

The average person on the street is an effect, not a cause. He is a victim of thoughts, moods, emotions, desire, appetites, his lower self, other people, biorhythms, his physical body, past lives, subconscious programming, heredity, the weather, astrological influences, vital forces, discarnate spirits, glamour, maya, illusion, and the environment, to name a few. The master rises above such elements and masters them. By the time of the sixth initiation and ascension, all of them have been transcended. The masters obey the causation of the higher planes, but they help to rule them on their own planes. At each level of initiation a master rises to another plane of consciousness, hence becoming a greater cause.

The key for most people on the Earth plane is to gain mastery over the mind, which leads to mastery over the emotions and desires and also to mastery over the physical body and appetites. Djwhal Khul has called this mastery over your three lower vehicles – the physical, astral, and mental bodies.

The basic causes of the details of your life are the thoughts and images you hold in your conscious and subconscious minds. By learning to be absolutely vigilant and allowing into your mind only thoughts of God, love, perfection, perfect health, prosperity, joy, oneness, and equanimity, you will create those qualities both inwardly and outwardly. Your thinking must be subservient to your soul and monad (spirit), instead of to your lower self and negative ego. When these lessons are mastered then there is no longer any reason to attend this school called Earth life, except for service to your brothers and sisters who have not yet mastered them.

Be the cause, be the master, be the cocreator with God that you truly are. Then you are using this principle instead of allowing it to use you. If you are not a master, you are a victim; that is the law of polarity. Change your polarization with the power of your mind and the power of your God-given free choice.

## VI. The Principle of Gender

"Gender is in everything; everything has its masculine and
feminine principles; gender manifests on all planes."

Everything has a yin and yang. On the physical plane each person has a male or a female physical body, however androgynous he or she might be in terms of thoughts and feelings.

In Chinese philosophy, foods are divided into yin and yang. This law applies not only on the physical plane, but also on the emotional, mental, and spiritual planes. Father God and Mother Earth; yang emotions and yin emotions; yang thoughts and yin thoughts. I have listed the yin and yang qualities at the close of this section.

The key point here is that the spiritual path is the path of balance and integration. Buddha called it the Middle Way. He demonstrated that the path to God was not the path of either self-indulgence or asceticism but was the path of balancing the male and female aspects within the self and also of balancing the Heavenly and Earthly aspects within the self.

The spiritual path also includes the balancing of the three minds, the four bodies, and the seven chakras. It also means proper balance between the soul and the ego. This is achieved by transcending negative ego, hence keeping the ego in its proper relationship to soul, allowing it to take care of the physical body but not to interpret your life.

As mastery is achieved this balanced state becomes more habitual and doesn't require as much time and energy. Balance is achieved by "knowing thyself" and understanding the universal laws that govern your being. To know God, you must understand God's laws.

## Yin and Yang Qualities that Should be Balanced

| Positive Yin | Positive Yang |
|---|---|
| Love | Personal Power |
| Compassion | Discipline |
| Forgiveness | Assertiveness |
| Joy | Discernment |
| Cooperation | Focus |
| Self-love | Self-mastery |
| Acceptance | Responsibility |
| Humility | Nonattachment |
| Gentleness | Patience |
| Peace | Faith |
| Flexibility | Decisiveness |
| Sensitivity | Organization |
| Receptivity | Perseverance |
| Openness | Givingness |
| Intuition | Logic |
| Feeling | Confidence |
| | Cocreativity |
| | Nonjudgmentalness |

| Negative Yin | Negative Yang |
|---|---|
| Hurt | Rigidity |
| Depression | Neurosis |
| Feelings of rejection | Anger |
| Moodiness | Violence |
| Defensiveness | Attack |
| Fear | Criticism |
| Insecurity | Superiority |
| Worry | Impatience |
| Laziness | Hate |
| Low self-esteem | Revenge |
| Guilt | Intolerance |
| Victim consciousness | Pride |
| Neediness | Selfishness |
| Self-pity | Resentfulness |
| Loneliness | Jealousy |
| Shyness | Addiction to work |
| Procrastination | |

## Balances of Life

| Feminine Energy | Masculine Energy |
|---|---|
| Earth Mother | Heavenly Father |
| Night | Day |
| Moon | Sun |
| Receptivity | Expressiveness |
| Play | Work |
| Silence | Speech |
| Inward energy | Outward energy |
| Flow | Organization |
| Hiding | Visibility |
| Feeling | Thinking |
| Passivity | Activity |
| Lack of focus | Focus |
| Sensitivity | Detachment |
| Processing | Goal-orientation |
| Orientation in space | Orientation in time |
| Continuous existence | Cause and Effect |
| Sensuality | Intellectuality |
| Intuition | Logic |
| Emotionality | Rationality |
| Heart orientation | Mind orientation |

| <u>**Feminine Energy**</u> | <u>**Masculine Energy**</u> |
|---|---|
| Slowness | Speed |
| Flexibility | Discipline |
| Openness | Inhibition |
| Allowingness | Willfulness |
| Receptivity | Assertiveness |
| Love | Firmness |
| Listening | Speaking |
| Water | Fire |
| Earth | Air |
| Personal orientation | Impersonal orientation |
| Matter | Spirit |

# 22

## *Akhenaton, the Egyptian Pharaoh*

*Every cause has its effect;*
*every effect has its cause; everything happens*
*according to law; chance is but a name for law*
*not recognized; there are many planes of*
*causation, but nothing*
*escapes the law.*

The Kybalion

King Akhenaton is most famous for reestablishing monotheism in Egypt in a civilization that was at the time of his reign very polytheistic. It was King Akhenaton's mother, an Egyptian Salemite physician, who taught her son the great teachings of Melchizedek which he adopted. No one since Abraham had had such a clear understanding of these teachings. Historians speak of him as one of the most remarkable persons in human history, a man who was in many ways ahead of his time. He kept alive on a vast scale the doctrine of El Elyon, the Most High God. He was the first king of any nation on Earth to try to move his entire country in this fashion.

According to channeled information from Vywamus through Janet McClure of The Tibetan Foundation, the same soul who was King Akhenaton was also Zoroaster and later was St. Peter, the disciple of Christ. He incarnated again in this present period as Brian Grattan who wrote *The Rider on the White Horse* and a double book, *Mahatma I & II.* According to these channelings, Peter was the first person incarnated on Earth to anchor into the physical the energy of the Mahatma, also known as the Avatar of Synthesis. According to his book, in this life Grattan has ascended.

From these incarnations it is clear that this soul has had a great influence on the evolution of Planet Earth. Just as Akhenaton was following in the footsteps of Melchizedek in his lifetime as King Akhenaton, he followed in the same footsteps again as Peter.

Akhenaton established monotheism by having his people worship the Sun God, Ra. All the other gods were absorbed into the one Sun God. Outwardly, before his people, he worshiped the Sun God, Ra; however, inwardly and with his more advanced associates, he worshiped the One God, the Creator, Aton. He actually wrote a book called *The One God*. The book was destroyed after his death when the more ego-oriented priests attempted to regain power.

In *The Rider on the White Horse*, Brian Grattan writes that during his life as King Akhenaton he wrote one hundred thirty-seven hymns, twelve of which were preserved in the Old Testament in the book of Psalms, although they have since been assigned Hebrew authorship.

King Akhenaton expounded a philosophy that said God created not only Egypt but the entire world and universe, including all people, animals, and things. This was a very advanced concept for the egocentric and poorly educated people of the time. His concept of deity was even more advanced than the later Hebrew religion, which also spoke of the One God.

King Akhenaton's skills in providing material security and prosperity for his people were not as advanced as his spiritual development. This would prove to be his Achilles' heel. Upon his death, the materialistic priests convinced the nation to go back to worshiping the old gods. The concept and ideal of the One God persisted in the minds of the people, however.

Some historians say that because of the reconversion that occurred after his death, he failed in his mission. I think a more appropriate historical perspective would be to say that he was quite successful in planting a great many seeds which sprouted in Egypt and had repercussions later in Palestine and Greece. The mass consciousness was ripened for developments that were to come. The *Cambridge History Book*, Volume II, says of King Akhenaton, "The modern world has yet to value this man who, in an era so remote and under conditions so adverse, became the world's first prophet of internationalism, the most remarkable figure in the ancient world."

# 23

## *Orpheus, Founder of the Greek Mystery School*

*I am a child of Earth
and of the starry sky, yet my origin
is in Heaven.*

The Golden Tablets of Orpheus

Orpheus founded the first Greek mystery school during the sixth century B.C. and established the science of initiation, having both studied and taught this ancient science during his wide-ranging travels. The name Orpheus actually means "he who heals with light." Both Pythagoras and Plato were strongly influenced by his teachings. The goal of the Orphic mysteries was to attain spiritual awareness. Orpheus was the founder of theology in Greece, and within that context he laid down the moral ideals of Greece for centuries to come. He was prophet, poet, and priest. He was also a past life of Gautama Buddha.

While still young he traveled to Egypt to study the Egyptian mysteries. When he returned he had attained mastery in medicine, astrology, and magic. He was also an accomplished musician.

The focus of Orpheus' work was to establish the divine nature of man. He emphasized personal responsibility and purification so that the divine nature could be revealed. Once an initiate lived these ideals he was said to be "living the Orphic life." He taught the truth of reincarnation, affirming that it was required by spiritual law that humans forget their past lives upon incarnation into a new body.

Orpheus wrote extensively, and among the works ascribed to him are *The Enthronings of the Great Mother*, *The Sacred Vesture*, and *The Rite of the Girdle.* The last writing tells of an ancient initiation ceremony in which the initiate is given a band or cord of gold. It is a ceremony much like the one all Hindu boys go through in which they are given a red thread that they carry with them for the rest of their lives. But Orpheus' best-known writing is called *Hymns of Orpheus.* Apollonius said that the followers of Orpheus should be called magicians because of the secret magic found in these hymns.

Orpheus also taught mantras and words of power. He composed an alphabet and a system of hieroglyphics. He gave prophecies and oracles. Legend has it that wild animals were tamed by his divine melodies as were the lower selves and animal natures of humans. He was a master healer who channeled his healing energies into his writings, his teachings, and his music. He spoke a great deal about divine essence, maintaining that all things have their source in divine essence and that everything returns back to it.

Legend also says that he sailed with Jason and the Argonauts to seize the golden fleece. (The film version of this story is one of my favorite movies of all time.)

Orpheus might be most famous for the golden tablets that were recently discovered in tombs in southern Italy. They date from the fourth to the third century B.C. Inscriptions engraved on the tombs give instructions for directing the deceased into the astral world after death. It is a sort of book of the dead similar to that used by the Tibetans and Egyptians.

On one of the tablets it says, "I am a child of Earth and of the starry sky, yet my origin is in Heaven." In the next part, the soul asks to drink of the waters of memory so it can remember how it existed before it fell under the illusion of matter. The goal of the Orphic mysteries was liberation from the wheel of rebirth which was achieved through a process of purification and initiation.

The golden tablets show the need to live a righteous, moral life and teach the need for confessions and self-discipline. Certain prayers were constantly repeated, and sacraments of communion and purification followed specific initiations. The Orphic initiates all wore pure white robes and were required to be vegetarians and to fast at certain intervals. The initiates of Orpheus were known throughout the country for their demonstration of the highest virtue and purity. Dionysus was considered the savior in the Orphic teachings just as Jesus is the Savior in Christianity.

On the day of initiation, the initiate carried a symbolic serpent which might have been a symbol for the raised kundalini. During the initiation ceremony the initiate performed a sacred dance and was then baptized in holy water. The skin of a young fawn was fastened over his clothes to symbolize his being spiritually reborn; the higher self had triumphed over the lower self. Each initiate was given the promise of immortality and of union with God at the time of his passing.

Orpheus taught that the body was a tomb for the soul and that the purpose of life was to seek liberation from this tomb. Such liberation was achieved through sacrifice of the lower passions and by living a life of the highest character, righteousness, and virtue. An initiate was taught that if he lived a pious life, his next incarnation, if he had to have one, would be on a much higher spiritual level.

Orpheus set the stage for a series of great future teachers in Greece, including Pythagoras (who was also Kuthumi), Socrates, Plato, and Aristotle.

# 24

## *Pythagoras and Biosophy*

*First honor the immortal gods, as the law
demands; then reverence thy oath, and then the
illustrious heroes; then venerate the divinities
under the Earth, due rites performing; then honor
your parents and all of your kindred. Among
others, make the most virtuous thy friend!*

The Golden Verses of Pythagoras

Pythagoras, one of Kuthumi's past lives, was born around 570 B.C. to Mnesarchus of Samos, a gem engraver, and his wife Pithais. An interesting story was told concerning his parents' visit to the Oracle of Delphi just prior to Pythagoras' birth. Mnesarchus asked a question concerning an upcoming voyage to Syria. The oracle did not answer his question but instead told them that Pithais would soon give birth to a son who was destined to pass all men in beauty and wisdom and who would be of great service to humankind.

Pythagoras had the benefit of the best possible education of his day. He had an insatiable thirst for knowledge which led him to travel extensively until the age of fifty-six. During these years he studied under the sages of Egypt and the wise men of Phoenicia, Babylonia, Chaldea, Persia, and India. Interestingly, Pythagoras lived at the same time Buddha was teaching his philosophy in India. While he was in Persia he studied the teachings of Zoroaster.

On returning from his travels, Pythagoras established a school in Crotona where he taught the many things had studied during his travels. From the Egyptians he had learned the science of mathematics. From the Chaldeans he had learned the science of astronomy. From the Magi of

Persia and the Brahmins of India he had learned the science of living.

Pythagoras was both a founder of new sciences and a moral reformer. He was one of the first philosophers in the West to recommend a vegetarian diet. The new religion he taught was called Biosophy, a word based on the Greek roots "bios," meaning life, and "sophia," meaning wisdom. Biosophy, hence, means the wisdom of living.

Pythagoras made a sharp differentiation among learning, knowledge, and wisdom. He saw wisdom as being far superior to the others. Learning is the information you memorize and what you are taught by your parents, teachers, and books; it is secondhand information. Knowledge comes from your experiences. Wisdom is the distilled essence of all that you have gained from life. The main goal of Pythagoras was the development of this wisdom of living. He was the first Greek to be called a philosopher.

Pythagoras was incredibly multifaceted in his understanding and his teaching. Among his most famous contributions was the Pythagorean Theorem, the forty-seventh proposition of Euclid, which says, "The square of the hypotenuse of a right-angled triangle is equal to the sum of the squares of the other two sides."

Pythagoras broke the science of numbers into four basic parts:

Arithmetic = number in itself

Geometry = number in space

Music or harmonics = number in time

Astronomy = number in space and time

Besides the mathematical sciences, Pythagoras was a master of numerology, believing numbers to be living, qualitative realities that must be approached in an experiential manner. He was the first to teach the principles of scientific astronomy; his statement that the Earth was spherical was bitterly opposed. He believed that all the planets and stars were actually alive and encased souls, minds, and spirits in the same manner that humans are encased in physical bodies. He saw the stars and planets as magnificent deities who were, however, subservient to the one God.

He was the originator of the diatonic musical scale on which music is based to this day. Pythagoras was also a master of medicine and naturopathic healing which was administered in the temples of Aesculapius. He considered geometry, music, and astronomy essential to arriving at a rational understanding of God.

The God of Pythagoras was the Monad, the one that is everything. He saw God as the supreme mind, distributed throughout all parts of the universe — the cause of all things, the intelligence in all things, and the power within all things. He taught that both man and the universe were made in the image of God. To understand one of these was to gain knowledge of the other.

He most definitely believed in reincarnation; he remembered a great many of his own past lives and had the ability to tell others about their past lives. He saw the purpose of life as being ultimately to ascend into the realm of the immortals where, by divine birthright, all belong.

Pythagoras divided the universe into three parts: the supreme world, the superior world, and the inferior world. The supreme world was the truest plane of the supreme Deity; the superior world was the home of the immortals; the material world was the home of those who were incarnated into the material universe.

At the age of sixty, Pythagoras married one of his disciples, and she bore seven children. After Pythagoras' death his wife continued to teach his doctrines. He was said to be six feet tall and to be as perfectly formed as Apollo. He was still in the prime of his life even when he neared the age of one hundred. Pythagoras had a persona of majesty and power.

Pythagoras was strongly influenced by the teachings of Orpheus (a past life of Gautama Buddha) who was the father of the Greek mystery school. Orphism taught that the soul is immortal but descends into the realm of matter during a long series of incarnations until it has purified itself and regained its true divine nature. Pythagoras taught his disciples, in his "golden verses," that they should honor the gods above geniuses, and heroes above men. Pythagoras divided people into three categories: men, gods, and beings like himself who stand in an intermediate position between both.

One of Pythagoras' senior disciples was Kleineas who, in a later incarnation, was none other than our dear friend, Djwhal Khul. One of Kleineas' disciples in that period was an early incarnation of C.W. Leadbeater of the Theosophical Society.

Pythagoras was holistic in his approach, for he taught the harmonious development of the body, mind, and soul. The main goal was the perfection of moral character, to which he gave priority over intellectual training in the sciences. Pythagoras was the first Greek to admit women into his school as freely as men, a breakthrough in the patriarchal Greek culture that predominated previous to that time.

In the center of Pythagoras' school at Crotona was a temple guarded by a statue of Hermes (who was a past life of Gautama Buddha and whom Egyptians knew as Thoth). The inscription on the statue read, "Let the profane not enter here." There were nine different temples for the arts and sciences. In the Pythagorean system, education, science, and religion were all perfectly unified. The subjects studied in the Pythagorean school included mathematics, geometry, astronomy, music, medicine, philosophy, politics, and an advanced form of ethics.

Music played an important part in the system of Pythagorean education. It was used to cure disease and to control desires and emotions. Pythagoras used music in the same way that a doctor uses medicine. He developed an exact science of what types of music healed which illnesses.

In terms of relations between the sexes, his attitude was that sexual association should never occur merely for pleasure, but only for the procreation of children. He was rather strict on this point, much like one of his followers six hundred years later by the name of Apollonius of Tyana, the incarnation of Jesus after his life in Palestine. The aim of the Pythagorean educational system was purification, with the goal of achieving assimilation with God.

An interesting story about Pythagoras demonstrates his remarkable powers. In his travels, he came across some fishermen drawing up their nets which were filled with fish. Pythagoras told the fishermen that he could tell them the exact number of fish they had caught. The fishermen thought that to be an impossible task, given how many fish were in the nets, so they said that if he was right, they would do anything he said. They counted all the fish and Pythagoras had been precisely accurate. He then ordered the fishermen to return the fish to the sea and for some mystical reason, none of them had died. Pythagoras paid the fishermen the price of the fish and left for Crotona. Incidents like this caused Pythagoras' fame to spread. During his time in Italy, it was said that he gained two thousand disciples from one lecture alone.

Pythagoras' advice to youth was that they should never revile anyone nor revenge themselves on those who did. He recommended that they devote themselves diligently to learning. According to historians, his words possessed such spiritual power that even wild animals became tame when he spoke to them.

Pythagoras taught a philosophy of moderation in all things, but there was an ascetic side to his teachings. His disciples were ordered to abstain from all animal food and wine. They were told not to eat too much and to sleep as little as possible. They were guided to suppress their speech and maintain silence as much as possible. They were taught to achieve contempt for fame and worship of money.

Pythagoras is acknowledged to have been the inventor and legislator of friendship, calling it the truest and most perfect of all relationships. He taught universal love toward all.

Pythagoras taught that no occurrence happened by chance or by luck but rather by divine providence, especially to good and pious people. He taught that it was much more holy to be injured than to kill another person; one circumstance incurs karma and the other doesn't. He taught the complete abstinence from all rivalry, competition, and contention among his disciples.

For breakfast Pythagoras would eat chiefly honey. For dinner he ate bread made of millet, along with barley and herbs, raw or boiled. Pythagoras also taught that special attention should be paid when going to sleep at night and when awaking in the morning. At each of these times his disciples were guided to consider their past and future actions. Therefore, he advised his disciples to repeat to themselves the following verses, as recorded in *The Pythagorean Sourcebook and Library* by Kenneth Sylvan Guthrie:

Upon going to sleep:

Nor suffer sleep to close thine eyes
till thrice thy acts that day thou hast run over.
How slip? What deeds? What duty left undone?

Upon rising:

As soon as e'er thou wakest, in order lay
the actions to be done that following day.

Pythagoras taught his followers, above all, to speak the truth. He said that, more than anything else, deifies man. Pythagoras was the first to call Heaven the cosmos, because it is perfect and adorned with infinite beauty and living beings. Pythagoras saw man as a microcosm, a compendium of the universe within himself.

He taught that there were eight parts of knowledge: sense, imagination, art, opinion, deliberation, science, wisdom, and mind. Art, prudence, science, and mind humans share with the gods. Sense and imagination humans share with animals. Opinion alone is solely a human characteristic.

Pythagoras was so admired that his disciples looked on all his sayings as being oracles from God. One time he criticized a disciple who took it to heart and actually committed suicide. Pythagoras was deeply saddened, and he vowed to be extremely careful in the future because of the hypersensitivity of some of his disciples.

Pythagoras saw the soul of man as being divided into three parts: intelligence, reason, and passion. He saw intelligence and passion in animals but taught that reason was found only in man whose greatest privilege was the ability to persuade his soul to be either good or bad. A person was seen as being happy when he had a good soul. He also taught that of all solid figures, the sphere was the most beautiful, and of all plane figures the circle the most beautiful.

## The Pythagorean Mystery School at Crotona

One of the most fascinating aspects of Pythagoras' life and teachings was his mystery school at Crotona. Admission to his school was dependent on the applicant's desire to learn. Pythagoras would not let a person into the school until he had tested him and interviewed him in a very in-depth manner. He would ask about a person's relationship to his parents and family. He would examine the candidate's laughter, speech, and silence, ask how he spent his leisure time and what brought him grief and joy. He examined form, gait, physical structure, and mannerisms to rate the invisible tendencies of the soul.

If the student passed this first test, he was then neglected for three years while Pythagoras secretly watched his disposition, studiousness, stability, and spiritual or egotistical tendencies. These students were called the akousmatikoi, or auditors. After that, the student was ordered to remain silent for the next five years so as to learn control of speech and the ability to listen. People in this group were called the mathmatikoi, or students. During this probationary period his property was put into a community trust. If he passed that test, he became an esoteric and was allowed to share in Pythagoras' doctrines. Prior to that time, he participated in the teachings only by hearing them; he was not allowed to see Pythagoras. If the student was rejected at that point, he was given double the wealth he had brought with him but had to leave the community.

According to Dr. Raymond Bernard in his book about Pythagoras, *The Immortal Sage*, the daily program of the school at Crotona began with a ritual observing of the rising of the sun. They wore white robes and offered a hymn to Apollo, the Sun God. After a morning walk, the students performed athletics, bathed, and went to the temple. At the temple they formed groups around the various masters. Their lunch consisted of bread, honey, and olives. In the afternoon they went to the gymnasium and then concentrated on their studies. They also worked in the communal gardens. At sunset, prayer was offered again and hymns were sung to the gods of the cosmos.

The Pythagorean school was divided into several degrees, or initiations. As the students developed, they would pass from initiation to initiation. The key word for the first degree was "preparation"; the key word for the second degree was "purification"; the key word for the third degree was "perfection."

It was in the third degree that the students gathered to study the teachings with Pythagoras himself. It was said that Pythagoras would on occasion teach all night.

The disciples of Pythagoras were trained first to know and master themselves so as to be able to intelligently and spiritually help to rule and serve others. Pythagoras' aim was to prepare future leaders for the new civilization.

## Pythagoras' Death

Pythagoras is said to have died at the ripe old age of one hundred and four years. Upon his death, his school at Crotona was passed on to his successor, Aristaeus, who carried on the school, educated Pythagoras' children, and also married his wife, Theano.

Pythagoras was said to have taught in his school for over thirty-nine years. This is rather an interesting synchronicity, for Buddha taught for exactly forty years after his illumination under the bodhi tree. When Aristaeus grew old, he turned the school over to Pythagoras' son, Mnesarchus. He was followed by Bulagoras in whose time the school at Crotona was plundered.

# 25

## *Plato*

*Love is the eldest and noblest and mightiest of
the gods and the chiefest author and giver of
virtue in life and of happiness in death.*

Plato

Plato is considered one of the great philosophers of Western civilization; in truth, he was also one of the great spiritual teachers. He
carried on the lineage of the Greek mystery schools that was started by
Orpheus (Buddha), Pythagoras (Kuthumi) and Socrates and that was carried on by Aristotle after Plato's death. Many of the great philosophers
were not what I would call spiritual in their orientation, but such was not
the case with Plato.

Plato became a disciple of Socrates at the age of twenty and studied
with him for approximately eight years. The night before Plato was
introduced to Socrates, Socrates had a dream that a young swan had flown
from Cupid's altar in the academy and had settled to rest in his lap. The
swan remained for a short time and then took wing again and flew back to
Heaven where it was received by the gods. When Plato arrived the next
day, Socrates exclaimed, "Friends, this is the swan from Cupid's altar."

Plato dedicated his life to the discovery of truth. He traveled to Italy
to study with the Pythagoreans and it was there that he learned of natural
and divine philosophy. From Socrates he learned grammar and rhetoric. In
the province of Sais, he studied with the spiritual teachers concerning the
immortality of the soul and the nature of creation. In Egypt, he studied
astrology and was initiated into the Hermetic rites (the teachings of Thoth).
He was also initiated into Mosaic practices and later into all the mysteries
of the Greek mystery schools.

When Plato returned to Athens he established his school, the Academy, in 386 B.C. Over the entrance of the Academy were these words: "Let none ignorant of geometry enter here." Geometry, to Plato, embodied the whole understanding of the mechanics of the universe. Plato's Academy is considered the first university in history.

Plato never married, and he died at the age of eighty-one on the same date on which he had been born. He is considered one of the great philosophers because knowledge came to him not as spiritual revelation but through the unfolding of his reasoning powers. The foundation of his beliefs lay in the teachings of Orpheus.

Plato had a high regard for reasoning but he was also very intuitive. It was Aristotle, one of his disciples, who worshiped reason to a fault. Plato referred to Aristotle as the mind of his school. Aristotle was often critical and argumentative with Plato. He had a brilliant mind but didn't seem to have the spiritual depth of his teacher. Upon Plato's death, Aristotle founded a second institute of learning in Athens called the Peripatetic.

During the trial of Socrates, Plato strongly defended his teacher and offered to pay the money needed to secure Socrates' freedom, but Socrates would not allow it. Upon the death of Socrates, Plato fled to Megara to avoid the prejudice of the Athenians who had brought about the fall of Socrates.

Plato did not have the opportunity to meet Pythagoras, for he had been dead for one hundred years when Plato lived. However, Plato was greatly influenced by Pythagoras and was even considered to be a disciple of his. He incorporated into his own teachings many of Pythagoras' theories of mathematics and numerology, and he saw God as the supreme geometrician. From Socrates he learned logic and ethics. Plato was truly holistic in his approach, incorporating the arts, the sciences, philosophy, and religion. The philosophers who followed never equaled his brilliance, except perhaps Apollonius of Tyana who lived three to four hundred years later. When Plato died, his school fell apart, but for the first twelve centuries of the Christian era, Plato's teachings dominated the Christian nations. Then in the thirteenth century Aristotle's more rational teachings began to overshadow Plato's teachings, which was really a move backwards in that Platonism was not just a philosophy but was a religion, too.

Plato's major focus was the unity of all things; division was seen as an illusion. For Plato, a life unexamined was a life not livable. He believed in using reason to decide moral questions, an approach he learned from Socrates, but the soul also played a crucial role in his overall philosophy. The soul was seen to function on three distinct levels: reason, assertion, and desire. Each of these parts had its virtue, its right exercise of function — wisdom, courage, and temperance. The fourth virtue was the balance of the first three virtues and was called justice or righteousness. The integration of the personality was said to come about when reason established control over instinct and emotion.

In *Phaedrus*, he described the soul as a chariot drawn by two horses, one good and one bad, with the charioteer being reason. The spirited and the desiring parts of the soul represented the two forms of the love principle, the attraction to eternal beauty and the attraction to physical beauty.

The soul was seen as being winged in its pre-existent state when with the gods and as losing its wings upon incarnation. The wings could sprout again upon the achievement of an awakened life. The concept of the soul as pre-existent came from the teachings of Orpheus; the soul was seen as a divine element imprisoned in a mortal body, a divine stranger inhabiting the world for a brief time and yearning for ultimate release, or liberation, so it can return to its true home. The incarnated soul could create good or evil according to its choices. The philosopher was the man who lived most for the soul and least for the body. Plato accepted the existence of an afterlife, including a period of discipline or purgatory upon passing into the spiritual world.

God was considered the Maker and Father of the universe, motivated solely by the desire to communicate His inherent goodness. The universe had been fashioned according to the eternal forms and patterns; all life forms were thought to have come into existence through the providence of God.

Plato did not acknowledge a principle of evil; it was only a form of truth that was not comprehensible. The inward nature of a person was of greater virtue than the physical body; it resided in the heart. An ignorant person was seen as being a slave to his animal nature; a partially ignorant person was seen as being a slave to his intellectual nature; an enlightened person was seen as being one with his spiritual nature. Plato believed all social ills could be resolved through education which should begin at the earliest possible time in childhood.

God was seen to have a threefold nature: the One, the Beautiful, and the Good. The One referred to the unity of all existence. The Beautiful referred to the harmony among people working toward the common good. The Good referred to the intrinsic nobility and integrity that were needed as a standard of community action.

Human identification with illusion and attachment to form prevented people from developing spiritual virtue. The goal of Platonism was to strive for and realize truth and virtue in every thought, word, and deed.

Plato delineated three orders of beings in the universe. The first was the gods, in whom truth manifested perfectly. The second order included the heroes, or enlightened men and women; they were not completely divine but were above the level of humans. The third category encompassed all mortals, average humanity whose souls were not awakened.

The physical body was seen as "the sepulcher of the soul." All people who were victims of astral and bodily desire were considered dead because truth was dead in their consciousnesses. Platonic thinking said all learning was remembering; science was the perfecting of reason, and the arts were the perfecting of passion.

Plato did his teaching outside under a tree. He accepted only disciples who came highly recommended and who were of great integrity. He usually gave lectures and then held discussions. In that, he differed from Socrates even though he often used the Socratic method of making students answer their own questions.

## Quotations from Plato

Love is the eldest and noblest and mightiest of the gods and the chiefest author and giver of virtue in life and of happiness in death.

Of all the things which a man has, next to the gods, his soul is the most divine and most truly his own.

Nothing in the affairs of men is worthy of anxiety.

Self-conquest is the greatest of the victories.

It is better to be unborn than untaught, for ignorance is the root of misfortune.

# 26

## *Zoroaster, the Avatar of Persia*

*Suffer no anxiety . . .*
*for this causes contraction to happen within*
*the body and soul. Form no covetous desire,*
*so that the demon of greediness*
*may not deceive thee.*

Zoroaster

Zoroaster was the great spiritual master who founded the religion of Persia which came to be called Zoroastrianism. It is interesting to note that he was an early incarnation of the Buddha and that his father, Zend, was an early incarnation of Jesus. (Zoroaster's name was actually Zarathustra, but the Greek pronunciation is Zoroaster.) Scholars believe he was born in about 660 B.C.

The Persian scripture known as the Avesta contains hymns called gathas which are attributed to Zoroaster. According to the teachings, the entire universe is a great battleground on which good and evil struggle for mastery. On the one side is Ahura Mazda, the manifested god of the universe. Ahura Mazda is supported by six vassals:

1. Good thought,
2. Right law,
3. Noble government,
4. Holy character,
5. Health, and
6. Immortality.

Against Ahura Mazda is poised Angra Mainyu, also known as the Lie Demon, with all his evil qualities. In the center point between the two stands the human being, who is seen as having free choice as to which side he chooses to serve. Once his choice is made, a person's every thought, word, and deed affects the outcome of the war, on both a personal and a collective level. This concept is reminiscent of the Armageddon of Christianity and of the Hindu view of life as a battlefield.

The teachings of Zoroaster focus on the need for work more than on the need for prayer. Ahura Mazda embodies the spirit of civilization, which was then attempting to create order and stability in the region. The most important ethical law is to help those in need, those who serve the forces of Light. This law applies even to animals; Zoroaster was against sacrifice. The one rite he did hold over from the past was the sanctification of fire, which was considered a symbol for Ahura Mazda. Even to this day, a small fire is kept burning in all Zoroastrian temples. (It is interesting that an automobile manufacturer has chosen the name Mazda. In fact, a number of companies use names of God; I have seen the words Ram and Brahma on trucks.)

Zoroaster said laziness is of the devil. In one of the scriptures, he said that every morning the demon of laziness whispers in the ear of man, "Sleep on, poor man, it is not time yet," but he alone who arises early will be the first to enter paradise. He described a heaven, a hell, and a judgment day. For every person there would be a trial at the time of death. The soul of each dead person would approach a bridge and would be commanded to march forward. If the person had lived properly, he would march straight to the heaven of Ormazd; if the person had led an evil and wicked life, he would fall into the hell of Ahriman, the devil, who was represented by a serpent, a noteworthy correlation with the Judeo-Christian tradition.

Today, Zoroastrianism is referred to as the Parsi religion. It is the only one of the world's great faiths that closes its places of worship to visitors of other religions; the Parsi's view is that each person should follow the religion he is born into. It is estimated that about one hundred twenty-five thousand people follow this religion today, mostly in Bombay and other areas in western India. Parsi women are seen as being equal with men.

Although called fire temples by non-Parsis, believers refer to their places of worship as the Doors of Mithra, Mithra being an ancient Persian god of Light. In these temples the sacred fire is always burning, but it is not worshiped. The temple is visited daily or weekly by its members. Shoes are removed at the door. Prayers and petitions are made in modern language; prayers are also said at home in the morning and at night.

## Zoroaster's Revelation

When Zoroaster was about forty years old he had a vision of a being nine times the size of a normal human. It was the Good Mind, Vohu Mana. The Good Mind led him into the presence of the wise lord, Ahura Mazda. It was there that Zoroaster heard the call to make known the divine teachings. He was put through a period of testing by Ahriman, much as were Jesus and Buddha.

Zoroaster denounced all idolatry and sinful living. He saw man as having been created by God and as eventually returning back to God.

Zoroastrianism is seen by some scholars as being dualistic because the two great powers of good and evil are viewed as being constantly at war. The eventual outcome was inevitable: Ahura Mazda and the people serving the good would win. Zoroastrianism clearly believed in life after death. Hell was considered to be a sort of purgatory but was also seen as a temporary punishment, an evolved understanding for its time.

Zoroaster prophesied that Ahriman would be defeated upon the coming of a savior from a virgin birth. There can be no doubt he was prophesying the coming of Jesus, especially as the being who was to be Jesus was Zoroaster's father in that lifetime.

The followers of Zoroastrianism call it "the good religion" the teachings of the good life. It has a strong moral code, and believers are taught the virtue of justice, service to others, and chastity. Later teachings emphasize moderation in all things and place a strong emphasis on preparing for future life, describing in great detail the heavenly beings and spirit guides who help humans on Earth.

Zoroaster is said to have had seven revelations, or divine visions, that formed the basis for his teachings. Many of the visions involved angels; in one, he beheld the amesha-spentas, also known as the angelic and archangelic hosts. It is interesting to note that angels were involved in Zoroastrian, Islamic, and Christian origins.

## A Deeper Understanding of the Zoroastrian God

The aspect of God that is the Unmanifest Creator is called Zeroana Akerne, whereas Ahura Mazda is the Manifested Creator. This concept is similar to mystical Judaism in which YHWH is the Unmanifest Creator and Jehovah, or Yod Hay Way Hay, is the Manifest Creator of the universe. Zeroana Akerne is said to have within himself the power of objectification out of his unmanifest state. Ahura means "eternal wisdom"; Mazda is the vehicle for that wisdom, so together, the name means "the Light of knowledge manifesting before the created world."

There was thought to be a constant struggle within the human between his higher and lower selves.

The Zoroastrians were very involved with astrology. As a matter of fact, one of the Christian Wise Men was an astrologer and a magi of Zoroastrian descent, if I am not mistaken.

In the teachings, it is said that Ahura Mazda caused to issue out of himself seven amesha-spentas. These beings were called the gods of the dawn, the world-builders, the elohim, and they were thought to have created the seven heavens and, descending downward, the seven octaves of energy. Ahriman was said to have seven vices that would oppose the seven cardinal virtues of Ahura Mazda who was also thought to have created twelve principles of Light, or the equatorial constellations. Ahriman would eventually be defeated by Ormazd and, through his repentance, restored to the Light. The seven amesha-spentas become manifest and are reflected in the human in his seven bodies, seven principles, and seven organs.

## Quotations from the Avesta

Suffer no anxiety . . . for this causes contraction to happen within the body and soul.

Form no covetous desire, so that the demon of greediness may not deceive thee.

I believe that purity is the first virtue, truth the second, and charity the third. Man must discipline himself by good thoughts, good words, and good deeds.

I believe that marriage excels continence, action excels contemplation, and forgiveness excels revenge.

I believe in God as seven persons — Eternal Light, Right and Justice, Goodness and Love, Strength of Spirit, Piety and Faith, Health and Perfection, and Immortality — and that they may best be worshiped through the representation of fire, the most sacred and single worshipful emblem.

Commit no slander so that infamy and wickedness may not happen unto thee.

May the Creator of wisdom teach me his ordinances through good thought, that my tongue may have a pathway.

# 27

## *Mohammed and Islam*

*I witness that there is no God but Allah and that Mohammed is the Prophet of Allah.*

The First Pillar of the Islamic Faith

I perceive a separation between the Western world and the Islamic world which has occurred, I believe, because of radical fundamentalists who have misinterpreted the true teachings and given the Islamic religion a bad name. I hope to help to correct that injustice and to show that the teachings of Mohammed and the Koran are as beautiful as those of Christ, Moses, Buddha, Krishna, Confucius, Lao-tzu, or Zoroaster. It is truly time to see all religions as spokes of the same wheel.

The Islamic religion takes a major step in this direction for it acknowledges that the God of the Hebrews and the Christians is the same God worshiped by Moslems. The teachings also acknowledge Jesus, Abraham, and Moses as prophets of God. Let us, however, start at the beginning.

Islam is the youngest of all the major religions. It is also one of the simplest and easiest to explain. It is monotheistic in nature, venerating a single and powerful God. Mohammed, the founder of the teachings of Islam, was a channel for Archangel Gabriel, and that is how he gained much of his information. It is interesting that he, unlike Krishna, Rama, or Jesus Christ, was not seen as a divine incarnation of God but as a prophet or a mouthpiece of God.

The word "moslem" means "one who submits." Its adherents encompass one seventh of the world's population. The sacred book of the Islamic religion is the Koran. Moslems acknowledge the truths of the Bible's Old and New Testaments but they see those texts as incomplete. The Koran is considered the final and absolute expression of the Will of God, or Allah, and Mohammed the greatest of all the prophets since Abraham.

One night Archangel Gabriel appeared to Mohammed in a vision and cried, "Recite!" With that initial revelation, the Koran was articulated, and Mohammed continued his channelings for over a decade. The people of Mecca heckled him and threatened his life because of his denunciation of idol-worshiping, so Mohammed left Mecca in 622 and went to the city of Yathrib. That year of Mohammed's flight is considered the first year of the Moslem calendar. Mohammed quickly became a religious leader and governor of the city. Then a war ensued between the two cities and he returned to Mecca in triumph.

The teachings of Islam are monotheistic and do accept a last judgment but do not acknowledge the trinity of God as Christianity does. The Koran is very detailed in its descriptions of Heaven and Hell. Mohammed prescribed five duties for every Moslem as Pillars of Faith:

1. Shahadah: to profess belief ("I witness that there is no God but Allah and that Mohammed is the prophet of Allah");
2. Salat: to pray five times a day;
3. Zakat: to give alms to the needy;
4. Saum: to fast in the month of Ramadan; and
5. Haj: to make the pilgrimage to Mecca.

Moslems believe that when all people submit to Allah and live by the teachings of the Koran, then peace will come to all. The Koran contains many legal and moral laws: there are rules about marriage and divorce and punishments for crimes; it disallows gambling, eating pork, and making images or sculptures of Mohammed. There is also a law that no non-Moslem may take the pilgrimage to or even enter Mecca.

Second only to Mecca as a sacred place is Jerusalem. Beneath the temple mosque called the Dome of the Rock is a hallowed rock long sanctified by the Moslems. According to Moslem teaching, it is where Abraham was about to sacrifice his son Isaac and where angels visited before the creation of Adam. Noah's ark was supposed to have sailed around it seven times. All the great prophets, including Elijah, went to pray there. It was from the rock that Mohammed was said to have ascended to Heaven. It is also the rock upon which the angel Israfil will sound his last trumpet on Judgment Day.

Near the Dome of the Rock are the holy places of Judaism and Christianity. In one of the Paul Solomon channelings of the Universal Mind, the Source predicted that this could be the starting point of a future war in the Middle East. He foresaw Jewish fundamentalists trying to rebuild their temple in an area that was sacred to the Moslems near the Dome of the Rock. This, he prophesied, was the instigation point for a possible conflict. Let us pray and hold the thought that this does not occur, for the future is in our hands to create at every moment.

At death, a Moslem's body is washed and the hands are placed in a praying position. Before the head is covered, the relatives say their good-byes. After prayers, a catechism is whispered into the ears of the dead: "Who is thy God? Allah. What is thy religion? Islam. Who is its prophet? Mohammed." This prayer prepares the departing soul for questioning by the angels Munkar and Nakir. Mourning may last as long as one hundred days.

Of all the religious duties of a Moslem, the fast of Ramadan is the most important. He must not drink or eat or perform any sexual act from dawn until dusk. He is supposed to pray, meditate, and read the Koran, which is the sacred scripture of Islam.

The Koran is made up of one hundred fourteen chapters called suras which are believed to have come to Mohammed as revelations from God. It is read daily in all schools and mosques. The opening of the Koran states, "In the name of Allah, the beneficent, the merciful! Praise be to Allah, Lord of the worlds, the beneficent, the merciful. Owner of the day of judgment, Thee we worship; Thee we ask for help. Show us the straight path, the path of those whom thou has favored, not [the path] of those who hear thine anger, nor of those who go astray."

The chapters of the Koran are not organized in the order in which Mohammed received the messages but with the longer chapters first and the shorter ones last. All but one of the suras begin, "In the name of Allah, the beneficent, the merciful!" The word Koran actually means "recitation," which is a form of the first word Mohammed received from Archangel Gabriel.

It is interesting that Archangel Gabriel was instrumental in the creation of the Islamic religion as well as playing a key role in the lives of Mary and Joseph in the Christian saga.

## The Five Pillars

Before praying, a Moslem must wash his face, arms, and feet. The prayers follow a fixed pattern of words and movements and may be recited in any clear place. Adult males are supposed to go to a mosque for noon prayers on Fridays.

Islam teaches its followers to be honest, generous, just, and ready to fight in its defense. Moslems are not allowed to lend money for interest. Moslems see these ordinances as being commandments from God that cannot be altered.

Islamic mosques are beautiful, always incorporating the unique feature of the minaret, or tall tower, from which the muezzin calls the people to prayer, using the following words: "God is most great. I bear witness that there is no God but Allah. I bear witness that Mohammed is the messenger of Allah. Come to prayer, come to your good, God is most great. There is no God but Allah." The mosque is a place for meditation, prayer, and teaching and it also serves as a meeting hall.

Ramadan occurs in the ninth month of the Moslem calendar which is holy because it is the month when Mohammed first started receiving revelations from God. Moslems are supposed to fast for all thirty days, but not during the evenings, and during that time they are not supposed to smoke or argue with friends or neighbors, and they are to be helpful, kind, and generous.

Moslems can eat meat only if it has been prepared in a certain way, a practice similar to the Jewish tradition of eating Kosher food. When an animal is being killed, the butcher must say, "Bismillah," which means "in the name of God," to show that life is taken only to provide food for the devout Moslem. Meat prepared in this way is called "halal," or permitted meat. Alcohol in any form is entirely disallowed. Eating the meat of a pig is forbidden, as in Judaism.

Once during life, a Moslem is supposed to go on a pilgrimage to Mecca — but only if he can afford it and it doesn't cause undue suffering to the family. Male Moslems wear, on this pilgrimage, only two seamless sheets of white cotton in order to make all people, regardless of status or wealth, equal in the sight of God.

During the pilgrimage, soap, perfumes, the cutting of hair or nails, the killing of any form of life, and sexual relations are not allowed. Upon reaching Mecca, the Moslem walks seven times around the Kaaba, tracing of the path of Mohammed (much as Christians and Buddhists trace the movements of Jesus and Buddha). Moslems have been undertaking the haj, or pilgrimage, for fourteen centuries. It is the world's largest spiritual gathering, and if you have never seen pictures of it, I recommend going to a library or a bookstore and looking at some pictures of it. It is quite a spectacle to behold.

There are many laws in the Koran concerning the misuse of wealth, such as the law that states that a Moslem may not cut his family out of his estate.

Moslems believe in the resurrection of the body after death; the dead are buried, not cremated. Moslems believe in direct communication between man and God; all are equal in the eyes of God, so priests or intercessors are unneeded. The Koran teaches that the soul is immortal. After being embodied on Earth, it then enters Heaven or Hell, depending upon Earthly conduct. The Koran also teaches the virtue of truthfulness, that it should be observed at all times and in all circumstances, even though it may incur injury or pain.

When a Moslem child is born, the first thing the child hears is the

Shahadah, the profession of faith: "I witness that there is no God but Allah and that Mohammed is the prophet of Allah." All Moslem boys are circumcised, another parallel with the Jewish faith. Parents have a special responsibility to teach their children what the Moslem faith requires of them. Schools in Moslem countries teach the principles of Islam, so there is no separation of church and state, as in the West. Teenagers are expected to work hard at school and to help around the house. Going to parties and discos is discouraged, especially for girls, who are treated more strictly than boys. Family life is very important to the Moslem, as is respect for elders.

The Koran encourages Moslems to marry and have children. Sexual relationships outside marriage are forbidden. Parents arrange marriages for their children, as in the Hindu faith, but the bride and groom do have the right to refuse, and unless both parties agree, the marriage will not take place. Islamic teachings consider the union to occur not just between two people but also between two families, so family opinion is very important.

Moslem men are allowed to marry as many as four wives, but that happens rarely. Islamic law requires that each wife be treated equally. The Moslem wife takes care of the family and home; providing for the family is the man's job. Divorce is permitted in Islamic teaching but is frowned upon. If a divorce does occur, the wife receives some money from her ex-husband and also takes all the household goods and furniture. The wife's maintenance then becomes the responsibility of her male relatives.

Women are seen as having equal rights but different duties. Women have the same right to own property and seek education. In actuality, however, men are often chauvinistic in this regard. Women often work in the fields of nursing, teaching, agriculture, and textiles.

Men are always to be covered from the navel to the knees, even when swimming or showering. Women are supposed to cover their entire bodies when out in public.

## The Prophet Mohammed

At the age of forty, Mohammed was seized by the conviction that he had been chosen by God to be the prophet of the true religion among the Arab people. Until that time, Arabs, unlike other peoples, had known no prophet. For days, Mohammed remained alone in a cave on Mount Hira, much like Moses' experience of climbing Mount Sinai to speak with God. In that divine moment, Archangel Gabriel spoke: "Recite! Speak out in the name of the Lord who created Heaven and Earth. Speak out, for the Lord is the most beneficent and has taught the use of the pen."

Moslem spiritual practices include repeating the ninety-nine beautiful names of God. When asked if there is a one hundredth, he answers, "Only the camel knows it and that secret which gives the camel his dignity."

Moslems use prayer beads much as all the major religions do. Moslems give great importance to angels; it is believed that Allah reveals his will through them. Azrael is the angel of death, and Israfil is the angel who will blow his trumpet on Judgment Day.

Allah was seen by Mohammed to occupy a throne in the Seventh Heaven, surrounded by a host of angels who wait upon him and do his bidding. Among them are Nakir and Munkar, who are entrusted with the job of subjecting every recently deceased person to an examination (similar to the period of bardo in Buddhism). Preparations for these tests have been made by the recording angels, two of whom are assigned to each person with the charge of listing the person's good and bad deeds.

Mohammed taught of the existence of Satan who became the devil when evicted from the Garden of Eden. Satan's task is to tempt men and impede the purposes of Allah, but he is considered doomed, for the will of Allah cannot fail.

Moslems believe that Allah has revealed himself in a progressive succession of one hundred twenty-four thousand prophets, of whom Mohammed was the culmination. If humankind fails to heed his revelation, then the end of the world will soon be at hand

Every occurrence in life, whether good or bad, is thought to have been determined far in advance by the immutable will of Allah. Many Moslem philosophers think that Allah is the author of evil, also, and that man has no free will. This is not true of all Moslems, but they do tend to face life with an innate fatalism. Moslems are warned that their wrongdoings will be balanced against their meritorious deeds on Judgment Day.

Because of Islam's formal and sometimes rigid nature (which, in some ways, is similar to Judaism), a new movement arose within it: Sufism. Abu-Hamid Mohammed Al-Ghazzali established Sufism, which emphasized the union of the soul and God here on Earth, not just in the afterlife. Sufis tend to be quiet, ascetic, and focused on the mystical aspects of Islamic teaching, much as Kabbalists focus on the mystical aspects of Judaism.

The Islamic faith has many sects (just as Christianity does), the major division being between the Shiites and the Sunnites. The two are linked in their belief in Mohammed, the Koran, and the Five Pillars, but that is about all. The Sunnites tend to be the fundamentalists, or traditionalists.

Another group with a heritage in the Moslem faith is the Sikhs. They tend to be tall, with impressive beards and turbans, and are sometimes seen wearing a knife. They revere the great spiritual master Kabir, who focused on the idea that love of God was enough to achieve salvation. He said, "Go where you will, to Benares or to Madura, if you do not find God in your own soul, the world is meaningless for you." (Kabir was also a past life of Sai Baba.) Kabir believed there was truth in all religions and that there was only one God, known variously as Allah, Krishna, Rama, and so on. Kabir was the creator of many beautiful songs that are incorporated into the Sikh scriptures.

A generation later, Guru Nanak taught the importance of repeating the true name of God as the main practice. The Sikh religion is a deliberate mixture of Hinduism and Islam. Guru Nanak had been married early in his life, but then he became an ascetic, wearing the robe of a Hindu and the turban and prayer beads of a Moslem. He had a vision of God holding out to him a cup of nectar and saying, "Go and repeat my name and make others do so." (This, of course, is a spiritual practice that Sai Baba has also strongly recommended.)

The nine successors of Guru Nanak are also called Gurus and they all are thought to be Guru Nanak reincarnated, much like the understanding of the Dalai Lama in Tibetan Buddhism. The tenth Guru, Govind Singh, instituted a ceremony of initiation in which all Sikhs took new names and the title Singh, which means lion. They swore to five rules: to leave the hair and beard uncut, to wear a steel comb, to wear shorts, to wear a steel bracelet on the right wrist, and to wear a steel dagger. All true Sikhs follow these rules, though the shorts may be under the trousers.

Today the Sikhs number about six million and are defined as those who believe in the ten Gurus and in the Granth Scripture, the primary book of Sikhism. The succession of Gurus came to an end with the tenth, Govind Singh. After that, the scripture became the Guru and teacher.

Sikhs believe that God is everywhere so there is no need to become an ascetic in order to find Him. (This is reminiscent of Buddha's espousal of the Middle Way.) Sikhs insist that God is personal and is revealed through their Gurus. Their model for living is the example of the ten Gurus, especially Guru Nanak.

## Summation

Mohammed died in the year 632. Within twenty-five years of his death, his followers had become masters of Arabia, Egypt, Palestine, Syria, Babylonia, and Persia. Within seventy-five years they had conquered the northern coast of Africa and almost all of Spain. In summation, there are very beautiful practices, ideals, and concepts in the Islamic teachings, but clearly, negative ego, glamour, illusion, and maya have infiltrated some of them. (The same can be said, however, about Christianity, Judaism, Hinduism, and Buddhism.) The teachings of the prophet Mohammed and Archangel Gabriel spiritually revolutionized the entire Arab world, providing a code of ethics and eliciting a devotion to God that has continued and is spreading rapidly even today.

# 28

## *Kabir, Sublime Poet*

*Whatever one's attachments were upon death,
that is where one's abode will be. Precious
human birth should be utilized in the form of
devotion, to escape the wheel of rebirth.*

Kabir

Kabir was a Self-realized master of soul travel and a master of Sabda Yoga (the yoga of the holy sound), so he was able to travel to the inner spiritual worlds at will. His writings are not scholarly; his knowledge comes straight from direct experience of the highest realms of spirit and of God. This being of such spiritual magnitude was a past life of Shirdi Sai Baba and Sathya Sai Baba. The similarities in their teachings are apparent.

### The Life Story of Kabir

Kabir was born in 1398 A.D., the son of a Moslem weaver living on the outskirts of the holy city of Benares. He was given the name Kabir, which means "most high." Kabir showed signs of interest in religion at a very young age, but because of his family's poverty he didn't have the opportunity to receive a formal education, so he focused his energy on learning the family trade and became a master weaver.

His spiritual hunger grew as he moved into adolescence. On one occasion his father wanted to sacrifice an animal at a particular festival. Kabir became so emotionally distraught that his father agreed to release the animal. On another occasion, a beggar was shivering in the cold, so Kabir gave him all the cloth he had with him, even though he and his family were exceedingly poor; he received a scolding from his parents on returning home.

Kabir's guru was a man named Ramanand, although it is clear from his writings that he visited many holy men. On one occasion Ramanand made a mistake in his religious practice while inside the temple. From outside the temple Kabir clairvoyantly saw what had happened and called to him to make him aware of the problem. Afterwards, Ramanand embraced Kabir, having gained new respect for his spiritual powers. It is even believed that Ramanand later came to be greatly influenced by Kabir's teachings.

Kabir married and had a son, Kamal, and a daughter, Kamali. Kabir recommended a family life rather than enforced celibacy and renunciation. He preached the practice of the Middle Way in all things. In his writings it can be seen that his wife was often angry with him for his hospitality to holy men. He worked regularly at his loom and sold his cloth in the weekly market. Kabir had very lofty ideals and would never compromise his principles. The small family lived a life of devotion and spiritual practice, inspired by Kabir's example. Kabir initiated his wife into the practice of Sabda Yoga. Kamali, his daughter, also became his disciple.

As Kabir matured he began to attract disciples from all walks of society. One of his disciples was the King Vir Singh Baghela, who was the ruler of a neighboring state. Their first meeting occurred when Kabir happened to be in town at the celebration of the king's new palace. When the king asked Kabir if he liked his beautiful new palace, Kabir said he liked it but it had two blemishes. The king was surprised by the comment and asked Kabir what he meant. Kabir said that the first blemish was that the palace would eventually crumble and fall; the second blemish was that the one who had built it would have to leave it. The king was annoyed by these comments but recognized Kabir as a holy man. Kabir said, "Oh King, the law of this world is such that the sun that rises must set, the day that comes must go, whatever is created has to crumble, and whoever is born has to die." Of course, Kabir was referring to the impermanent nature of worldly attachments. The king became his loyal disciple.

There was a great scholar of the Vedas and scriptures named Sarvanand who had defeated many learned men in debates about points of theosophy, metaphysics, and the six systems of philosophy. He was so egotistically prideful that he changed his name to Sarvajit, which means "conqueror of all." His mother had recently been initiated by Kabir whom she saw as a true holy man. She told her son that she would accept him as the conqueror of all only if he defeated Kabir in a debate.

He thought to himself that it would be easy, for Kabir was nothing more than a lowly weaver. On arriving at Kabir's home with a load of books, he found that Kabir was not home and his daughter, seeing the load of books, said, "Kabir's home is on a peak. The path is slippery and hard. Where even an ant's foot finds no hold, the pundit wants to reach there with a bullockcart of books!"

When Kabir finally arrived, he was challenged by Sarvajit to hold a debate on any subject. Kabir replied, "I am grateful that you have given me the honor of talking to a great scholar. I am only an illiterate weaver who has never before even seen such a large number of books." Sarvajit told him why he had to hold the debate, and Kabir admitted defeat before hand, agreeing to sign any statement of defeat, for his name was the only thing he could write.

Sarvajit wrote a document that said, "Sarvajit has defeated Kabir" and had Kabir sign it. Triumphantly, he marched off to see his mother. However, when he gave it to his mother, the paper read, "Kabir has defeated Sarvajit." Sarvajit went back to Kabir's home and had him sign a new document. He took it to his mother but again it read, "Kabir has defeated Sarvajit." Sarvajit made a third trip and the same thing happened. After the third time Sarvajit was exasperated and accused Kabir of being a magician. His mother said, "Son, he is a saint, a man of God, not a magician. See how humble he is, not ashamed to admit his humility." Sarvajit finally understood and went back humbly to Kabir. On his return to his mother he said, "Kabir is truly great. I fell at his feet and owned my defeat. He initiated me and took me into his fold." Sarvajit's mother said, "Yes, my son, you have now found the path to real knowledge. One who owns defeat at the saint's feet is the real victor. He wins his heart."

Kabir had his own unique way of dealing with people. A Moslem dervish whose name was Jahan Gasht Sha heard that Kabir was a great holy man and went to Benares to meet him. While he was waiting for an audience, Kabir told one of his disciples that the man, though a noble soul and true seeker, had not freed himself from certain deeply rooted prejudices which had become a hindrance in his spiritual progress. He asked the disciple to get a pig and tie it near the door of his hut. When Jahan Gasht Sha arrived, he was deeply disturbed to see the pig, which he considered an impure being, especially at the door of a holy man. He severely judged Kabir for his unholy act before storming out in anger. Kabir said to him, "Friend, I have kept the impure outside my house. You have given it shelter within your heart. Did not your eyes flash with anger and hatred for me? Are anger and hatred pure and within the tenets of religion? In God's creation no being should be despised. In the eyes of the Lord, no being is filthy, for He has created each one of them to fulfill His own design."

Kabir taught the path of God-realization to Hindu and Moslem alike for over seventy years despite slander and criticism from the orthodox believers of his time. Kabir is quoted by V.F. Sethi as saying, "If you say God dwells only in the mosque or He dwells only in an idol, then who dwells in the rest of the world? You say, in the south is the home of Hari, or in the west is the abode of Allah, but not one of you has found the truth. Search for Him in you heart, search for Him deep within yourself. This is the place where He lives; this is His true abode."

Kabir was a proponent of repeating the name of God. He said, "Take refuge in the One; repeat His name. Only then will you cross the ocean."

In regard to those who believed in the caste system he had this to say: "In the womb the soul has neither caste nor clan. All souls have sprung from the seed of Brahm. No one is high, no one low. All are nurtured by Him who has given them form. . . . Only he is low whose heart is adverse to God's name."

He was a revolutionary for his time. Because of his direct experience of God, he saw through the shallow practices of idol worship, pilgrimages, fasting, penances, and ritual baths. He viewed the priests who were involved in such external worship devoid of inner understanding as being the blind leading the blind.

Kabir taught a dynamic, living faith based on the actual experience of God. That view was extremely threatening to all those holding positions of power in the churches and mosques of his time. It was no different from what Jesus Christ encountered during his ministry. The priests were selling religion and filling their pockets with money in the name of God.

Kabir said the "true Brahmin is one who realizes Brahm; he is the true priest who fights with his mind and subdues it." He went on to say to the Hindu and Moslem accusers, "Realize, oh ignorant men, the one who speaks and dwells in the body is neither a Hindu nor a Turk; the imperceptible Allah is present within every vessel. Seek within your heart and know it. Within the Hindu and the Turk dwells the same One Lord." This was blasphemy to the ignorant religious orders of his time.

At one point, the sultan ordered Kabir drowned for his unorthodox spiritual beliefs. Kabir responded by saying, "Lord, I live and have always lived under thy shelter. The world looks upon thy lovers as its enemies. In life and death, dear Lord, Thou alone art my support and my succor." Finally the sultan realized Kabir's exalted nature and said to him, "I did not realize your greatness. You are a man of God, a great dervish. . . . Please forgive me." Kabir bore no grudges. One of his favorite sayings was "Forgiveness is a game that only the saints play."

When Kabir was close to physical death he chose to spend his last days in the unholy city of Maghar. The pundits and orthodox priests said that he should spend his last days in the holy city of Benares if he wanted to realize God. Kabir's reply was, "A hardened sinner will not escape the fires of hell even if he dies in Benares, but a saint of God, even if he dies in Maghar, emancipates the entire fold of his disciples. . . . Listen friends, let no doubts remain; he who has true faith in the Lord, for him, holy Benares and barren Maghar are the same."

He went on to say, in another passage, "I have ascended the divine throne and met the Lord. God and Kabir have become one. No one can distinguish who is who." Elsewhere, he said, "What I was once, I am not now. I have reaped the benefit of my precious birth; as water once mixed in water can never be taken apart, so has this weaver flowed and merged into the Lord. One who is always absorbed in God's love and devotion, what is there to wonder at when he attains this high state? Through the blessings of his Master, through the company of the saints, this weaver marches onward. He has conquered Kal's [the devil's] domain."

Upon his death, the Hindus and Moslems continued their ignorant arguments over what should be done with the body; the Hindus wanted to cremate the body and the Moslems wanted to bury it. A great argument ensued. Suddenly, a disciple came running in and pointed out that the body had disappeared, and in its place was a bouquet of flowers. They divided the flowers. Kabir had resolved the argument.

## Kabir's Sublime Teachings and Poetry

Kabir saw the spiritual path as being the complete absorption of the lover in the beloved, the merger of the flame within the flame. In one of his poems, it is as if spirit itself is writing: "Kabir, I have him as my companion, who is beyond pleasure and pain; I will revel with him, I will merge with him and never be parted again!"

He often described himself as "the bride of God" or "the wife of Ram." He imagined himself as a new bride would feel when away from her husband and then when union was achieved. He wrote about how the bridegroom had come to wed the bride and take her to his divine abode.

Kabir urged, "Attach yourself to that Lord whose devotions will end all pleasures, all pains, who will redeem you from your state of orphanhood."

In another stanza he says, "Having recognized the Lord within, my thoughts rest only in Him. Now wherever I cast my eyes, I see none else but Him. Since realization came, here, there, everywhere the Lord alone I see."

On the subject of staying on the spiritual path, Kabir says, "He who is near, within your own body, why forsake him and run far and wide? For whom the world wanders about, him I found close to my heart." He searched for Him in all directions, even on the peaks of lofty mountains, but failed to find Him. When he looked within, he found "the one who raised the citadel within the citadel itself."

Kabir refers to the name of God as a thing beyond the comprehension of the mind or senses. The name of God that cannot be written or spoken is "Sat Nam," which means "the true name." That is also the name of God the Sikh religion uses. In the teachings of Eckancar, interestingly enough, Sat Nam is the cosmic being who governs the soul plane. Kabir goes on to say about this name, "This is the Satguru's message: Sat Nam is the real essence of His being. It is the bearer of the tidings of your liberation. Friends, listen to this name with true devotion."

Kabir believed it was only the inner practice of repeating the name of God that would lead to liberation. He saw the name of God as being indivisible, permanent, and indestructible, whereas everything else in the universe was perishable.

In *Kabir, the Weaver of God's Name*, Sethi says, "All heavens and astral worlds, all continents and even the domain of Brahm are subject to destruction, but not the name of God. Those who merge into the perfect name will become perfect. Never again will they come and go who realize the secret of the true name." Kabir described the repetition of the name of God as the invisible string along which the soul can climb back to the Lord.

On getting out of the ego, Kabir said, "Beyond words is the Shabd [the holy word, or the holy sound], that word of ours. Oh Kabir, when one eliminates his I-ness under the Master's guidance, only the word remains. . . . The firmament where He abides is flooded with the Light of Shabd. There the Shabd blooms in its white resplendence and there the pure souls revel in bliss."

On the qualities of saints, Kabir had the following to say: "He has ill will for none. He has overcome all desires. Only the Lord does he love. He is far above the reach of pleasures and passions. Such, oh Kabir, are the traits of a true saint."

Kabir saw the true guru as Shabd and Shabd as the true guru: "Adopt that guru who is himself Shabd; all other gurus are false. . . . Shabd is mine; I am of Shabd. Realize that Shabd if you crave salvation. Don't let this chance slip by."

On the subject of dying to worldly attachment, Kabir said, "If one dies while living, for him death is sweet. Death is sweet for him who has experienced it through the Master's grace. . . . Those who, while living, die by merging into the Lord become immortal, oh Kabir. . . . rare are they who while living die; free from all fear, they merge in the Lord's qualities, and wherever they look, only Him they see. . . . To kings and paupers, to emperors and fakirs [renunciates] to one and all, I give the call: If you long for eternal bliss, come and dwell in my home! No-grief land is my abode, oh friend."

Learning to soul travel to higher spiritual regions begins by seeking the perfect spiritual master, then adopting the practice of Nam (repeating the name of God) and withdrawing the consciousness to the third eye. He never advised the continued focusing of consciousness below the third eye center. Kabir was a master of the Light and sound of God. Through the repetition of God's name he would soul travel from one of the two highest chakras and experience the Light and sound of God in the higher heavens.

Kabir referred to the mind as a thief and the biggest obstacle because it would steal the disciple's spiritual wealth through its negative qualities of "lust, anger, attachment, greed, avarice, jealousy, hate, and, above all, ego." He called the mind a wild beast. It was an enemy with no head, form, or shape. He also referred to it as "a monkey; not a moment does it stay still."

Kabir said that a devotee could be free of the bondage of mind only upon reaching a state of consciousness called unmani, the region of the Universal Mind, the realm of Brahm. In a brilliant exposition on the nature of dealing with the mind, Kabir said, "When the devotee grasps the original source of mind, the mind becomes still. He who knows this secret will know what mind is. Let no one's mind delude and hinder him from realizing the truth, for only he who is attuned to the Lord will obtain true peace." It is necessary to accept the help of the mind, for only on controlling the mind will one attain perfection and it is only through mind that the mind can be controlled. "There is none other like the mind. This mind is energy; this mind is power; this mind is made of the five elements. He who takes his mind and fixes it in the region of Brahm, to him the mysteries of the three worlds are revealed." In Hinduism, the mind is controlled by the intellect and the intellect is subservient to the atman, or Eternal Self.

Kabir saw that the mind in the physical world was not free because it was in bondage to the five physical senses. Only when the soul eclipses the mind can soul liberation be achieved. Kabir said, "If you conquer the mind, you will conquer the world and will become indifferent to sense pleasure. . . . When the mind becomes pure, the soul will merge in the Pure One." Mind becomes still through the practice of Nam or Shabd. Unless put under the shackles of the true name, mind will run about wherever it pleases. "Mind is stubborn and mighty like a mountain, but the moment the crowbar of Shabd strikes it, it yields a mine of pure gold. Explore the Shabd, oh, Kabir, and through it control your mind; this is the way to union."

Kabir said that to give in to the cravings of the mind is to add fuel to the fire. The mind's cravings will not dry up if they are watered. By going within and enjoying inner bliss, the lower-self pleasures of the outer world become abhorrent. The mind transformed becomes like "a pure swan and savors only divine pearls."

Kabir advocated the development of character and virtue. He saw the need to replace lust with modesty, purity, and chastity. He sought to replace anger with gentleness, affection, tolerance, and forgiveness.

Kabir said, "What use is it to scrub the body when the dirt is within? The bitter gourd may bathe in all the eighty-eight holy spots, but its bitterness will not depart. . . . Men roam the shores picking up empty shells; they do not dive into the sea where priceless jewels await them."

On praising the power of simran (repeating the name of God), Kabir had this to say: "In the seven islands and nine worlds, such is the power of my Nam [the name of God], that Yama [the lord of death] and all evil forces shudder in fear, and my victorious drum resounds in the entire Brahmand [land of Brahm]."

On the subject of attachment, Kabir said that whatever a person's attachments are, that is where his abode will be upon death. Precious human birth should be utilized for devotion in order to escape the wheel of rebirth. "The saint's physical form is the mirror of the Formless One. If you long to see the Invisible, see him in the saint."

With the practice of meditation the devotee can learn to hear the Shabd (holy sound) without having to do anything but listen. The object of meditation is to merge the soul into the Shabd. In terms of the outcome of successful meditation, Kabir said, "When the body is motionless and the mind is still, and the surat [hearing faculty] and the nirat [seeing faculty] are still, too — oh Kabir, the glory of such a moment not a billion years' happiness in the heavens can equal. The soul will merge into Shabd and then transcend the bounds of kal [time and death]." Kabir went on to say that the effects of a million sins are wiped out by practicing the Nam [the name of God]. Faith and absorption in the true name dispel all delusions and eliminate all karmas.

In terms of the law of karma, Kabir said, "Whatever one puts into a kettle, the same will pour out of the spout. Realize the one and only name and erase the stain of karma. Then will the soul become immaculate; then will it be free from fear and pain."

About the importance of love and mercy, Kabir said, "If a person is devoid of mercy and kindness and yet boasts of vast learning, he will go to Hell in spite of his knowledge even of saints' works."

On the subject of alcohol: "Oh wise ones, consider the curse of wine. You part with money that with effort you earn, in order to turn from man into beast. . . . Kabir is intoxicated with Nam [God's name], not with wine or with drugs. He who drinks from Nam's cup is the truly intoxicated one."

Kabir advocated the Middle Way: "Too much speaking is not good, nor is too much silence. Excess rain is no use, nor is excess sunshine. . . . Oh Kabir, remain aloof from the two; stick to the one. Things extremely hot and things extremely cold are both injurious, like fire."

Kabir was in favor of the life of the family man rather than that of the ascetic. He believed in renunciation and the performance of spiritual exercises but thought they should be maintained while simultaneously meeting life's obligations and responsibilities. He said, "Gradually and easily, all left my mind – son and wealth, wife and lust; and Kabir, the slave, and his beloved Lord fused into one. Such is the achievement of the lovers of Nam. With their body they do their duty, but within, they meditate in a bodiless state."

Kabir had the following to say about sexual promiscuity: "He who flirts with others' wives and he who cheats others of their profit might remain verdant for four days, but at the end will be destroyed from the roots. The adulteress does not control her mind and body; without chastity she ruins her human birth. . . . Those who are engrossed in sensual pleasures are like a grain whose core has been devoured by weevils; the sprout of knowledge will not grow in them, however much they try."

On worldly pursuits: "Nights you have wasted in sleep, days in pursuit of food and pleasure; the priceless pearl of human birth you have exchanged for a bunch of shell."

About procrastination, Kabir said, "Today you say, I'll meditate tomorrow. When tomorrow comes you say, Not now, next day. Saying tomorrow, tomorrow, this golden chance will pass away. . . . False, false, I declare false is the world."

Kabir said not to call Vedas and holy books false. "False are they who do not ponder and practice what the scriptures teach." If your knowledge of scriptures is true then you should be able to see the Lord in every being.

In speaking about the nature of God, Kabir said, "He cannot be seen by the eyes nor perceived by the senses; He cannot be heard by the ears nor described through words; He is beyond the reach of physical efforts; yet, for the convenience of expression, we call Him the ultimate Creator of all."

About seeking God he said, "Day and night I looked for Him. I looked and looked and my eyes turned red. When thus looking for Him, I found Him; the seeker and the sought became one. When the drop mingles with the drop, the drop does not part from the drop. He who becomes a slave and adores the Lord, the Lord becomes his protector and cherishes him. One should be so absorbed in his love for the Lord that he goes not elsewhere; then he will attain the highest truth. If he loves God with such unwavering absorption, he will obtain the Lord and merge in His lotus feet."

Kabir spoke about transcending physical appearances: "Even if the faithful wife be ugly and ungainly, before her inner beauty and grace a million beauties of the world will fade. Even if she be without ornaments, amidst all women she will shine like the sun during the day, like the moon at night."

On surrender to God's will, Kabir said, "Whatever happens is Thy will, oh Lord. He who realizes this merges into sahaj [the natural state of the soul]. Then, oh Kabir, all sins vanish and the mind becomes absorbed in the life of all life. . . . Do not be envious, do not complain. Stick to the righteous path. The man of God lives within the Lord's will and is at peace within. Whatever pleases God, he accepts as true and final. He has absorbed God's will in his heart."

On the subject of the Light of God, Kabir had the following to say: "I have filled the vessel of my body with the ambrosia of pure Light. I drink and drink, yet want more and more. Such is the thirst of Kabir."

The following poem by Kabir sums up the wisdom of this enlightened being.

## To Attain Truth

You may not get the human body again. Keep remembering the Lord with ardor and joy. If your mind discards not its vile ways, how will you cross the dreadful ocean? If mind will give up its wayward trend, the Lord Himself will come and meet you.

Since you were born, you will one day die. Be not dejected on this account. But one who willingly dies while living will never have to face death again.

When one merges in the Master's words, he will be attached to the Lord's name; when he is attached to the Lord's name his delusions depart, his fears end.

When the moon becomes one with the sun, the unstruck melody resounds within; when the melody of the bagpipe resounds [the sound of the higher celestial spheres], the soul shares the throne with the Lord.

Keep constantly the company of saints; then your mind will be dyed in the Lord's hue. Have firm faith in the saints' lotus feet and you will take abode where there is no fear

It is not a game for the unripe to play; the rare valiant one alone plays it well. When he plays the game with audacity, the firmament within he makes his home.

Hold your restless mind; keep it still and taste the elixir of His love. When you drink this elixir within, death dies and you begin truly to live.

Thus singing, Kabir, the Lord's slave, through mind controls his wayward mind. When he stilled his mind within, he became one with his Master; he realized the truth.

# 29

## *Apollonius of Tyana*

*His noble countenance,*
*his winning presence, his pure doctrine,*
*his unsullied life, his ardent advocacy of the*
*immortality of the soul, as well as his miracles, led*
*men to believe, wherever he went, that*
*he was more than mortal.*

W. B. Wallace

In my study of the Alice Bailey books, I came across the understanding that the being who was Jesus had two subsequent incarnations after his life as Jesus Christ. This was a great surprise to me. According to Djwhal Khul, Jesus took his fifth initiation as Apollonius of Tyana, and then he came back one more time in the 1600s in a Syrian body. It is in that body, according to Djwhal Khul, that Jesus ascended in this century. Not much information is available on the most recent incarnation, but there is quite a lot of information about his life as Apollonius of Tyana. An encyclopedia had a short article which said, to my surprise, that the teachings of Apollonius were very similar to those of Jesus Christ. Little did the writer of the encyclopedia know that they were the same soul!

Much of the available information about Apollonius comes from a biography by Flavius Philostratus, *The Life of Apollonius of Tyana*. The actual date of his birth is unclear; what is clear is that this being again incarnated on Earth very soon after his life as Jesus.

At the age of twelve he was sent to Tarsus where he studied literature, rhetoric, and all forms of philosophy. He was initiated there into the healing arts in the temple of Aesculapius, and he committed himself to following the philosophy of Pythagoras. He became a vegetarian, abstaining from alcohol and from all sexual activity. He dressed only in a white robe, and he walked barefoot. His handsome features are said to have resembled those of Jesus; he had a long beard and hair to his shoulders.

It was during those early times that Apollonius committed himself to the pursuit of knowledge and philosophy. He gave his money to his poor relatives and traveled to Antioch, where he began receiving disciples and teaching. He studied there in the temple of Apollo and later traveled to India and Egypt in search of knowledge. His travels were similar to those he took as Jesus.

There is much confusion among Apollonius, Jesus, and the Lord Maitreya, who resurrected Jesus' physical body after the crucifixion. For one thing, Jesus and Apollonius were so similar and lived so close together chronologically (it seems he was born about nine years after the death of Jesus), that some historians have confused the two. Secondly, Lord Maitreya traveled around India and the Americas during the thirty-one years following the resurrection, which has also confused people. There is even a group of historians who believe that Jesus didn't exist and that it was Apollonius who was the Messiah. This, of course, is not true. Confusion arises because Jesus and Apollonius were the same soul, so their teachings were similar.

Upon returning from his travels in India and Egypt, he went to Greece to restore the mystery school. Along with the teachings of Pythagoras, he also taught the teachings of Krishna and the Buddha to which he had been exposed while in India studying under the Himalayan spiritual master Iarchus.

During his early years of training with the Pythagoreans he maintained silence for five years and continued to be an ascetic throughout his entire life.

He was extremely psychic and had the ability to see into the future. He believed in the immortality of the soul and in God the Creator. He was a great healer, a religious reformer, a social leader, a philosopher, and a teacher of morals. He traveled throughout the Roman Empire and wherever he went, divine honors were given to him. He was one of the great spiritual masters who has worked on the Earth, so it is curious that he is not nearly as well known as Jesus, Buddha, Krishna, Pythagoras, or Saint Francis.

Over seventeen temples were built in his honor. He was an example of human perfection, physically, emotionally, mentally, and spiritually. It is said that the Essenes were his followers, which is fascinating, given that he initiated the Essene movement in a past life as Melchizedek and then was the Messiah of the Essenes in his past life as Jesus Christ. The name of his religion at the time was Essenian Christosism, a fitting name in that he had been both an Essene and the Christ in his past life.

Constantine directed his armies to murder all the descendants of Apollonius after his death which probably explains why the Essene movement disappeared so quickly from historical records.

Emperor Aurelian called Apollonius "the most God-like, holy, and venerable of all mankind, endowed with more than mortal powers." Emperor Alexander Severus had a statue of Apollonius made and placed in his private chapel with Orpheus (formerly the Buddha), Abraham (also El Morya), and Christ (Jesus and the Lord Maitreya).

Apollonius had great modesty and virtue. He traveled the world, counseling, teaching and helping wherever he could. There arose the belief that he was the second Christ which, in truth, he was. At one point in his life, he was imprisoned and sentenced to death, but by using brilliant oratory skills at his trial, he secured his own freedom.

The country people of the Roman Empire said that he was the son of Zeus, but he claimed to be the son of Apollo, as his name indicates. He was considered to be the "true friend of the gods."

W.B. Wallace writes in his book about Apollonius that "his noble countenance, his winning presence, his pure doctrine, his unsullied life, his ardent advocacy of the immortality of the soul, as well as his miracles, led men to believe, wherever he went, that he was more than mortal."

J.A. Froude, in his book, says, "According to Philostratus, he was a heathen savior who claimed a commission from Heaven to teach a pure and reformed religion, and in attest to this, he went about healing the sick, curing the blind, raising the dead, casting out demons, stilling tempests, and prophesying future events, which came afterwards to pass."

After his death his followers were called Apollonians, and the sect flourished until some time during the fourth century.

William Lecky, in his book *History of European Morals*, says that Apollonius "obtained a measure of success second only to that of Christ." G.R.S. Mead writes that "Apollonius of Tyana was the most famous philosopher of the Graeco-Roman world of the first century, and he devoted the major part of his long life to the purification of the many cults of the empire and to the instruction of the ministers and priests of its religions. With the exception of Christ, no more interesting personage appears upon the stage of Western history in these early years."

Apollonius was actually at a higher level of spiritual initiation than Jesus was, as Jesus took his fourth initiation at the crucifixion, and Apollonius took his fifth initiation in that lifetime. The crucifixion was one of the most poignant moments in the history of the Earth, for Jesus on the cross was taking his fourth initiation at the same moment that Lord Maitreya was ascending. You can just imagine the enormous amount of spiritual energy that was constellated in those moments. Lord Maitreya was the highest being to graduate from the mystery school called Earth.

Arnobius, the teacher of Lactantius at the end of the third century, classes Apollonius among the great prophets, side by side with Zoroaster (who was also Buddha). Philostratus compared Apollonius to Pythagoras. Apollonius wrote many books, including *The Mystery Rites Concerning Sacrifices, The Oracles Concerning Divination, The Life of Pythagoras, The Will of Apollonius*, and *A Hymn to Memory*, but unfortunately, they have all been lost.

Apollonius never married and he remained chaste even though he was one of the handsomest men of his time. He perceived two paths in life: the path of hedonism and the path of philosophy and wisdom. He taught harmlessness to all living beings, including animals. He was, of course, opposed to the cruel sports practiced throughout the Roman Empire. Apollonius considered healing the most important of the divine arts. Of all the systems of philosophy he studied, the Pythagorean philosophy was his favorite, and he referred to Pythagoras as his spiritual ancestor, even though he was greatly influenced by the Brahmin sages with whom he studied in the Himalayas.

Iarchus, a great Buddhist religious reformer, became the teacher of Apollonius when he was in the Himalayas. When they first met, Apollonius was immediately given a psychic reading of his entire life and it amazed him; Iarchus and the Brahmin sages were able to see directly into the soul. They saw themselves as gods among men because of their goodness and their commitment to knowing themselves. According to Philostratus, Brahmin sages were able to levitate at will, and Iarchus was capable of performing many miracles. Apollonius was instructed by Iarchus in the sciences of medicine, astrology, and soul divination, and he developed an in-depth understanding of Buddhism.

Upon Apollonius' departure from the Himalayas, Iarchus gave him seven rings which were named after the seven planets and each of which was to be worn on a particular day of the week. They were to give Apollonius good health and a long life.

Many believe he might have returned to the Himalayas, but that has never been ascertained. Iarchus prophesied that Apollonius would attain the honors of divinity, and it was from Iarchus that he received his mission to restore the ancient mysteries to their former purity. He remained in telepathic communication with Iarchus for the rest of his life.

Apollonius spread the Eastern teachings along with his foundation in the Grecian mysteries of Orpheus and Pythagoras. On his return to Greece he was regarded as a divine personage with miraculous powers.

Much of Apollonius' work involved unifying the various religious philosophies and demonstrating their common origin. He also worked diligently to abolish all animal sacrifice and to replace idolatry with the worship of the living God within each person. He traveled throughout the Roman Empire and to Syria, Egypt, Greece, and Spain in his mission.

He saw each person as having a higher self which considered to be an angel that inhabited the Heavenly world. Apollonius was very politically and socially active during his life and he stirred up much trouble because of his outspoken views, although his main work was that of a religious reformer.

At the advanced age of one hundred, Apollonius disappeared without leaving a trace.

# 30

## *Appearances and Teachings of the Virgin Mary*

*Hail Mary full of grace, the Lord is with thee.*

The Rosary of the Virgin Mary

For the past one hundred fifty years, the Virgin Mary has been making documented appearances in her spiritual form all over the Earth. The first documented case was in 1858 when she appeared to a fourteen-year-old peasant girl, Bernadette Soubirous, in Lourdes, France. The Virgin Mary appeared eighteen times. She instructed Bernadette to dig a hole in a certain spot and holy water poured out from it. A grotto was built which eventually became one of the world's most famous healing shrines. To this day, thousands of people make spiritual pilgrimages to Lourdes, and many are still experiencing miraculous healings.

### The Lady of Fatima

One of the most famous appearances of the Virgin Mary was in Fatima, Portugal, in 1916. Here Mary appeared to three small children whose names were Jacinta, Francisco, her brother, and Lucia dos Santos. The children were tending sheep when an angel appeared and said, "Do not fear, I am the angel of peace. Pray with me." The angel requested that the children recite the following prayer: "My God, I believe, I adore, I hope, and I love you. I implore your pardon for those who do not believe, do not adore, do not hope, and do not love you."

Two of the children heard the inner words whereas one was able to just see, clairvoyantly, what was happening. The angel appeared again a couple of months later and said, "Pray very much. The most holy hearts of Jesus and Mary have designs of mercy on you. Offer prayers and sacrifices constantly to the Most High." The angel turned out to be the guardian angel of all of Portugal.

On May 13, 1917, the children were tending sheep again when there appeared on top of an oak tree a woman of luminous, transcendent beauty. She was wearing a dress of white and her hands, holding a rosary, were pressed together in prayer. She asked the children not to be afraid and told them she came from Heaven. She requested that the children go to the same physical spot at the same hour on the thirteenth day of each month until October. She told the children, when asked, that they would all go to Heaven, but they would need to say many rosaries.

Mary was true to her word and appeared when she had said she would. She told the children many things, among them that World War I was the karmic result of humankind's selfishness and materialism.

One of the requests she made through the children was to have Russia be consecrated to the Immaculate Heart. Through that process, she said, it was possible that Russia would be converted to the ways of God. If it was not done, Russia was in danger of spreading the scourge of Communism and the lack of belief in God around the planet.

During one particular appearance, on September 13, thirty thousand people were present. They witnessed the darkening of the sun's light to such an extent that stars became visible. On that occasion, thousands of people were able to see the Virgin Mary, not just the children.

She appeared to one priest first as a white globe of Light moving from east to west in the sky, heading for the oak tree. Many were unable to see her with their normal vision but witnessed a shower of white flowers falling from the sky. Most of the people saw the globe of Light but not Mary herself. She requested the people who were there to say the rosary to hasten the end of the war.

## Her Most Famous Appearance at Fatima

On October 13, 1917, a rainy day, the most extraordinary appearance of Mary occurred. It has been called the Miracle of the Sun and it was witnessed by over one hundred thousand people, for Mary had prophesied that a miracle would occur on that day.

It began when a cloud of white Light that everyone could see moved through the sky. The Virgin Mary then appeared to the children at the oak tree and requested that a chapel be built in that place in her honor. She prophesied that the war would soon end. She told the children that men must amend their ways and stop offending the Lord. At about one o'clock the rain stopped. The sun began to appear as a shining silver disk that grew and expanded until it broke through the clouds. It then began to whirl rapidly, like a gigantic firewheel. There appeared on the sun's rim a border of crimson. Blood-red light was flung across the sky. Then a full spectrum of brilliant colors washed across the heavens. All one hundred thousand people were able to see the display, and thousands of them fell to their knees, weeping and praying. The sun began to dance in the sky. Then it seemed to plunge down toward the Earth. People began to scream, thinking that the end of the world had come. As people prayed, the sun began to climb back into the sky and return to normal.

People began to shout, cry, laugh, and weep with joy over what they had just experienced. Then they became aware that their clothes were completely dry and that the mud caused by the earlier rain had also dried up. All who were present had the profound knowingness that they had witnessed a miracle. For many years the Catholic Church disavowed the experience, but I don't think it is possible that all one hundred thousand people were hallucinating.

During the series of apparitions, Lucia was given three secrets by Mary. The first was a vision of Hell. The second was a vision of a strange light in the sky that was a prophecy of the Second World War. The third was a sealed envelope which was given to the Pope, to be opened in 1960 and shared with the world.

Mary also told Lucia of five scourges that were to transpire upon the Earth: the first was the beginning of the Second World War; the second was the militant rise of Communism; the third and fourth scourges were karmas involving the Catholic Church itself; the fifth scourge was the potential for several entire nations to be completely annihilated. She did not say exactly how that was to happen, but a vision was given of Communism dividing the world into two heavily armed, angry camps. This prophecy turned out to be accurate, given the Cold War that existed for much of this century.

The most interesting secret was the letter that was given to the Pope and opened in 1960. The Vatican apparently sent excerpts from the letter to President John Kennedy, to Premier Nikita Khrushchev of Russia, and to Prime Minister Harold McMillan of England in 1963.

According to Earlyne Chaney's book *Revelations of Things to Come*, a newspaperman was able to obtain part of the letter, and it was published in a European newspaper in October of 1963. The following is a direct quote from that newspaper article:

> Don't worry, dear child. I am the mother of Jesus speaking to you and begging you to proclaim in my name the following message to the entire world. In doing this, you will meet with great hostility but be steadfast in the Faith and you will overcome this hostility. Listen and remember what I say to you. Men must become better. They must implore the remission of the sins which they have committed and will continue to

commit. You all may understand the words which, through you, I address to mankind. You have just seen the prodigy of a short while ago, the great miracle of the sun. Everyone has seen it, believers, nonbelievers, country and city dwellers, scholars and journalists, laymen and priests. And now proclaim in my name:

A punishment will befall the entire human race. It will not come today nor even tomorrow but in the second half of the twentieth century [after 1950]. What I revealed at La Salette through the children Melanie and Maxamin, I repeat today before you.

Mankind has not developed as God expected. The human race has been sacrilegious and has trampled underfoot the gifts which were bestowed on it. Nowhere does order reign. Satan has reached the very highest positions. It is Satan who governs and decides the march of events. He will succeed in introducing himself into and reaching the highest summit of the Church. He will succeed in sowing confusion in the minds of great scholars who invent arms with which it will be possible to destroy half of mankind in a matter of a few minutes. He will have powerful nations under his empire and he will lead them to the mass production of these weapons. If mankind does not take steps to restrain him, I shall be obliged to let my Son's arm fall. If those at the top in the world and in the Church do not oppose these acts, it is I who shall do so.

And I shall pray God my Father to visit His justice on men. Then it is that God will punish men more harshly and severely than He punished them by the Flood. The great and powerful will perish thereby as well as the weak and small.

But a time of severe trials will also come for the Church. Cardinal will oppose cardinal and bishop oppose bishop. Satan will put himself in their midst. In Rome also there will be big changes. What is rotten will fall and what falls must not be maintained. The Church will be darkened and the world plunged into confusion.

If mankind does not change, the big, big war will happen in the second half of the twentieth century. Then fire and smoke will fall from the heavens and the waters of the oceans will be turned to steam, hurling their foam toward the sky. And everything that is standing will be overthrown. Millions will lose their lives by the hour and those who are left alive will envy those who have died. There will be tribulation wherever the eye can see, and misery over all the Earth and desolation in all countries.

The time is continually approaching. The abyss is growing wider and there is no end. This will be a time which neither king nor emperor, cardinal nor bishop is expecting. But it will come nevertheless, in accordance with my Father's plan to punish and avenge.

Later, however, when those who survive all things are still alive, God in His glory will once more be invoked and will once more be served as He was so long ago, before the world was so corrupted. I call on all true imitators of my son, Jesus Christ, all true Christians and latter-day apostles. The Time of Times is coming and the end of all ends if mankind is not converted. But . . . if this conversion does not come about. Go, my child, and proclaim it. I shall remain always at your side to help you.

Interestingly enough, when this letter was printed in the newspaper, the Vatican never denied its authenticity, which is their usual policy.

## The Virgin Mary at Medjugorje

One of the more recent appearances of the Virgin Mary has occurred in Medjugorje in the former Yugoslavia, where she is first appeared to six children on June 24, 1981, which was the day of the feast of John the Baptist. Since then she has appeared every day, and people from all over the world have traveled there to see her. One of her main messages has been this: "I am the Blessed Virgin Mary. I come here because there are many devout believers here. I have come to convert and reconcile people." The children described the Virgin Mary as the most beautiful of all women.

When the appearances first began and news of them started to spread, the Communist authorities forbade the children to travel to the hill where the appearances were taking place. The children asked Mary if she would come into their church where the authorities had no control, and she agreed.

The church held six hundred people and was always filled. The service began with the rosary and then the children would go into a small sideroom. The Virgin Mary began every communication with the words "Praise be Jesus." The children's vision lasted for two to forty-five minutes. Then the children remain after the mass to answer questions.

On a particular hill in Medjugorje there is a large cross and it is there that the Virgin Mary first appeared. Many people in the community have seen lights rising from the cross and have seen the Virgin Mary suspended above the cross with her arms outstretched. Visions like this sometimes last for as long as thirty minutes. Since the appearances began, the entire community has manifested a collective and ongoing religious fervor.

Earlyne Chaney states, in *A Book of Prophecy*, that Mary has made the following appeal: "The Madonna brings an appeal, a warning from Heaven to all mankind to turn from materialistic ways and cease offending God and nature. If people do not respond by prayer and penance, both offended God and violated nature will allow man to reap the justice of his own dark deeds and thoughts. She pleads for seven Our Fathers, the Lord's Prayer, seven Hail Marys, seven Glorias and one Credo, the Apostles' Creed."

I have enclosed the rosary prayer here. You may change a word or two in it if you are not comfortable with the Biblical version from the Catholic Church.

In the above-mentioned book, on pages 137 to 141, Earlyne Chaney has included a New Age version of the rosary which she channeled. Even though I don't believe in the Catholic doctrine, I find this prayer to be one of the most powerful on the planet.

## Prayers of the Rosary

### The Sign of the Cross

In the name of the Father, and of the Son, and of the Holy Spirit. Amen.

### The Apostles' Creed

I believe in God, the Father Almighty, Creator of Heaven and Earth; and in Jesus Christ, His only Son, our Lord; who was conceived by the Holy Spirit, born of the Virgin Mary, suffered under Pontius Pilate, was crucified; died, and was buried. He descended into Hell; the third day He arose again from the dead; He ascended into Heaven, sitteth at the right hand of God the Father Almighty; from thence He shall come to judge the living and the dead. I believe in the Holy Spirit, the Holy Catholic Church, the communion of Saints, the forgiveness of sins, the resurrection of the body, and life everlasting. Amen.

### The Our Father

Our Father, who art in Heaven, hallowed by Thy name: Thy kingdom come; Thy will be done on Earth as it is in Heaven. Give us this day our daily bread: and forgive us our trespasses as we forgive those who trespass against us. And lead us not into temptation: but deliver us from evil. Amen.

### The Hail Mary

Hail Mary, full of grace; the Lord is with thee: blessed art thou among women, and blessed is the fruit of thy womb, Jesus. Holy Mary, Mother of God, pray for us sinners, now and at the hour of our death. Amen.

### Glory Be to the Father

Glory be to the Father, and to the Son, and to the Holy Spirit; as it was in the beginning, is now, and ever shall be, world without end. Amen.

### The Hail, Holy Queen

Hail, holy Queen, Mother of Mercy! Our life, our sweetness, and our hope! To thee do we cry, poor banished children of Eve; to thee do we send up our sighs, mourning and weeping in this valley, of tears. Turn, then, most gracious Advocate, thine eyes of mercy toward us; and after this our exile show unto us the blessed fruit of thy womb, Jesus; O clement, O loving, O sweet Virgin Mary.

V. Pray for us, O holy Mother of God.

R. That we may be made worthy of the promises of Christ.

**Let Us Pray**

O God, whose only begotten Son, by His life, death, and resurrection has purchased for us the rewards of eternal life, grant, we beseech Thee, that meditating upon these mysteries in the most Holy Rosary of the Blessed Virgin Mary, we may imitate what they contain, and obtain what they promise: through the same Christ our Lord. Amen

## Messages From the Virgin Mary at Medjugorje

The Virgin Mary's main messages have to do with the importance of maintaining peace, praying, reconciliation, fasting, penance, and conversion. She encourages people to pray every day and to fast every Friday as a form of penance. She suggests that people pray for thirty minutes in the mornings and evenings, asking that the Holy Spirit descend and become one with their consciousnesses. She prophesies that humanity is going through a critical stage  and says that conversions from materialism to spirituality are of the utmost importance for all people on Earth.

When one of the children asked about the purpose of fasting, Mary said it would produce "joy and availability to God, a more total trust in Him, and a more vital prayer. The world has forgotten the value of fasting and prayer. With fasting and prayer, wars could be stopped and natural laws suspended."

Mary suggests carrying a blessed object or spiritual amulet of some kind for protection. She also suggests having blessed objects in the home, such as spiritual statues, pictures, lighted candles, and so on. She says that such statues can become the repositories of great spiritual power, thus helping to generate that power within.

The six children have been given ten secrets by the Virgin Mary, but only the girl named Mirjana has been given all ten. The children are not allowed to release these secrets until permission has been given. One of the secrets has to do with the time in the future when the appearances at Medjugorje will end. At that time there will appear on the hill at Krizevak, near the cross a spiritual sign for all the world to see, one that is beyond the destruction by mortal man. The children know when that will occur but have not yet been allowed to release the information.

According to the children, the eighth secret was to be a terrifying chastisement of the world, but that has been avoided through prayer and conversion. Mary has also given all six children a vision of Heaven and Hell. In this regard she said the following: "I am showing you Heaven and Hell so that you can see for yourselves what reward God has prepared for those who love Him and what punishment awaits those who offend Him."

Another message that was sent through the children was a message to the Pope in which she requested that he consider himself the father of all people, not just of Catholics.

## The Virgin Mary in San Damiano, Italy

On September 24, 1961, Rosa Quatrini was discharged from the hospital and sent home to die after a nine-year illness connected with the birth of her third child. The doctors had given up on her and said she had only a short time to live. Five days later an unknown woman visited Rosa's home and asked her aunt for an offering of one thousand lire. The aunt, having almost no money, gave her five hundred lire, and the unknown visitor asked to see Rosa. She told Rosa to get up, but she couldn't. Then she took both of Rosa's hands and told her again to get up. Suddenly Rosa felt an exceptional sense of well-being said, "I am cured." She placed her hands on Rosa's wounds and they were healed instantly. They then recited the rosary together.

Rosa clearly recognized the woman as the Virgin Mary, which was confirmed. She was told to meet with Padre Pio and was later given instructions to care for the sick for the next two years. Then she would receive further instructions from Mary.

One day while saying the rosary, she heard a voice from within say, "Come, I am waiting for you." She went outside and saw a large gold and silver cloud surrounded by stars and roses of many colors. A red globe descended upon the pear tree near her home, and the Madonna stepped off the globe. She gave Mama Rosa the following message: "My daughter, I come from very far away. Announce to the world that all must pray because Jesus can no longer carry the cross. I want all to be saved – the good and the wicked. I am the Mother of Love, the Mother of All, and you are all my children. This is why I want everyone to be saved. It is for this reason that I come: to call the world to prayer because the chastisements are approaching. I will return each Friday and I will give you messages which you must make known to the world."

Mama Rosa tried to protest, but Mary said she would leave a sign. On October 16, the pear tree burst into bloom and filled with fruit, even though it was autumn and the rainy season had begun. The Virgin Mary appeared to Mama Rosa every Friday afternoon from then on, giving messages through Mama Rosa to the many people who flocked to experience the miraculous presence.

In one message Mama Rosa asked why she had come. Mary responded by saying, "My dear child, I have come to tell you that you gave me a great consolation, and I have also come to shower down many graces. I am here in your midst in the name of the Eternal Father, because I am the Mother of Heaven and the Mother of Earth and of my children. The Eternal Father has given me this name – Miraculous Madonna of the Roses – because I shower down many roses. These roses are the many graces that I shower upon you and your road, so that your life will be a life of grace, mercy, and forgiveness, always in my arms. My dear children, don't worry about the things of this world, but rather be concerned with the salvation of your soul."

## The Virgin Mary in Egypt

In 1924, a Mr. and Mrs. Khalil were grieving deeply for the death of their only son. Mrs. Khalil turned to her picture of the Virgin Mary and said, "The only thing left is prayer." Suddenly, there before them was a vision of the Virgin Mary. She told them not to grieve, for their lives could still have meaning. She requested that they donate their land to build a church in her honor and that she would appear there for one full year if they would do so.

The church was built and was called the Church of St. Mary Coptic Orthodox Church. Mary kept her promise, but her visitations didn't begin until forty-two years later. It was on April 2, 1968, in the evening that two mechanics saw what appeared to be a nun standing on the top of the church. She looked as though she might be ready to jump, so the priest was summoned. He immediately knew what had begun to occur.

Mary began making nightly appearances. Often there would be a formation of doves around her. She was also seen holding an olive branch which she seemed to offer to the many people who would sit and wait for her nightly appearance. On other occasions she appeared with the baby Jesus in her arms and  occasionally with Saint Joseph (who was also Saint Germain). Many miracles of healing began to manifest. Word of her appearances spread all over the world.

In Earlyne Chaney's book *Revelations of Things to Come*, there are some absolutely fabulous photographs of these appearances, and I highly recommend looking at them the next time you are in your local metaphysical bookstore. They are so beautiful that I have cut them out and hung them on my personal altar. They show her totally illuminated as she walked back and forth on top of the domed church. She often appeared with a crown of Light suspended above her head and forming a beautiful halo.

The appearances occurred throughout 1968 and 1969 and then less frequently in 1970. They stopped completely in 1971. Each night, hundreds of thousands of Christians, Moslems, and Jews would all kneel in adoration of the blessed occurrence.

## The Virgin Mary at Garabandal, Spain

On June 18, 1961, four girls had hiked up to an apple orchard that was referred to in their village as the Pines. All of a sudden they heard a loud clap of thunder. Shortly after that, all four girls went into an ecstatic trance and had a vision of an angel. That night, one of the girls heard an inner voice that told her not to worry, for she would see the angel again. Two days later the four girls were saying the rosary when they were engulfed by a dazzling Light. Approximately eleven days after that, the angel came again and said, "Do you know why I have come? It is to announce to you that tomorrow, Sunday, the Virgin Mary will appear to you as Our Lady of Mt. Carmel."

The next day, with a gigantic following of people, the children walked back up to the Pines. Suddenly, all four fell to their knees and their heads were thrown back as they went into another ecstatic trance. The Lady of Mt. Carmel appeared to the children and taught them how to say the rosary in a very slow manner. Then she disappeared. One of the children described her as gleaming most brilliantly like a crystal of great beauty through which the sun's rays glistened.

The four girls began to develop an inner sense of when the apparitions were going to occur. That gave them about three hours to prepare and to go up to the Pines. All four girls would always fall into the rapturous at the exact same moment. Sometimes they would enter the rapturous state while running to the Pines, but they would continue running, even though their heads were thrown back.

Once one of the girls fell and injured her head quite seriously but, being in an ecstatic trance, felt nothing and didn't even know it had happened. During every trance session they would all say the rosary. The Virgin Mary requested that they say the rosary daily in a slow manner as a kind of meditation. The visions continued almost daily through 1962.

When the girls were in the trance state, their faces were radiant with joy, and their bodies became extremely heavy. Once four men tried to lift one of the girls and couldn't do it. As the appearances began to occur more often, certain religious objects such as rosaries, crucifixes, medals, and wedding rings were kissed and blessed by the Lady of Mt. Carmel.

In 1965 the girls began to experience an ecstatic oscillation of their physical bodies. From a kneeling, standing, or sitting position, their bodies would gradually tilt backwards until they were lying on the ground. Their bodies would then levitate. These changes occurred only while they were in the trance state. As soon as the trance ended, the children immediately returned to normal.

On October 18, 1961, Mary gave the following message: "Many sacrifices must be made and much penance. Visit often the blessed sacrament but above all, it is necessary to be very good. If this is not done, a chastisement will come upon us. Already the chalice is filling, and if we don't change, the chastisement will be very great."

On June 18, 1965, the following message came from the Virgin Mary: "As my message on the 18th of October, 1961, has not been complied with, and as it has not been made known to the world, I am telling you that it is the last one. Previously, the cup was filling. Now it is brimming over. Many priests and bishops are following the road to perdition and with them they are taking many more souls. Even less importance is being given to the Holy Eucharist.

"We should turn the wrath of God away from us by our own efforts. If you ask His forgiveness with a sincere heart, He will pardon you. I, your Mother, through the intercession of St. Michael, the archangel, wish to tell you that you should make amends. You are now being given the last warnings. I love you very much, and I do not want your condemnation. Ask us sincerely and we shall grant your pleas. You must make more sacrifices. Reflect on the passion of Jesus."

# 31

## Mother Teresa, Modern-Day Saint

*Do it unto the least of these, my brethren,*
*and you do it unto me.*

Master Jesus

One of the most extraordinary women on the Earth today is Mother Teresa of Calcutta whose life is totally dedicated to Master Jesus. She was the winner of the Nobel Peace Prize in 1979, and there are few people who are not deeply moved by her service to the poorest of the poor.

She was born in Albania and her early training was as a Catholic nun, but she now considers herself to be a citizen of India; in truth, she belongs to the whole world. She was twelve years old when she decided to turn her life over to God. Her mother, who was a holy woman herself, set an example. At the age of eighteen she decided to leave home and become a missionary and she never once doubted her decision.

It was in 1946 that she received the inner calling to leave her mission and instead go to the slums to serve the poorest of the poor. The message she received was quite clear: she was to leave the convent and help the poor while living among them. Jesus wanted to be cared for in the slum-dwellers, the abandoned, the homeless, the uncared-for. Mother Teresa went not only to serve; she also took on the poverty of the people she was helping. She had no money but relied solely on divine providence and a simple faith that God would provide for her and for those she was helping. She felt it was the only way she could put her love for Christ into action.

On her first trip into the streets of Calcutta she had five rupees. She gave four of them to the poor, and then a priest asked her for a donation to the Catholic press. Mother Teresa proceeded to give away her last rupee.

She was on the streets of Calcutta with nothing. Later that day the same priest came back and gave her an envelope containing fifty rupees. A man had heard about her service work and wanted to help her. To this day Mother Teresa and her organization, the Missionaries of Charity, have no regular salary but rely entirely on divine providence to supply all they need for themselves and their service work.

When the first twelve sisters joined her mission they took the vows of poverty, chastity, obedience, and charity, and those vows remain the same today. When a new sister joins, she spends six months as an aspirant, six months as a postulant, and two years as a novice. After that there are six years of temporary vows and then one year before final vows. They cannot accept a woman younger than seventeen years of age.

Their mission is one of total and unconditional love. Their mission is to bring Christ to the people and to bring people to Christ. The key to their work is that they see Jesus in every person they serve, regardless of the distressing disguises he might be wearing. Mother Teresa's view is that the world has turned its back on the poor and in doing so has turned its back on Christ himself. Did not Jesus say, "Do it unto the least of these, my brethren, and you do it unto me."

The sisters walk together in pairs with a rosary in hand. The Virgin Mother is their mother, strength, and protection. Help is given to all people, Christians and non-Christians alike. Everything the sisters do — prayer, work, suffering — is for Jesus. It is Jesus who gives them the strength to carry on this life and to do it with great joy and happiness. It is Christ they tend in the poor. It is his wounds they bathe, his sores they clean, his limbs they bandage, They are taught to see beyond appearance and into the true reality of their brothers and sisters.

The sisters wash, sweep, tidy, mend, and cook for those who are unable to do so. In a beautiful story in a book called *My Life for the Poor* by Jose Luis Gonzalez-Balado and Janet N. Playfoot, Mother Teresa tells of a very sick old man whom the sisters were helping. One day the old man said, "Sisters, you have brought God here. Now bring the priest also." The priest heard his confession, which he had not made for over sixty years, and the next day the man died in the peace of God.

Mother Teresa teaches the sisters to accept everything that happens in life with joy, for that is the best way to show gratitude to God. She believes in action, not just words, and she teaches that each person should give until it hurts, otherwise it is not true giving.

There is a poignant story about an atheist who went to the home for the dying in Calcutta. A man who had been picked up from the streets unconsciousness and covered with maggots was brought in. The sister did not realize she was being watched as she was touching him and soothing him as though Jesus Christ himself were in her arms (which he was, in truth). The atheist stood there and watched in amazement. Then he went to Mother Teresa and said, "I came here Godless and full of hatred. I am leaving full of God. I have seen God's love in action. I have seen it through the hands of that sister, through her face, through her tenderness, so full of love for that man. Now I believe."

The day begins for the sisters at 4:30 a.m. with prayer, meditation, mass, and holy communion. Each Sister owns only two saris so one has to be washed each morning. At 7:30 a.m. they go out into the streets. At 12:30 they gather for spiritual reading and then have a cup of tea. At 3:00 the sisters go out into the streets again. They return at 6:30 for adoration of the blessed sacrament. Dinner is at 7:30 and from 8:30 to 9:00 there is recreation. Then at 9:00 they say night prayers and make preparation for meditation the next morning. Once a week there is a Day of Recollection, including confessions and adorations.

The Missionaries of Charity is a means of putting their love for Christ into living action. Mother Teresa has said that others might not be able to do what they are doing in the slums, but that they cannot do what others are doing in their families, their work, and with their friends. It does not matter where a person is or what he is doing; all that matters is that a person is putting his love for God or Christ into action wherever he happens to be. The sisters believe they are the ones who are privileged in being able to serve the poor, for in serving them they are serving God Himself.

Mother Teresa believes that the poverty in the West is actually much worse than the poverty in India, Ethiopia, and the Middle East. A plate of rice can satisfy the people there, whereas people in the West are dealing with a kind of poverty that involves being lonely, unwanted, unloved, and shut in rooms and old-age homes with no visitors.

Another touching story involves a man who was picked up from the streets in Melbourne, Australia, after having been an alcoholic for many years. He was taken to the Home of Compassion in Melbourne, and the sisters treated him like Christ himself. The man suddenly exclaimed, "God loves me!" After a few weeks he was released and he never touched alcohol again.

Mother Teresa tells of hearing a child's cry at the gate in the middle of the night. When she went downstairs she saw a little boy not more than seven years old. He was crying. He told her that he had gone to his father who had said he didn't want him. He had gone to his mother, and she didn't want him either. Then he said, "But you want me."

At one time a group of sixteen sisters were given permission by the government of India to come and help Mother Teresa in her work. A couple of months later, on leaving, one of the sisters said, "I have received much more than I have given and I can never be the same person again because I have touched Christ, I have understood what love is, what it is to love and to be loved!"

Part of the work of the Missionaries of Charity is to take care of lepers. The sisters are trained properly so there is little possibility of infection, but the dangers are obvious. When the sisters are asked who will volunteer for this work every single hand in the congregation goes up.

Mother Teresa has gone to those infected with leprosy and said that what they have is a gift of God, that God has a very special love for them, that they are very dear to Him, and that what they have is not a sin. An old man who was very disfigured came close to Mother Teresa and said, "Repeat that once more. It did me good. I have always heard that nobody loves us. It is wonderful to know that God loves us. Please say that again!"

In Calcutta alone the sisters take care of seventeen thousand lepers. The greatest suffering for the lepers results from their being shunned by everyone and wanted by no one. Recently, the Missionaries of Charity were given land by the government to rehabilitate lepers, so now fifty-five thousand lepers are being cared for.

The sisters of the Missionaries of Charity do not preach their religion to people in words. Their preaching is done by the example of putting God's love into action, by serving the dying, the homeless, the abandoned, the destitute. The majority of people who go to India to help in this great and noble work are not even Christians.

A man was picked up from an open drain, and his body was covered with wounds. He was brought to the home for the dying and cared for. Three hours before he died he said, "I have lived like an animal in the streets, but I am going to die like an angel, loved and cared for." He died with a big smile on his face.

Mother Teresa picked up a woman from the streets who was being eaten alive by worms and maggots. Mother Teresa did everything in her heart and soul she could do for the woman. When Mother Teresa put her to bed that night the woman took hold of her hand. There was a beautiful smile on her face and she said only two words: "Thank you!" Then she died. Mother Teresa said she had never seen a smile like that on another human face.

One time during the early days of her work, Mother Teresa became very sick. She had a high fever and was in a delirious state when she saw Saint Peter in a vision. He said to her, "Go back! There are no slums in Heaven!" Mother Teresa got very angry with him and said, "Very well! Then I will fill Heaven with slum people and you will have slums then!"

The meaning of Mother Teresa's life is the love of God. It is Christ she serves, who is every human being, regardless of race, creed, or color. She has accepted the responsibility for representing the poor of the world. She tells the sisters, "Let your Light shine before men, that seeing your good deeds they may praise your Father in Heaven! So let men see your good deeds. It is Christ who does them through you. When people praise us for what we are doing, I do not mind it at all. Rather, I rejoice because it all leads to the glory of God."

# 32

## *Joseph Smith and the Mormon Religion*

*Love the Lord your God
with all your heart, and soul, and mind,
and might, and love your neighbor
as you love yourself.*

Master Jesus

The *Book of Mormon*, which is similar to the New Testament in that it is about the teachings of Jesus, is said to have been written by many ancient prophets; their words were inscribed on golden plates. The words of the prophets were said to have been written down by a prophet-historian whose name was Mormon.

*The Book of Mormon* gives an account of two great civilizations: one came to North America from Jerusalem in 600 B.C. and then split into two nations, the Nephites and the Lananites; the other had arrived much earlier and its people were known as the Jaredites. After many years all civilization was destroyed except for that of the Lananites, who the Mormon gospel says are the principal ancestors of the American Indians. The most important segment of *The Book of Mormon* is thought to be the part concerning the ministry of Jesus Christ.

When Mormon had completed his writings, it is said that he gave them to his son, Moroni, who is thought to have added some teachings of his own before hiding the plates in the hill of Cumoran. In the year 421 A.D. Moroni, who was the last of the Nephite prophet-historians, is believed to have sealed the sacred tablets and hidden them with the Lord, to be brought forth in the latter days.

The Mormon gospel states that on September 21, 1823, Moroni appeared to the prophet Joseph Smith in the form of an ascended being. Smith had been in his room praying when a Light appeared and formed itself into the resurrected Moroni. He said Moroni was floating in the air, his feet not touching the ground, dressed in a robe of exceedingly bright white Light.

Moroni said that he was a messenger sent by God and that Joseph Smith had a mission to perform in the service of God. Moroni proceeded to tell Joseph that there existed a book written on golden plates that gave an account of the inhabitants of the North American continent and where they had come from. The everlasting gospel was contained within it. With the book were two stones in silver bowls that Joseph could use in translating the book. He was told that when the time was right to receive the book, he shouldn't show it to anyone except those people he was guided to show it to. Joseph was given a vision as to where the golden plates were hidden, and Moroni then disappeared.

A few minutes later the room lit up again and Moroni returned, repeating the same story and adding to it a prophecy of great destruction by famine, sword, and pestilence that was destined to occur in the twentieth century. Moroni then disappeared again.

He returned a third time and retold exactly the same story, adding that Satan would tempt Joseph to use the golden tablets to get rich. He warned Joseph that he should use the tablets for no other purpose than to glorify God, and he disappeared again for the last time.

As Joseph got up to do his farm work that day, he found himself to be incredibly weak and unable to work. His father sent him back to the house to go to bed, but on the way home he passed out. When he awoke, Moroni had appeared again and had again told him the whole story. He then guided Joseph to tell his father of his experience. Joseph did as he had been bidden and related his experience to his father. His father said that it had been of God and that Joseph should do as he had been commanded.

Joseph went to the physical location he had seen in his vision to find the golden tablets. He said the tablets were hidden on the west side of a hill near the village of Manchester in Ontario County, New York. They were in a stone box underneath a large boulder. Everything was as it had been described to him and as he had seen it in his vision. Joseph was about to remove the golden tablets from the box when Moroni told him that the time was not right for them to be removed. He was told that he would have to wait four years. He was guided to go to the same spot once a year every year until the four years had passed.

Each year Joseph returned and was met by Moroni and given instruction. At the end of four years he was given the golden tablets and the stones for interpreting them. He was told to protect the tablets at all costs until the time when Moroni would return to take them back.

Joseph kept the golden tablets for eleven years and then returned them to Moroni on May 2, 1838. Eleven people testified that they had seen the golden tablets and wrote their testimonies to the fact in the beginning of *The Book of Mormon.*

The book is seen by the Mormons to be an additional witness to the fact that Jesus Christ is the son of God and that all who follow His commandments can be saved. Joseph Smith is seen to be a revelator and prophet in these last days. The church is referred to as the Church of Jesus Christ of Latter Day Saints. Integral to the teachings is the belief in the second coming of the Messiah.

# 33

## *Madam Blavatsky and the Theosophical Society*

*As soon as anyone
pledges himself as a probationer
certain occult effects ensue. Of these, the first is
the throwing outward of everything latent in the
nature of the man: his faults, habits, qualities, or
subdued desires, whether good or bad.*

Madam Blavatsky

Madam Helena P. Blavatsky was one of the most extraordinary women
of the nineteenth century. She was the first person to bring forth an
awareness of the Great White Brotherhood and its teachings. She is one of
the finest channels of spiritual information who has ever existed on this
planet.

Her two books, *Isis Unveiled* and *The Secret Doctrine*, are classics in
the same way that the Alice Bailey books are classics. It was Madam
Blavatsky who established the first dispensation of the Spiritual Hierarchy's teachings; the second dispensation was given by Djwhal Khul in the
Alice Bailey books. Soon there will be a third dispensation of teachings,
again led by Ascended Master Djwhal Khul. It was Madam Blavatsky who
began the whole process.

Her main teacher was El Morya, but she was also a channel for Kuthumi,
Djwhal Khul, Saint Germain, and many other members of the occult hierarchy. The masters said they had waited a long time for someone of her
caliber. She was not only an extraordinary channel, she also had psychic
powers such as few other people on Planet Earth had ever known.

Madam Blavatsky was born in 1831 in Russia, and even as a young child she was clairvoyant, and she spent a great deal of time playing with invisible playmates. She often walked in her sleep. From the beginning, her family knew that she was no average child, for she lived in two worlds simultaneously. She was educated in modern languages, music, and painting. She married at the age of seventeen, but within three months they had separated. That allowed her to travel to Constantinople and Egypt and finally to London where she physically met her master, whom she had seen in her visions since childhood. Of course, it was Ascended Master El Morya who at that time was living in Tibet with Master Kuthumi and Djwhal Khul.

El Morya had gone to London as part of a delegation from Nepal. Although they met in the physical at that time, her true esoteric training did not occur until fifteen years later. Madam Blavatsky tried to travel to Tibet to find El Morya but was unsuccessful since the timing was not yet ripe, so she went back to Russia and her family.

As she matured, her psychic abilities became more and more pronounced. Everywhere she went she seemed to be followed by a hoard of spirit guides that would use her vital force or the vital forces of the group with which she was involved to create all kinds of amazing psychic phenomena. Wherever she went there would be all kinds of raps, whisperings, mysterious sounds, and the moving of furniture and pictures. As she reached her late twenties, these phenomena became more and more pronounced. In these early years, most of the occurrences were beyond her control. She seemed to be a sort of walking psychic vortex. People constantly asked her to demonstrate her amazing psychic powers. On one occasion, she asked one of the young men present in the room to test the weight of a certain small chess table. Then she stared at it intently and asked him to pick it up again. He and another burly man tried to pick it up but it was as if glued to the floor or as though it had a ten-thousand-pound weight on it. Madam Blavatsky had never left her seat.

On another occasion, a certain colonel went into another room and wrote down the name of his favorite war horse, the one he had used in his first military campaign. He put the piece of paper into his pocket and went back into the main room. During the type of seance she was holding at that time, raps on the table would spell out words. The raps accurately told him the name of his horse. Madam Blavatsky's methods of communication with her unseen friends later evolved into automatic writing. Her hand would begin moving without her volition.

At one time, Madam Blavatsky developed a large open wound in her heart area, and was experiencing intense pain and convulsions. A doctor was called while Madam Blavatsky lay unconscious on the bed. As the doctor was treating her, a hand materialized right in front of him and began moving energy from her neck to her waist. The room began to be filled with noises and sounds coming from the ceiling, floor, window, and every piece of furniture. The doctor was scared to death and ran out of the house.

When she had first met El Morya, while sitting on a bench in Hyde Park, London, he had told her that some day she would be living in Tibet, training for the special work she was destined to do. True to his word, El Morya went to Constantinople and took Madam Blavatsky back to his home in Tibet near Trashi Lhunpo. She actually lived for two years in the home of Master Kuthumi Lal Singh. With the help of her guru, she gained entrance to the convents for lamas where no European, male or female, had ever before set foot.

Master Kuthumi had actually been educated at European universities and he spoke English, whereas Madam Blavatsky's English was rather poor. Every day for two months, Master Kuthumi would put his hand on her third eye and have her pull out of his mind all the knowledge he had of the English language. She would feel a cold shiver pass through her; her English greatly improved. At that time, he was training a group of teenaged boys. A boy of fifteen was his most outstanding student; his name was Djwhal Khul. They had been together in a past life when Kuthumi was Pythagoras and Djwhal Khul was his senior disciple, Kleineas.

During that period of Madam Blavatsky's life, her family had no idea where she was. They had not heard one word from her for five years and actually feared she might be dead. On November 7, 1870, a man of Asiatic appearance came to Madam Blavatsky's sister's home with a letter. It was not postmarked and only the name of the city appeared on the envelope. As she took the letter, the Asiatic man disappeared right before her eyes. The letter said, "The noble relations of Madam H. Blavatsky have no cause whatsoever for grief. Their daughter and niece has not left this world at all. She is living and desires to make known to those whom she loves that she is well and quite happy in a distant and unknown retreat which she has selected for herself. She had been very ill but is so no longer, for under the protection of the Lord Sangyas (Lord Buddha) she has found devoted friends who guard her physically and spiritually. The ladies of her house should therefore remain tranquil. Before eighteen new moons shall have risen, she will return to her family." It had been written by the Master Kuthumi.

Master El Morya led Madam Blavatsky out of Tibet and back to Europe. On her travels home she also met Master Hilarion. Her esoteric training was then complete and she was ready to begin her mission. She arrived home before eighteen new moons, as Kuthumi had prophesied, and her family was very happy to see her.

It was long afterwards that she received a letter from her master, El Morya, who ordered her to travel to America. It was there she would meet Henry S. Olcott and found the Theosophical Society in 1875. On her way to America she met a woman with two children who had received money from her husband so she could meet him in America. While in Hamburg, she had bought the tickets but was swindled and lost all her money. Madam Blavatsky boiled with anger at hearing this story and stormed off to the shipping office. The office refused to do anything, so she proceeded to trade in her first class ticket for a third class ticket so her three new-found friends could travel with her. She had to travel in filth, with bad smells and rats in the overcrowded steerage quarters, but she found it to be well worth it, for she had warm companionship. When they arrived in New York the woman's husband was there to meet her.

When Madam Blavatsky needed money she would ask her masters for help and money would magically materialize in one of the drawers of her cabinet. The only problem was that this money, because of occult law, could be used only for her mission and not for her own personal needs. On one occasion she received twenty-three thousand French francs in this manner. El Morya told her to await his orders. She was finally told to take the money and give it to a man at a certain address in Buffalo, New York. Upon doing as she was ordered, she found a man who was about to commit suicide because of a severe financial crisis. He had intended to kill himself within an hour of her arrival.

Soon after that she was telepathically ordered to go to a certain house in Vermont where a seance was being held. There she was to meet a man who had been selected by the masters to be her future partner: Colonel Henry S. Olcott.

Colonel Olcott had a profound interest in psychic and spiritual matters. It wasn't hard for Madam Blavatsky to win him over with her amazing occult and psychic abilities. Olcott soon began to receive letters from certain adepts, fifth degree initiates of the Egyptian Lodge of the Great White Brotherhood. Letters would appear to him magically, materializing right out of the ethers.

Madam Blavatsky received orders to found a philosophical and religious society. The name they decided upon was the Theosophical Society, "theos" meaning divine and "sofia" meaning wisdom. Colonel Olcott became the president because of his excellent administrative abilities. He was the perfect balance for Madam Blavatsky and just the right physical anchor she needed. For a period of time they lived together, even though they were never romantically involved. He became an accepted disciple of Master El Morya.

Colonel Olcott soon began to see how incredibly extraordinary Madam Blavatsky really was. On one occasion, when she was beginning to write *Isis Unveiled*, they were both sitting at a particular table. She asked to borrow a certain type of pencil he had. He hesitated because every time in the past when he had lent her pencils and the like he never saw them again. While he was hesitating, Madam Blavatsky looked at him sarcastically, as if the ascended masters were reading his mind. Suddenly, a dozen of the pencils she wanted materialized right out of thin air. Colonel Olcott had just been taught a little lesson.

Olcott would watch with fascination while the various masters channeled through her to write the book. All of the masters were still physically incarnated on Earth except one discarnate entity who was a Platonist. Madam Blavatsky described her channeling process in the following manner in Howard Murphet's book, *When Daylight Comes*: "It is as if I were asleep or not quite conscious – not in my own body but close by, held only by a thread which ties me to it. However, at times I see and hear everything quite clearly. I am perfectly conscious of what my body is saying and doing, or at least its new possessor." In another letter she said, "Well, Vera, I am writing *Isis*; not writing, rather copying out and drawing that which the personality is showing me."

Whenever Madam Blavatsky would need a quotation from some ancient text it would appear before her in "astral light," and she would just write it down as she saw it. She did not go into full trance but was a conscious channel. Upon the publishing of *Isis Unveiled*, one thousand copies sold within the first nine days. It was through this first set of books that Theosophy began to spread. She was receiving letters from around the world thanking her for her great work.

On one occasion when Colonel Olcott was with Madam Blavatsky and a group of people, she asked the group which spiritual master they would like a portrait of. William Q. Judge asked for Tiravalla, an Indian yogi who was held in high esteem by Madam Blavatsky and the masters. She proceeded to take a blank piece of paper and place on it "a grain of plumbago from a lead pencil." She made a circular motion with her right hand, and after about a minute a stunning picture of the master in samadhi appeared. The great American portrait painter Le Clear was later to say that no living artist within his knowledge could have produced such a masterpiece.

On one occasion she showed her close friend, Belle, a drawer filled with gold bracelets, rings, lockets, and precious stones. Belle picked up the jewelry, handled it, and tried on various pieces. Then Madam Blavatsky closed the drawer. Belle asked her to open it again, and the jewelry had disappeared.

On another occasion Madam Blavatsky materialized a plain gold ring. As it lay in Belle's hand, without touching the ring, Madam Blavatsky closed Belle's palm around it. When Belle opened her palm the plain gold ring had three small diamonds imbedded into the gold.

On yet another occasion Madam Blavatsky materialized for Belle a beautiful necklace with carved beads, telling her to not let anyone else wear it but herself. Later, Belle forgot the warning and let a sick child wear the beads. A medium happened to be present who told her to take the necklace back immediately. She quickly did so, but many of the beads had already disappeared and the other beads were quite hot. What is amazing is that these are the kinds of things Sai Baba can do, but he is the Cosmic Christ, while Madam Blavatsky was still only a third or fourth degree initiate, at best. It just illustrates the abilities that are available to everyone. You don't have to be an ascended master or galactic avatar to do these things; Madam Blavatsky is living proof of that.

On another occasion, Madam Blavatsky fell unconscious and remained so for over a week. Colonel Olcott and Belle were very worried, needless to say, but then they received a cable from Master El Morya, from Bombay, that read, "Fear nothing. She is neither dead nor ill, but has need of repose. She has overworked herself. She will recover." Madam Blavatsky gave much of the credit for her abilities to the masters. However, the masters were later to say that many of her supernatural miracles were created by herself without the masters' help.

Master Kuthumi, commenting on Madam Blavatsky's occult powers in Murphet's book, said, "She can and did produce phenomena owing to her natural powers combined with several long years of training, and her phenomena are sometimes better, more wonderful, and far more perfect than those of some high, initiated chelas whom she surpasses in artistic taste and purely Western appreciation of art as, for instance, in the instantaneous production of pictures and her portrait of the kabir [renunciate] Tiravalla."

Once six Theosophists went on a picnic. A seventh person joined them soon after they had left the house, but that meant they were missing one teacup. The group challenged Madam Blavatsky to materialize another teacup so with the help of an invisible brother, she did, and it perfectly matched the rare set of English cups and saucers Mr. Sinnett had packed for the picnic.

On the same occasion, a Mr. Henderson was impressed but still suspicious. He challenged Madam Blavatsky to produce a diploma of membership in the society already made out in his name and fully completed with the date and the president's signature, even though he had never actually joined. He said that if she could do that he would join the organization and become a believer. Madam Blavatsky materialized his exact wish right before everyone's eyes.

What happened after that was quite interesting and was typical of Madam Blavatsky's entire life. Even though she had done exactly what Mr. Henderson had requested, thus fulfilling her end of the agreement, at a later time Mr. Henderson reneged on his end and wanted more proof. Madam Blavatsky got angry with his failure to keep his word and refused; he resigned and became her enemy.

No matter how many demonstrations Madam Blavatsky would give, ignorant people always wanted another miracle. If she didn't do as she was requested they would turn against her. She often got angry and impatient with people's ignorance and unfair treatment of her, which ended up making things worse.

It was very difficult for most people to believe that she could actually materialize whatever she wanted right out of the ethers. It defied all of modern science. Indeed, the scientific world was always trying to destroy her and her reputation, because if she was legitimate, everything their materialistic beliefs were founded on was undermined.

Madam Blavatsky often did not handle in a detached manner the onslaught of abuse that chronically followed her throughout her life. At the end of her life, when asked about her anger and temper, she replied, "That is my loss and your gain. If I did not have that temper, I should have become an adept [a fifth degree initiate] by this time and would no longer be here among you." Her lack of control of her emotional body was slowing down her spiritual progression even though she was one of the most extraordinary psychics, channels, and instruments of the Great White Brotherhood the world has ever known.

Mr. A.P. Sinnett once approached Madam Blavatsky with a request to be directly put in contact with the Trans-Himalayan Brotherhood. She told him to write a letter and she would send it to them, which she did by holding the sealed envelope against her third eye and then warning the masters to be ready for a communication. Several days later, Mr. Sinnett found a letter from the Brotherhood in his locked desk drawer. It was from the Master Kuthumi. That began a four-year correspondence with Master Kuthumi and occasionally Master El Morya. Based on what Sinnett learned from the letters, he wrote a book called *Esoteric Buddhism*. Later the letters were published in a book called *The Mahatma Letters*. The originals are now in the British Museum.

Madam Blavatsky and Colonel Olcott were guided to transfer their head-quarters to Adyar, Madras, India, where the work continued to expand. According to Colonel Olcott, Master El Morya went there every day in his subtle body. They created a special room for attunement to the masters.

A reporter from the *India Mirror* wrote the following story for his newspaper, which I am quoting from Murphet's book:

A correspondent who has just been visiting the headquarters of the Theosophical Society at Madras sends us particulars of some wonderful phenomena that are occurring there almost every day.

It appears that, under special instructions from the Higher Authorities who preside over the destinies of the society, a special room has been constructed on the house roof, to which few visitors are admitted. In it is a small, splendidly carved cabinet, or almirah, standing upon a pedestal. In it are two portraits of adepts and a figure of the Buddha. If letters addressed to the mahatmas be placed in here and the door is closed for a few moments, the letters will be found to have disappeared, and replies written upon Chinese or Tibetan paper to have come mysteriously from the addressed adepts.

On one occasion, Madam Blavatsky had just finished an eight-page letter expressing her anger with a particular disciple whom she felt had been very disrespectful to the mahatmas. All of a sudden a hand materialized in front of her and tore up the letter. It was Master El Morya.

Several times, Madam Blavatsky became very ill and was close to death, but she was always miraculously healed by the mahatmas.

Once while they were with a group of people, her sister Vera received a letter from one of their relatives. Madam Blavatsky was curious about its contents so Vera challenged her to use her psychic powers to read the letter without opening it. Madam Blavatsky took up the challenge. She held the letter to her forehead and read it word for word without opening it. What she said was written down. Then she took the paper on which her words had been written and made two red marks: one underlined a word; the other was a double triangle beneath a different word. She then said that she would cause those marks to appear on the unopened letter in the exact places she had inserted them on the transcript. When Vera opened the letter, Madam Blavatsky's transcript was shown to be completely accurate and the red marks appeared exactly where she had placed them on the transcript.

On another occasion she asked a group what psychic phenomena they would like to see. One man said he wanted a letter giving him advice from the masters about how to deal with his son who was in America. Above a picture on the wall, a ball of Light started to form and a letter flew forth from the picture. The letter was addressed to the man who had made the request, and its contents gave him the advice he'd been looking for.

During the writing of *The Secret Doctrine*, a Swedish countess who was a good friend of Madam Blavatsky lived with her. The countess was quite clairvoyant, and as she watched Madam Blavatsky write *The Secret Doctrine* she could see the various masters in their subtle bodies. She was also able, at times, to hear clairaudiently what they were saying.

One night after Madam Blavatsky had gone to bed, the countess went over to her bedside to turn out a lamp that had been left on. As she walked away, it went right back on again. This same sequence of events occurred three times in succession until she finally tuned in more deeply, using her clairvoyant abilities, and saw a brown hand turning the knob of the lamp back on. For some strange reason, she called to Madam Blavatsky, who woke up with a start, experiencing fibrillations and a near heart attack. She said that she had been out of her body with her master, and the shock of calling her astral body back so suddenly, especially in her weakened physical condition, had almost killed her.

Soon after that, a report from the Society of Psychical Research came out, saying that Madam Blavatsky was the greatest impostor of the age. She was devastated for a time, and many people turned against her. The fact was that she had never faked a single psychic event in her entire life, but no matter how many demonstrations she gave they were never enough because her abilities were a threat to the very core of everything Western science stood for. Look what happened to Jesus: despite all the miracles he performed, people wanted to crucify him.

I believe that was one of Madam Blavatsky's tests for passing the fourth initiation, which is liberation from the wheel of rebirth. No matter how many miracles she had performed, nothing would ever have been enough. She would always be under attack, and that was something she had to come to terms with.

On this subject, Master Kuthumi has said the following: "I pledge you my word of honor, she was never a deceiver, nor has she ever willfully uttered an untruth even though her position often becomes untenable and she has to conceal a number of things, as pledged to by her solemn vows. She can and did produce phenomena, owing to her natural powers combined with several long years of regular training, and her phenomena are sometimes better, more wonderful, and far more perfect than those of some high, initiated chelas." This should put the matter of Madam Blavatsky's credibility to rest. She was extraordinary!

Toward the end of writing *The Secret Doctrine* she became very ill and again almost died. El Morya came to her on her deathbed and gave her a choice between dying and being free or living to complete *The Secret Doctrine*. He warned her that if she chose to live there would be great suffering and calamities in store. Madam Blavatsky chose to live and be of service to her students and the Theosophical Society.

After *The Secret Doctrine* was published, a review copy was sent to a Mr. W.T. Steac, a famous London editor. He sent the copy to Annie

Besant to review it for his newspaper. Annie Besant gave the books a most admirable review and very shortly thereafter went to visit Madam Blavatsky. Upon looking at her, Madam Blavatsky immediately knew that before her was a great soul. Annie Besant wanted to join the Theosophical Society. Madam Blavatsky took from a shelf the Society of Psychical Research report that said she was the biggest fraud in history and handed it to Mrs. Besant, saying, "Study this well before you take the important step of joining us." Annie Besant did join and eventually became president of the Theosophical Society after Madam Blavatsky's death.

Madam Blavatsky went on to write a shorter book called The *Voice of Silence* and another small book called *The Keys to Theosophy*. The purpose of the second book was to make the Theosophical teachings easier to read and understand.

Shortly after that, a Theosophist by the name of Annie Jaques came to see Madam Blavatsky who said to her, as recorded by Howard Murphet, "We will never meet again in these bodies."

Miss Jaques was startled and asked, "Will I soon pass on, then?"

Madam Blavatsky said, "Not you, but when you return, I shall be gone."

Miss Jaques asked, "Who will take your place?"

Madam Blavatsky said, "Annie Besant, but do not speak of this. I have the word from the Master."

Jaques asked, "How can that cold, intellectual woman ever fill your place?"

Madam Blavatsky said, "She will unfold in spirit and become soft and beautiful, and she will be able to reach the people and do a greater work that I could ever do, as she has command of languages, especially English."

In 1891, Madam Blavatsky finally passed over. Meanwhile in Russia, her aunt, not knowing of her death, was concerned because the agate ring which she had received from Madam Blavatsky twelve years earlier had turned completely black. Katherine, who was with her, said, "I am sure she will recover." As she said that there came a tremendous crash as if a wall of the room had shattered or a table of glasses had crashed. The ladies ran around the house to find out what had happened but they couldn't discover any damage. Katherine, who was somewhat clairvoyant, exclaim-ed, "I see her! There she is!" In a dark corner of the room she could see Madam Blavatsky clad in white with great white flowers on her head. In truth, two days earlier in her coffin, that was exactly how she had looked. When word of her death finally arrived, there were no more strange noises and the ring had turned back to its normal color.

Madam Blavatsky was cremated and her ashes were divided into three parts, one for each of the three main world centers of Theosophy: one part for Europe, one part for America, and the third part for India. Colonel Olcott was busy lecturing in Australia but upon hearing the news of her death, he canceled his lecture tour and steamed back to England. He was the one who took her ashes back to Mother India.

Madam Blavatsky had made an extraordinary mark on the world and she had performed an incredible service to the Great White Brotherhood by making their presence known and by spreading their teachings. She had earned astonishing praise from the likes of Einstein and Thomas Edison.

Strangely enough, Mahatma Gandhi's life and mission were, in part, attributable to Madam Blavatsky. In his autobiography he tells of how, as a law student, he went to London and met two Theosophists who introduced him to the *Bhagavad-Gita.* Strange as this may seem, it is the truth. They also took him to meet Madam Blavatsky and Annie Besant. Gandhi read *The Key to Theosophy,* and it stimulated him to read books on Hinduism. Her teachings literally revolutionized the entire spiritual movement. The continued work of Leadbeater and Annie Besant carried her legacy forward and set the stage for Djwhal Khul to use Alice Bailey in a similar manner in the twentieth century. The writings of Earlyne Chaney also followed Blavatsky's initial thrust.

Madam Blavatsky's classic books, *Isis Unveiled* and *The Secret Doctrine,* stand as a monument to the important work she performed for the Great White Brotherhood and for humanity.

# 34

## *Colonel Henry S. Olcott and the Theosophical Society*

*The strength of the Society
has been derived from the Masters of
Compassion who stand behind us. Its stupendous
growth is due to the willing cooperation of many
unselfish workers in many lands.*

Henry S. Olcott

olonel Henry S. Olcott was an important figure in the New Age spiritual movement and in the beginning stages of the externalization of the Hierarchy in the nineteenth century. He was the perfect male balance for Madam Blavatsky, even though they were never romantically involved. He had been chosen by the Great White Brotherhood to be her partner in the founding of the Theosophical Society before he and Madam Blavatsky ever met and was president of the Society for over thirty-one years, from 1875 to 1906. He traveled and lectured extensively, had miraculous healing powers, and was a great writer which allowed him to be instrumental in helping Madam Blavatsky to write *Isis Unveiled*. It was Colonel Olcott who carried all the administrative responsibilities of the Theosophical Society which the thoroughly mystic Madam Blavatsky had very little to do with. The Society would never have gotten off the ground without his efforts.

Henry Olcott was born in 1832. As a young man he became interested in mesmerism which was kind of a combination of laying on of hands and hypnosis. He had a natural talent for it and it provided a foundation for the later development of his healing talents. As a young man he became involved in scientific agriculture, served in the Civil War, and later found his calling in journalism. In 1874, he began investigating the mysterious world of spirits for a New York newspaper, and it was shortly after that time that Madam Blavatsky was guided to go and meet Colonel Olcott, whom her master had said was going to be her future partner.

Madam Blavatsky amazed him with her enormous psychic and spiritual powers, and a friendship and partnership were begun. She told him that the Brotherhood was using the upsurge in spiritism in the modern world for the purposes of expanding their work.

In 1875 Colonel Olcott received his first letter from the Brotherhood. As described in Howard Murphet's book *Yankee Beacon of Buddhist Light*, the letter said, "From the Brotherhood of Luxor [Serapis Bey's retreat] to Henry S. Olcott: Brother neophyte, we greet thee. He who seeks us finds us. Try. Rest the mind, banish all foul doubt. We keep watch over our faithful soldiers. Sister Helena is a valiant, trustworthy servant. Open thy spirit to conviction, have faith and she will lead thee to the golden gate of truth. She fears neither sword nor fire, but her soul is sensitive to dishonor and she hath reason to mistrust the future."

He was to receive another letter shortly thereafter that read, "Beware, Henry, before you pitch headlong into it. . . . You can decline the connection as yet. But if you keep the letter I send you and agree to the word neophyte, you are cooked, my boy, and there is no return from it. Trials and temptations to your faith will shower on you first of all. Remember my seven years' preliminary initiations, trials, dangers, and fighting with all incarnated evils and legions of devils, and think before you accept. On the other hand, if you are decided, remember my advice . . . patience, faith, no questioning, thorough obedience, and silence."

A short while later he received another letter that said he was to be given esoteric instruction by an initiate named Jack. In an interesting letter sent by the mahatmas to Mr. A.P. Sinnett (one of four years' worth of correspondence which later became known as the Mahatma letters), the following was stated: "One or two of us hoped that the world had so far advanced intellectually, if not intuitively, that the occult doctrines might gain an intellectual acceptance, and the impulse given for a new cycle of occult research. . . . So casting about we found in America the man to stand as leader — a man of great moral courage, unselfish, and having other good qualities [Olcott] . . . with whom we associated a woman of most exceptional and wonderful endowments [Madam Blavatsky]. . . . We sent her to America, brought them together — and the trial began. The chiefs wanted a Brotherhood of Humanity, a real universal fraternity started, an institution which would make itself known throughout the world and arrest the attention of the highest minds."

Master El Morya was later to say to Sinnett in another letter, "There is more of the movement than you have yet had an inkling of, and the work of the Theosophical Society is linked in with similar work that is secretly going on in all parts of the world."

As the Theosophical Society started up, Colonel Olcott was elected president and he made the following statement in his opening address: "If I understand the spirit of the Society, it consecrates itself to the intrepid and conscientious study of truth and binds itself, individually as well as collectively, to suffer nothing to stand in its way. . . . Come well, come ill, my heart, my soul, my mind, and my strength are pledged to this cause, and I shall stand fast while I have a breath of life in me, though all others shall retire and leave me to stand alone."

Colonel Olcott was to receive the education of an ordinary lifetime in a short two-year period as he helped Madam Blavatsky with the English language in her writing of *Isis Unveiled*. Often when Madam Blavatsky needed a quotation from an obscure book, the actual book would materialize from a distant library somewhere in the world. When she was finished with it, it would dematerialize.

Colonel Olcott was greatly tested, for he had stepped onto the path of discipleship. He is quoted in Howard Murphet's book as saying, "No one knows, until he really tries it, how awful a task it is to subdue all his evil passion and animal instincts and develop his higher nature."

Olcott was later to say about *Isis Unveiled*, "If any book could ever have been said to make an epoch, this one could. Its effects have been as important in one way as those of Darwin's first great work have been in another. Both were tidal waves in modern thought, and each tended to sweep away theological crudities."

Early in Colonel Olcott's training, Master El Morya materialized himself from the Himalayas. Murphet says he saw a flash of light out of the corner of his eye and turning his head, he saw a man.

> I saw, towering above me in his great stature, an Oriental clad in white garments and wearing a head cloth, or turban, of amber striped fabric. Long raven hair hung from under his turban to his shoulders. His black beard, parted vertically on the chin in the Rajput fashion, was twisted up at the ends and carried over the ears. His eyes were alive with soul fire, eyes which were at once benign and piercing in glance, the eyes of a mentor and a judge, but softened by the love a father who gazes on a son needing counsel and advice.
>
> He was so grand a man, so imbued with the majesty of moral strength, so luminously spiritual, so evidently above average humanity, that I felt abashed in his presence and bowed my head and bent my knee as one does before a god or god-like personage. A hand was lightly laid on my head, a sweet, though strong voice bade me to be seated, and when I

raised my eyes, the presence was seated in the chair on the other side of the table. . . . He told me that it lay with me alone whether he and I should meet often in this life as coworkers for the good of humanity and I had the right to share in it if I wished; that a mysterious tie, not now to be explained to me, had drawn my colleague and myself together, a tie which could not be broken, however strained it might be at times.

As El Morya was about to leave, it occurred to Olcott that he could be having a hallucination. He inwardly wished for tangible proof that he wasn't just under hypnosis and that the experience was real. El Morya read his mind and left his turban on the table. The turban remained permanently in Olcott's possession, and over one hundred years later, it is still in one piece at the headquarters of the Theosophical Society in India.

When Colonel Olcott went on a special mission for the mahatmas that involved traveling and leaving his business, it resulted in a loss of about $1000 of income, a lot of money at that time. When he returned, that exact amount of money had been deposited into his account by an impressive-looking Hindu man. When Olcott asked Madam Blavatsky where the money had come from, she said that there were hoards of hidden wealth on the Earth to which the masters had access. It apparently belonged to no one. This money often had "bad karma" attached to it and would thus bring harm and misfortune to any ordinary person who found and used it, but the mahatmas knew where it was and could use it in their work for humanity.

At one point he and Madam Blavatsky were having financial problems themselves. They decided to create a magazine which they called *The Theosophist*. Through it they earned a modest but steady income.

Madam Blavatsky was often rude and quite nasty because of her lack of mastery over her emotional vehicle. When Colonel Olcott was asked about it he said, as quoted in Howard Murphet's book, "Do you think I could stand going about with that mad French woman if I did not know what lies behind her!"

On other occasion an Indian man by the name of Thibaut casually remarked to Madam Blavatsky, "These pundits tell me that in ancient times there were yogis who had actually developed the siddhis described in the shastras. They could do wonderful things, such as making a shower of roses fall in a room like this; but that nobody can do such things now." Madam Blavatsky muttered something and swept her right hand through the air. Onto the heads of the pundits fell a dozen roses. As he was about to leave, he asked for another dozen, thinking it might have been a trick. Sure enough, twelve more flowers rained down upon them.

Madam Blavatsky wasn't finished yet, however. One of the Theosophical initiates named Damodar was carrying an oil lamp to light the way.

Madam Blavatsky pointed her right forefinger at the flame and said, "Go up!" The flame proceeded to rise until it reached the ceiling. Then she said, "Go down." She then did it a second time and the same process occurred. The stunned Thibaut nodded farewell and left.

Colonel Olcott was deeply committed to the Buddhist path. He wrote a well-known book called *Buddhist Catechism* which later became a bestseller. Olcott also went through a certain phase during which he was doing literally miraculous healings. A crippled man named Cornelius went to see him and somehow convinced him to try to do some healing on him. He made a few mesmeric passes over the man's arm. Later that day, the man thanked him for the miraculous improvement. News began to spread and by the end of the week his house was packed from the dawn till late at night.

People called him the White Buddhist. He performed a great many of what could only be called miraculous healings, although everyone he worked on was not miraculously healed. He set up a test to determine who would be most open to his mesmeric healings. It was thought by some that the masters were working through Colonel Olcott, but not being clairvoyant or clairaudient he couldn't say for sure. He healed a boy who had had epilepsy of a very serious nature for over seven years. In ten sessions, he healed a man who was blind and had been pronounced incurable by the doctors. He never charged a fee for his healings.

He seemed to wield this superhuman power for over a year, during which time he treated over eight thousand patients in one two-thousand-mile circuit in India while at the same time giving lectures and starting new Theosophical Society branches in the cities he visited. He was a man of enormous physical energy and stamina.

During the last half of 1883, his remarkable healing powers began to wane. He then received a message from the mahatmas to stop performing healings until further notice. It seemed that healing was meant to be a phase of his life but not his total life's work.

At one point, Colonel Olcott had a visitation from Master Kuthumi. He was sleeping when all of a sudden he found himself rushing back to external consciousness. He felt a hand being laid upon him. Kuthumi materialized a letter for him and then left. The letter gave him much personal advice and prophesied the physical death of two active enemies of the Theosophical Society. It went on to say that he would return for a conversation the following night.

The next night a white-clad figure appeared in front of Olcott's tent. It was none other than Djwhal Khul. Olcott was taken some distance from the tents where they would not be bothered, and they spoke for approximately thirty minutes. He was warned of the grave difficulties that lay ahead. He was requested never to lose his faith and confidence. Djwhal Khul said that the mahachohan had ordered him to come and speak with Colonel Olcott and that the mahachohan wanted Olcott to know, through Djwhal Khul, that he was well satisfied with his fidelity to the great cause.

At one point Colonel Olcott was speaking to Madam Blavatsky about a certain Theosophical Society member who had donated five hundred rupees for convention expenses from his own personal account even though he did not actually have the money. Madam Blavatsky reflected on the matter and five minutes later asked Damodar to go to the shrine room and look into the cabinet that was serving as an astral post office. Five minutes later Damodar came back with a sealed envelope in which were found government promissory notes adding up to five hundred rupees and initialed by Master Kuthumi. Also enclosed was a kind letter thanking the member for his service.

The Theosophical Society went through many trials and tribulations. The work they were doing was a great threat to many materialistically minded people as well as to many egotistical "spiritual" people. Madam Blavatsky's psychic powers were always being questioned. Very few people believed it was possible for any person to do the things she did. Because of Madam Blavatsky's explosive emotional nature, even she and Colonel Olcott didn't always see eye to eye. On a deeper level he believed that he and Madam Blavatsky had worked together in former lifetimes and could work well together.

One day when he was sailing on the Ionian Sea toward the heel of Italy, he was sitting in his cabin feeling particularly distraught and discontented. An envelope dropped suddenly onto the table before him. It was from Master Kuthumi. The following is a quote from this letter, as described in Howard Murphet's book:

> Just now on deck your thoughts about her [Madam Blavatsky] were dark and sinful, and so I find the moment a fitting one to put you on your guard. . . . [Of the masters' agents] for the past thirty years, the chief has been the personality known as Madam Blavatsky to the world. Imperfect and very troublesome, no doubt, she proves to some, nevertheless, there is no likelihood of our finding a better one for years to come. Her fidelity to our work being constant, and her sufferings having come upon her through it, neither I nor either of my brother associates will desert or supplant her. . . ."

> To help you in your present perplexity: Madam Blavatsky has next to no concern with administrative details and should be kept clear of them, so far as her strong nature can be controlled. But this you must tell to all: With occult matters she has everything to do. In the adjustment of this European business, you will have two things to consider — the external and the administrative, and the internal and the psychical. Keep the

former under your control and that of your most prudent associates, jointly; leave the latter to her. You are left to devise the practical details with your usual ingenuity.

This letter helped greatly to clarify his thoughts and put his relationship with the Theosophical Society and Madam Blavatsky in the proper perspective.

Soon after that he had the opportunity to meet Annie Besant who had become a student of Madam Blavatsky and was deeply involved in the work. In his dairy, Olcott wrote the following: "Mrs. Besant I find to be a natural Theosophist. Her adhesion to us was inevitable from the attraction of her nature toward the mystical. She is the most important gain to us since A.P. Sinnett." Upon hearing her lecture he said, ". . . a very able and facile discourse. She is a power, indeed, a magnificent lecturer and a chivalrous defense of Madam Blavatsky."

During another difficult period of power struggles within the Theosophical Society, Colonel Olcott sent out a letter of resignation. On the morning of February 10, 1892, as he lay in bed between sleep and wakefulness, he heard clairaudiently the voice of Master El Morya. He was told that he must not resign until given permission to do so by the Brotherhood. They were in great support of him and they would be sending him a messenger to help him in his great work.

It is important to note here that Colonel Olcott was usually not a channel and was certainly not as psychic as Madam Blavatsky was, so periods of time would go by when he had no contact with the masters. During times of great struggle, doubts would come into his mind because of his inability to commune with them whenever he wanted to. The experience mentioned above was a strong confirmation for him, so he rescinded his resignation

Soon after that experience, early one morning he again heard the voice of El Morya telling him that the great messenger they were sending him to help in the work was none other than Annie Besant who was later to become the president of the Theosophical Society.

Colonel Olcott had a high opinion of Charles Leadbeater, whom he saw as a reliable man who put the cause of the mahatmas before his own interests. He was a great seer and a prolific writer, and Colonel Olcott considered him a potential president of the Society. Leadbeater and Annie Besant became the two great leaders of the Theosophical movement after the deaths of Madam Blavatsky and Colonel Olcott.

Marie Russak also played a role in the Society. She had sent a letter to Olcott telling him how her father had appeared to her soon after his death, telling her to study books about Theosophy. He told her to learn to meditate in the manner taught by the Theosophical Society because he

wanted to be able to converse with her while she slept and he wanted her
to remember the meetings. She studied Theosophy, practiced meditating,
and soon attained the ability her father had spoken to her about. Then
during one of their meetings, her father told her to go and meet Colonel
Olcott. After that, Olcott came to call her "Little Mother." As Marie got
more involved with the Theosophical Society she became greatly troubled
by the ego battles and power struggles that were going on. She wondered
what had happened to peace, love, and brotherhood. That night her father
told her, "Base your Theosophic life on the principles of Theosophy, not
on the conduct of the personalities."

One day after Madam Blavatsky had passed on to the spirit world,
Colonel Olcott was visiting with a fellow Theosophist who was quite gifted
psychically. He asked her to give him a reading concerning his future and
that of the Theosophical Society. Suddenly she said that in the air above
his head she could see the word "come." Colonel Olcott leaped into the air
in great amazement; "come" was the secret word he and Madam Blavatsky
had agreed upon early in their friendship. Whichever one died first would
use it as a sign, or password, to prove that a communication from the other
world was genuine.

On October 3, 1906, while traveling aboard a ship, Olcott caught his
foot on the edge of a step and went tumbling to the lower deck. He was
hospitalized for a whole month, and it was found at that time that he also
had heart disease. Annie Besant came from Benares to fill the role of
acting president.

Again, there was some confusion and conflict over procedural and
administrative matters, and Colonel Olcott sent out a telepathic call to the
masters for help. El Morya and Master Kuthumi appeared astrally in
Olcott's bedroom when Marie Russak and a Miss Renda were both in the
room to confirm the conversation. The masters disappeared by fading into
the wall of the room after having confirmed that Annie Besant should be
the next president of the Society with no conditions attached, and Olcott
thus appointed her.

On January 11, 1907, El Morya and Kuthumi paid another visit to
Colonel Olcott and he asked if Annie Besant had been deluded by her work
with Charles Leadbeater. The masters said there had been no delusion
whatsoever. They said they didn't agree with Leadbeater's teachings about
sex, but if they had to wait for perfect human instruments before giving out
esoteric information, then no knowledge would ever be given out. They
went on to say that he had been a "light to the Society."

Leadbeater, who had resigned from the Society because of his sexual
teachings, was reinstated with a letter from Colonel Olcott as approved by
Master El Morya.

Close to death, Olcott lay in a reclining chair one day when Marie Russak was present. Suddenly, he cried out, "Old horse!" Marie clairvoyantly saw Madam Blavatsky and their friend Damodar in astral form.

On February 3, 1907, four of the masters came to visit and told him that his work was over. They thanked him for his loyal service. Colonel Olcott was overcome with joy and he jumped from the bed and prostrated himself at their feet. Two weeks later, on February 17, 1907, Colonel Henry S. Olcott passed on to the spirit world. The three masters he was closest to were all present in astral form, as was Madam Blavatsky. At 7:27 a.m., Madam Blavatsky said, "The cord is broken." He was cremated and half his ashes were put into a casket and dropped into the Ganges River, while the rest of his ashes were given to the sea, at his request. He had completed his mission in service of the first dispensation of the externalization of the Hierarchy.

# 35

## *C.W. Leadbeater and the Theosophical Society*

*Before the man can proceed
to the second initiation, the initiator chosen
by the king demands evidence as to how the
candidate has used the powers acquired
by him at the first initiation.*

C.W. Leadbeater

Charles Webster Leadbeater was one of the great clairvoyants and master occultists of the twentieth century. He was a clear channel for the Great White Brotherhood at a time when very few people were acquainted with it. He was also a master of astral travel; he said he had visited and explored most of the planets in this solar system while his physical body remained on Earth. He had penetrated the depths of the atom with his psychic powers. He could take disciples in their astral and mental bodies to see the masters in the Himalayas and had almost total recall of everything that happened.

He was a prolific writer on occult matters and without his books, Theosophy would scarcely be understandable. He was a controversial figure and although not a saint, he performed a great service for humankind in bringing forth the teachings of the Great White Brotherhood and the Spiritual Hierarchy.

Leadbeater was able to see thought forms and was an authority on the chakras and the human aura. He was quite proficient at communicating with the dead, and he often told of visiting the states of existence known as Heaven, Hell, and Purgatory. He was able to see into the inner aspects of anything he looked at. His disciples considered him the world's greatest seer and psychic. Annie Besant, president of the Theosophical Society at that time, called him "a man on the threshold of divinity" and continued to hold him in high esteem even when he was under attack by many members of the Theosophical Society. He wrote over forty books; *The Masters and the Path* is one of the classics in the field.

He popularized Theosophy because his books were so easy to read, which was not true of the books of Madam Blavatsky or even of those of Annie Besant.

Leadbeater was the man who found Krishnamurti. It was also Leadbeater, not Alice Bailey in the Djwhal Khul channelings, who first announced that Lord Maitreya would be reappearing in the world.

C.W. Leadbeater was born on February 17, 1847. It was in 1883 that an old school friend who was the captain of a British steamer told him some extraordinary stories about Madam Blavatsky. He had seen her strike a match and light a cigarette in a howling gale and she accurately predicted that he would be appointed captain of the ship even though at the time he was only the second officer; when the ship reached Calcutta her prophecy proved accurate.

Leadbeater immediately read A.P. Sinnett's book, *The Occult World*, which was dedicated to Master Kuthumi and which contained many of the Theosophical teachings. It also spoke of Madam Blavatsky's ability to materialize things at will, right out of the ethers, and made reference to letters Sinnett had received from the mahatmas, or ascended masters. Leadbeater eventually became initiated into the Theosophical Society and began attending meetings regularly.

When he attended a seance through another organization, the spirit guide spoke of the Masters of Wisdom and said that he could take a letter to them. Leadbeater took him up on the offer and wrote a letter to Master Kuthumi, requesting to become his disciple. It wasn't until he met Madam Blavatsky that he got his reply. She told him one evening that Master Djwhal Khul had just given her a message saying that a reply to his letter would be forthcoming. Master Kuthumi did respond and he requested that Leadbeater go to the main Theosophical Center in India for a few months.

Leadbeater was willing to devote his life to the masters, but he needed three months to clean up his affairs and he didn't know if that would be acceptable. Madam Blavatsky told him to stay close to her for the next forty-eight hours and a reply would be forthcoming. Sure enough, that evening, right before his eyes, a letter materialized in her hand out of the etheric substance. The letter was addressed to Leadbeater and it said, "Since your intuition led you in the right direction and made you understand that it was my desire you should go to Adyar [the location of the

Theosophical Center in India] immediately, I may say no more. The sooner you go, the better. Do not lose one day more than you can help. Sail on the fifth if possible. Join Madam Blavatsky at Alexandria. Let no one know that you are going, and may the blessings of our Lord and my poor blessings shield you from every evil in your new life. Greetings to you, my new chela. KH [Master Kuthumi]."

Leadbeater immediately resigned from his position as a bishop of the Church of England. Madam Blavatsky later materialized another letter for Leadbeater as he traveled to India, which read, "Tell Leadbeater I am satisfied with his zeal and devotion." He was later to have another remarkable experience in the presence of Madam Blavatsky when Master Djwhal Khul materialized right out of the ethers. Madam Blavatsky proceeded to scold Leadbeater, saying, "A novice occultist! You will not go far on the path of occultism if you are so easily startled at a little thing like that."

Blavatsky requested that Leadbeater be officially initiated into the Buddhist faith. Djwhal Khul, Kuthumi, and El Morya were Tibetan Buddhists, although very universalistic in their approach. These three great masters were all physically incarnated in the Himalayas and lived close to each other.

Leadbeater went through the Buddhist initiation and renounced the Christian faith as he had once understood it, although later in his life he was to reconnect with it in a new and innovative way, becoming a bishop in the Liberal Catholic Church. He took the following vows:

> I reverence the Blessed One, the Holy one, the Perfect in Wisdom.
> I take the Lord Buddha as my guide.
> I take his law as my guide.
> I take his order as my guide.
> I observe the precept to refrain from the destruction of life.
> I observe the precept to refrain from taking that which is not mine.
> I observe the precept to refrain from unlawful sexual intercourse.
> I observe the precept to refrain from falsehood.
> I observe the precept to refrain from using intoxicating liquors or stupefying drugs.

A lock of hair was cut from his head and he was officially initiated into the Buddhist faith. One day, Leadbeater was on the roof of the headquarters when Master Kuthumi materialized right before his eyes. Leadbeater prostrated himself before his master, but Kuthumi said that that kind of devotion was not necessary for European devotees, for it was not part of their culture to give salutations in that manner.

Now it must be understood that up until that time, Leadbeater had had
no clairvoyant abilities. The story of how he obtained these abilities is a
fascinating one. His own writings describe the process:

> One day, however, when the Master Kuthumi honored me with a visit,
> he asked me whether I had ever attempted a certain kind of meditation
> connected with the development of the mysterious power called kun-
> dalini.

> I had, of course, heard of that power, but knew very little about it, and
> at any rate supposed it to be absolutely out of reach for Western people.
> However, he recommended me to make a few efforts along certain lines,
> which he pledged me not to divulge to anyone except with his direct
> authorization, and told me that he would himself, watch over those
> efforts to see that no danger should ensue.

> Naturally, I took the hint and worked away steadily, and I think I may say
> intensely, at that particular kind of meditation day after day. I must
> admit that it was very hard work and sometimes distinctly painful, but,
> of course, I persevered, and in due course began to achieve the results
> that I had been led to expect. Certain channels had to be opened and
> certain partitions broken down. I was told that forty days was a fair
> estimate of the average time required if the effort was really energetic
> and persevering.

After Leadbeater had practiced the exercises for forty-two days, Master
Kuthumi visited him again. It was Master Kuthumi who "performed the
final act of breaking through which completed the process and enabled me
thereafter to use astral sight while still retaining full consciousness in the
physical body." This is equivalent to saying that the astral consciousness
and memory became continuous, whether the physical body was awake or
asleep.

Many masters came to help Leadbeater train in his new-found clairvoyance. His principal teacher at that time was Master Djwhal Khul. Leadbeater had been Djwhal Khul's student in a past life when Djwhal Khul had
been the chief pupil of Pythagoras. One subject the masters advised him
about was his younger brother who had been murdered in South America.
They told him that his brother had reincarnated as a Singhalese boy, and
Leadbeater eventually found him as a thirteen-year-old Buddhist boy
named Jinarajadasa.

One of the many books Leadbeater wrote was *The Astral Plane*. On an
eventful morning Master Kuthumi came to Leadbeater and asked for the
original manuscript. He went on to say, according to Gregory Tillet's book
*The Elder Brother*, "that he desired to deposit it in the Museum of Records
of the Great White Brotherhood." The master explained that *The Astral
Plane* was an unusual production and a landmark for the intellectual
history of humanity.

Soon after that Leadbeater began an intensive investigation into the past lives of many of the members of the Theosophical Society. His most famous research concerned Krishnamurti, also known as Alcyone, and was recorded in *The Lives of Alcyone*.

During this early period Annie Besant started working intensively with Leadbeater in his clairvoyant research. She was not very psychic initially either, but after meeting with Leadbeater, she developed psychic abilities almost overnight.

Leadbeater was a rising star in the Theosophical Society when there occurred a sequence of events that led to his fall from grace. Misunderstandings and accusations are almost inevitable when moral standards are as rigid and judgmental as they were in 1900. Even though his so-called infraction involved no one else, because of all the nasty gossip, at least half of the Theosophical Society looked at him in a very harsh manner. However, he was later to be given the full support of the Masters of Wisdom, who criticized Colonel Henry Olcott for having made the matter public, when the whole affair should have been kept private. Colonel Olcott was deeply apologetic at the end of his life for this grave mistake which had thrown the entire Theosophical Society into an uproar.

After that incident, Leadbeater led a rather paradoxical life in terms of public opinion. He was considered either a god because of his incredible occult powers or a criminal because of the alleged events to which those who didn't like him held on tightly. Many people in the Society used the events for their own egotistical purposes to gain power by judging and defaming Leadbeater. Although it was a controversy that followed him throughout his life, it is to his credit that he seemed to handle the negativity with a great deal of detachment and evenmindedness, looking at the whole affair as one of the tests involved in going through the fourth initiation.

With that matter behind him, there began the saga of Krishnamurti. Krishnamurti, of course, was the Indian boy Leadbeater found, who, according to Leadbeater, was going to be the next vehicle for the Planetary Christ, the Lord Maitreya. Krishnamurti was going to repeat the same function that Jesus Christ had performed for Lord Maitreya two thousand years earlier. Leadbeater and Annie Besant became his main teachers and tutors to prepare him for this mission. I have dedicated a whole chapter to the story of Krishnamurti so I am not going to repeat it here; however, I would like to mention some of the details as they were seen by Leadbeater.

Leadbeater's amazing clairvoyance allowed him to see many things that Krishnamurti, himself, had no idea were going on. On one occasion he was instructed to take Krishnamurti and Nitya, his brother, to Kuthumi during the night in their astral bodies to formalize their stepping onto the

path of probation. I would like to record here Leadbeater's experience of
the occasion.

> We found the Master Kuthumi seated on the veranda of his house, and
> as I led the young ones forward to him he held out his hands to them.
> The first boy dropped gracefully to one knee and kissed his hand, and
> thence forward remained kneeling, pressing against the master's knee.
> Both of them kept their eyes upon him, and their whole souls seemed to
> be pouring out through their eyes.
>
> He smiled on them most beautifully and said, "I welcome you with
> particular pleasure. You have all worked with me in the past, and I hope
> you will do so again this time. I want you to be one of us before the Lord
> comes, so I am beginning with you very early. Remember, this that you
> wish to undertake is the most glorious of all tasks, but it is not an easy
> one, because you must gain perfect control over these little bodies. You
> must forget yourselves entirely and live only to be a blessing to others
> and to do the work which is given us to do. . . . Then I take you as my
> pupils on probation, and I hope that you will soon come into closer
> relationship with me, and therefore I give you my blessing, in order that
> you may pass it on to others." As he spoke, the boys' auras increased
> wonderfully in size, and their colors of love and devotion glowed with
> living fire. [Krishnamurti] said, "Oh Master, make me really good. Make
> me fit to serve you."

Leadbeater continued training Krishnamurti and his brother in a
mixture of orthodox Hindu practices, English education, and occult discipline and one day received a message requesting that he, along with Annie
Besant, Krishnamurti, and Nitya, go that night in their astral bodies to
Kuthumi for Krishnamurti to be officially accepted as a disciple. Once
they had all arrived at Master Kuthumi's house, and Krishnamurti had
expressed his desire to work under him, Kuthumi said, "Come with me. I
must present you in your new character for official recognition and
registration." He took them to the mahachohan who looked at them
carefully, noting how young they were and congratulating them on reaching such a position. He admonished them to live up to the levels they had
reached and entered their names into the permanent records.

The next account from Gregory Tillet's book gives Leadbeater's experience of Krishnamurti's first initiation in his astral body:

> When I left my body the first night, I went at once to the Master's house
> and I found him there with the Master Morya and the Master Djwhal
> Khul.
>
> The Master talked to me very kindly for a long time and told me all about
> the initiation and what I should have to do. Then we all went together to
> the house of the Lord Maitreya where I had been once before. There we
> found many of the masters – the Venetian Master, the Master Jesus,
> Count St. Germain, the Master Serapis, the Master Hilarion, and the two

Masters Morya and KH.

The Lord Maitreya sat in the middle and the others stood around him in a semicircle. Then the Master took my right hand and the Master Djwhal Khul my left and they led me in front of the Lord Maitreya, you, Mrs. Besant and Uncle Leadbeater standing close behind me. The Lord smiled at me, but he said to the Master, "Who is this that you bring before me?" And the Master answered, "This is a candidate for admission to the Great White Brotherhood."

Then the Lord turned away from me and called toward Shamballa, "I do this, Lord of life and Light, in Thy name and for Thee." And at once the great silver star flashed out over his head and on each side of it in the air there stood a figure, one of the Lord Gautama Buddha and the other the Mahachohan. And the Lord Maitreya turned and called me by the true name of my ego [soul], and laid his name upon my head and said, "In the name of the One Initiator, whose star shines above us, I receive you into the Brotherhood of Eternal Life."

As I mentioned earlier, there were friction and ego battles in the worldwide Theosophical Society. One of the lodges that broke away from Adyar, the Theosophical Lodge in India that was the main headquarters, was the German lodge, which was under the leadership of Rudolph Steiner. Steiner was a great mystic and to this day he has a large following, although I find his books to be extremely difficult to read because they are so intellectual, technical, and scientific.

In the chapter on Krishnamurti I refer to an experience he had later on in his discipleship when Lord Maitreya first began to overshadow him while he was giving a lecture. Leadbeater happened to be in the audience and he explains in Gregory Tillet's book what he saw clairvoyantly when that happened for the first time.

A great circle of the characteristic blue fire of the Lord Maitreya appeared some feet above our Krishna's head and then stretched down into a funnel. Just above the funnel floated the rosy cross of the Master Jesus, and high above all, near the ceiling of the lofty hall, flashed the star of the Lord of the World.

Down through the funnel poured a torrent of blue fire tinged with rose and all permeated by the indescribable electric glow of the star. This stream rushed into our Krishna's head through the highest of the force centers, and poured through his hands upon each person he blessed. Round the hall stood a circle of great green devas, with forms twenty feet high. And as Krishna gave that final blessing the Bodhisattva himself stood in the air above him, smiling benignly on those who had done him reverence through the person of his disciple.

Krishnamurti and Leadbeater had a very strained relationship except for a few brief periods. The antagonism seemed to be coming mainly from Krishnamurti who later rejected all that he had learned from the Theosophical Society and the masters and even rejected his role as the instrument of the Lord Maitreya. He chose to go out on his own and not be a part of any organization or occult overshadowing. Leadbeater considered it to be Krishnamurti's personality and ego obstructing his clarity, but that was something he said privately, not openly to the Theosophical movement as a whole.

One of the other projects Leadbeater became involved with was a revised ritual mass of the Catholic Church. He had the help of the masters in this regard and later rejoined the Church that had been his roots. He also spent some time exploring and researching the hidden side of Freemasonry.

There were certain members of the Theosophical Society who were claiming openly to have taken all the initiations, which seemed to be their egos talking more than being an occult truth. To his credit, Leadbeater claimed that he and Annie Besant had not achieved more than the fourth initiation and they both hoped to take their fifth initiations in a future lifetime.

In his books, Leadbeater claimed to have met Master Jupiter of the first ray, and to have dined with him and Master Subba Row while working at Adyar. He also said he had met the Count Saint Germain in Rome and had conversed with him often on the inner plane.

When Krishnamurti finally resigned from the Theosophical Society and rejected all of its teachings along with his role, Leadbeater's only public statement was, "The coming has gone wrong." He considered Krishnamurti's new Zen-like teachings destructive and dangerous.

During Annie Besant and Leadbeater's reign, the Theosophical Society grew in membership to over forty-five thousand members in 1928. Leadbeater passed away on February 29, 1934. His final words to his dear friend Morton were, "Well, if I do not see you again in this body, carry on."

Annie Besant had died five months earlier, having been one of his closest friends and even a disciple. Upon her death, George Arundale became president of the Theosophical Society, but it never reached the same level of success it had enjoyed under Madam Blavatsky, Annie Besant, and C.W. Leadbeater.

I want to acknowledge that the quotations in this chapter are from a biography of Charles Webster Leadbeater by Gregory Tillet called *The Elder Brother.*

# 36

## *Krishnamurti and the*
## *Theosophical Society*

*Hold a mirror constantly before you
and if there is anything you see there which is
unworthy of the ideal you have created for
yourself, change it.*

Krishnamurti

The story of Krishnamurti is among the most fascinating of the past two millennia because it was two thousand years ago that Jesus was overshadowed by the Lord Maitreya, the Planetary Christ, and it was Krishnamurti's destiny for approximately twenty years of his life to be the next initiate to perform that service for the Lord Maitreya, two thousand years later.

He chose not to perform that service after going through the training and guidance of C.W. Leadbeater, Annie Besant, and the Theosophical Society, but to follow his own path.

Krishnamurti was born on May 11, 1885, in Madanapalle, India, into a strictly vegetarian Brahmin family. His father was a worshiper of Krishna and a member of the Theosophical Society. His mother had a psychic premonition that her eighth child, Krishnamurti, was to be remarkable in some way and insisted that he be born in the puja (prayer and meditation room).

At his birth, an astrologer cast his horoscope and said that he was destined to be a great man. As Krishnamurti grew, he developed a strong bond with his younger brother Nitya, a clever and left-brained child, while he himself was more right-brained, and even as a youth had some clairvoyant abilities, for he often saw the spirit of a dead girl at a special place in his garden.

In 1909 Krishnamurti's father moved to the Theosophical complex in India to take a job there, and he took Krishnamurti and his brother with him. When Charles Leadbeater first saw Krishnamurti he said that he had one of the most wonderful auras he had ever seen, that it was without a particle of selfishness in it. He predicted that Krishnamurti would one day become a great spiritual teacher. This amazed one of the Theosophical teachers, because having worked with Krishnamurti on his homework, he considered him particularly stupid.

Leadbeater began to meet with Krishnamurti and to clairvoyantly access his past lives. The name Leadbeater gave Krishnamurti throughout all his past lives was Alcyone. It was Leadbeater who went on to predict that Krishnamurti would be the next great world teacher, the initiate the Lord Maitreya would use for his reappearance into the world.

Many people were surprised because not only was Krishnamurti not very bright, but he was scrawny, undernourished, and covered with mosquito bites, with lice in his eyebrows and crooked teeth. The people in the Theosophical Society who knew Krishnamurti at a young age would have predicted that he was the least likely of all to have any kind of spiritual mission. Leadbeater was adamant in his belief, however. Krishnamurti was in such bad shape on all levels that even he admitted later in his life that had Leadbeater not discovered him, he would certainly have died.

Leadbeater said that the Master Kuthumi had directed him to train Krishnamurti for his future destiny. Leadbeater had actually chosen another boy for this great mission, a fourteen-year-old boy from Chicago named Hubert, but he changed his mind after meeting Krishnamurti.

Krishnamurti refused to do anything without his brother Nitya, so they were trained together by four tutors and Leadbeater. Krishnamurti had a bad habit of staring off into space with his mouth hanging open, and no matter how many times he was reminded not to do it, he continued. One day Leadbeater slapped him on the chin and Krishnamurti finally stopped, but later in life he said their relationship had never been the same again.

Soon after that, while Krishnamurti and Nitya were sleeping, Leadbeater took them, in their astral bodies, to the house of Master Kuthumi in Tibet where they were initiated. It was then that they were placed on the path of probation, the first step before moving onto the path of initiation.

For the next five months, Leadbeater took Krishnamurti to Kuthumi's house for instruction every night for fifteen minutes. Every morning Krishnamurti wrote down what he remembered. This later became his famous first book called *At the Feet of the Master* which is actually channelings from Master Kuthumi. It was later that year that Krishnamurti first met Annie Besant, president of the Theosophical Society, and that meeting marked the beginning of an undying love between them.

Leadbeater received guidance from Master Kuthumi that he was going to accept Krishnamurti as his disciple, and he requested that Krishnamurti, Annie Besant, and Leadbeater all be present in their astral bodies the following night. Leadbeater and Krishnamurti remained out of their bodies for two nights and a day, coming back only occasionally for some warm milk.

Krishnamurti later said that El Morya had been there with the three of them and they had all gone to Lord Maitreya's house. It was then that Krishnamurti was welcomed officially into the Great White Brotherhood. The next night he was taken to see the Planetary Logos, Sanat Kumara, whom Krishnamurti described, as recorded by Mary Lutyen in her book *Krishnamurti, His Life and Death,* in the following manner: "It was the most wonderful experience of all, for he is a boy not much older than I am but the handsomest I have ever seen, all shining and glorious, and when he smiles it is like sunlight. He is strong like the sea, so that nothing can stand against him, and he is nothing but love, so that I could not be the least afraid of him."

In 1911, C.W. Leadbeater and Annie Besant started an organization called the International Order of the Star, and Krishnamurti became its leader. The purpose of the organization was to prepare the world for the coming of the World Teacher. Krishnamurti's training was intensified. His natural clairvoyance had continued into adulthood; on one occasion he described seeing nature spirits in the garden.

Meanwhile, Leadbeater had compiled all of Krishnamurti's past lives in a book called *The Lives of Alcyone.* Krishnamurti had been enrolled in a special high school to prepare him to go to London University, but on three different occasions he was unable to pass his final exams. He finally gave up on college.

Leadbeater is said to have received a message from Kuthumi for Krishnamurti that stated, "Of you two, we have the highest hopes. Study and widen yourself, and try more and more to bring the mind and brain into subservience to the true self within. Be tolerant of divergencies of view and of method, for each has usually a fragment of truth concealed somewhere within it, even though oftentimes it is distorted almost beyond recognition. Seek for that tiniest gleam of Light amid the stygian darkness of each ignorant mind, for by recognizing and fostering it you may help a baby brother."

Krishnamurti had passed the second initiation and was moving strongly toward the third initiation when one night, while sitting under a tree, he had a visitation from the Lord Maitreya. One of the women of the

Theosophical Society witnessed the event and was greatly moved. That began a whole strange phase of Krishnamurti's life during which the masters worked on his physical body to prepare it for inhabitation by the Lord Maitreya. The masters took him, in his soul body and consciousness, to travel in other dimensions, leaving his body vacant except for what is referred to as the body elemental, a subpersonality that is very childlike and takes care of the physical vehicle when the incarnated personality is soul traveling.

While the masters worked on his physical body to electrically rewire it in preparation for the supremely high vibration of the Lord Maitreya, his body and the body elemental went through enormous pain and suffering. The body elemental would cry and speak like a child while it went through this suffering every night. This process seemed to go on intermittently for almost two years. The pain was almost unbearable at times. In essence, Krishnamurti was undergoing major surgery on his spiritual bodies in a most intensive fashion. He was told by the masters that it was the first time in the history of the world that such an experiment was being carried out in such a manner.

When the process finally stopped, he received a message from the Lord Maitreya: "Learn to serve me, for along this path alone you will find me. Forget yourself, for only then am I to be found. Do not look for the Great Ones even when they may be very near you. You are like the blind man who seeks sunshine, you are like the hungry man who is offered food and will not eat. The happiness you seek is not far off. It lives in every common stone. I am there if you will only see. I am the helper if you will let me help."

During this period Krishnamurti had an experience that is quoted in Mary Lutyen's book: "On the first day while I was in that state and more conscious of the things around me, I had the first most extraordinary experience. There was a man mending the road. That man was myself. I also could feel and think like the road mender and I could feel the wind passing through the tree, and the little ant on the blade of grass I could feel. The birds, the dust, and the very noise were a part of me. Just then there was a car passing by at some distance. I was the driver, the engine, and the tires. As the car went further away from me, I was going away from myself. I was in everything, or rather everything was in me. I was inanimate and animate, the mountain, the work, and all breathing things. All day long I remained in this happy condition."

A disconcerting event occurred in Krishna's life when he was told by Leadbeater and Annie Besant that his brother Nitya was not going to die even though he was very ill. Some time later Nitya did die and a bit of a schism was created, especially with Leadbeater and even with the masters.

He still was accepting his role as the vehicle for the Lord Maitreya, however.

To show how far the process had gone, Annie Besant announced to the Theosophical Society the names of seven of the chosen apostles of the coming Planetary Christ, the Lord Maitreya. At the end of one of the major Theosophical conventions, which over three thousand people attended, Krishnamurti spoke. For the first time, Lord Maitreya was clearly felt and seen by clairvoyants to descend into Krishnamurti as he was speaking. This was considered a monumental occurrence by the Theosophical community.

Soon after that, Annie Besant issued a statement to the Associated Press of America stating, "The Divine Spirit has descended once more on a man, Krishnamurti, one who in his life is literally perfect, as those who know him can testify. The World Teacher is here."

The Theosophical Society, as a worldwide organization, was very fragmented. There seemed to be a lot of infighting and ego battles. Krishnamurti was becoming more and more conflicted and was feeling like a fish out of water. The general secretary of the Theosophical Society for Wales said, "He told us that he had never been able to read a Theosophical book in his life, could not understand our Theosophical jargon and, although he had heard many Theosophical lectures, none of them had convinced him of their knowledge or truth." Here was a man who had been trained by the leaders of the Theosophical movement and who was representing the ascended masters and their teachings, yet he didn't understand or believe in them. This, of course, was a foreshadowing of things to come.

Krishnamurti began describing himself as having achieved "union with the Beloved," but many of the people in the Theosophical Society didn't believe he had achieved such union, for his teachings were not consistent at all with basic Theosophical beliefs. He began to claim there was no such thing as the seven levels of initiation, or stages, along the path, and went so far as stating disbelief in the ascended masters. At one point he even said he didn't believe in God.

Krishnamurti closed the Order of the Star. Leadbeater and Annie Besant agreed that he clearly did not have the omniscience of the Lord, and that was eventually stated in the Theosophical newspaper when Krishnamurti resigned from the Theosophical Society and went his own way. He did not want disciples or apostles or even to be a vehicle for the Lord Maitreya.

The final blow had come when he had ordered Annie Besant to close the esoteric section of the Theosophical Society. She had done so but later changed her mind and when she reversed her decision, Krishnamurti resigned.

His new philosophy was a rather Zen-like philosophy that was very abstract and difficult to understand, but nonetheless, he became an influential world teacher in his own right and affected an enormous number of people.

I do not relate to his later philosophy, for I feel the teachings of Madam Blavatsky and Leadbeater and later those of the Alice Bailey material are some of the clearest teachings on the planet. Krishnamurti, however, rejected it all. He was to have a great following, but I think it was in large part because of how the Theosophical movement had built him up to be the next Jesus Christ.

There are many paths to God and his decision not to be the vehicle for the Lord Maitreya was a mutual one. Lord Maitreya, seeing what was going on, decided that it was not meant to be, and there was no judgment in this. The path of being a vehicle of the Christ was one of free choice; he was not required to it. In retrospect, it can be said that Krishnamurti did the world a great favor, for because of his decision, Lord Maitreya later decided to come here himself and not overshadow an initiate. As you probably know, he is on the planet right now, living in London in a materialized physical body.

To understand how far Krishnamurti departed from the Theosophical Society's thinking, consider the following quotation from Lutyen's book: "We have invented God. Thought has invented God; that is, we, out of misery, despair, loneliness, anxiety, have invented that thing called God. God has not made us in His image. I wish He had. Personally, I have no belief in anything. The speaker only faces what  is, what are facts, the realization of the nature of every fact, every thought, all the reactions. He is totally aware of all that. If you are free from fear, from sorrow, there is no need for a God." In a later address he said he considered the ascended masters as having no objective existence, saying they were mental images shaped by belief and imagination. (Leadbeater's explanation, stated in private, was that Krishnamurti had let his personality, or ego, obscure his clarity.) Krishnamurti went on to discount all paths, all religions, and all spiritual organizations, saying, "I maintain that truth is a pathless land, and you cannot approach it by any path whatsoever, by any religion, by any sect. That is my point of view, and I adhere to that absolutely and unconditionally. Truth, being limitless, unconditioned, unapproachable by any path whatsoever, cannot be organized; nor should any organization be formed to lead or coerce people along any particular path."

Again, I disagree. It is not the path, religion, or organization that is the problem; the problem occurs when ego infiltrates an organization. It is possible to have a path to God that is free of ego. However, in Krishnamurti's defense, it is true that the Theosophical Society was rife with ego battles to the extreme, but I think he was throwing out the baby with the bath water in rejecting all their teachings along with their politics.

Krishnamurti's place in history is quite extraordinary. He established eight schools in Europe, America, and India that focused his special interest in educating children. The single object of his teaching was to set humanity free from the distinctions that divide man from man, such as race, religion, nationality, class, and tradition.

Although his teachings might not have been completely clear of ego and personality, he was most definitely a world teacher who influenced an enormous number of people for the positive through his lectures and books. He will always be best known as the one initiate on Earth who almost became the next vehicle for the coming Messiah and Planetary Christ, the Lord Maitreya.

# 37

## Count Saint Germain — the "Wonder Man" of Europe

*I AM the Scepter of Dominion,
the Quenchless Flame, the Dazzling Light and
Divine Perfection made manifest!*

The I AM Discourses of Saint Germain

One of the most amazing spiritual masters this world has ever known is Ascended Master Saint Germain. He is currently living in the spiritual world as Chohan of the Seventh Ray. He is so gifted a master that he has recently been offered the position in the spiritual government of Mahachohan of the Third Ray, which also governs rays four, five, six, and seven. He has not taken this position yet, for he still has one final mission to fulfill as the seventh-ray leader: to bring in and ground the New Age on Planet Earth. Doing so is primarily his job, for the sixth ray is now passing away from this planet and the seventh ray is replacing it. The seventh ray is the ray of ceremonial order and magic and the violet transmuting flame.

Saint Germain has lived an interesting variety of past lives. He was Joseph, the husband of the Virgin Mary. He was Columbus, the explorer. He was Francis Bacon, who wrote under the name William Shakespeare. He was Merlin in King Arthur's court. He was the Jewish prophet Samuel. And he was Prince Rakoczy. It was, however, in his life as Count Saint Germain that he ascended. He lived for over three hundred fifty years; Emperor Frederick the Great called him "the man who never dies."

Because Saint Germain lived for such a long time, he was constantly staging and, in truth, faking his own death so as to not give too much notice to the important work he was doing as an adept of the Great White

Lodge. His true name was Francis Tudor, for he was the son of Queen Elizabeth I.

The name under which he was known during the early part of his life was Francis Bacon. It was Bacon who wrote all of William Shakespeare's plays. If you break down the name, you will note that it reads "Will-I-AM" and "Shaking the spear" of wisdom. He made reference to this in his books, *The "I AM" Discourses*, which he wrote in the 1930s through Godfre Ray King. Francis Bacon's writings also appeared under the assumed names of Christopher Marlowe, Edmund Spenser, Montaigne, Robert Burton, Cervantes, Valentine Andraes, and Comte de Gabalis.

Napoleon was so taken with Saint Germain's activities in Europe that he formed a special commission to investigate the truth of all the extraordinary stories that were circulating about him.

It is believed that Saint Germain was born in 1561. As he grew into adulthood, he mastered all the European languages and spoke them fluently without any foreign accent. He was one of the best swordsmen of his day. He was a master violinist. He had extraordinary powers of mind and a photographic memory. He could write two letters at the same time, using both his hands simultaneously, each copy being a duplicate of the other so exact that when placed over each other and held up to the light, they were found to be identical!

Frederick the Great referred to him as "one of the most enigmatic personages of the eighteenth century." During that century, Saint Germain was on intimate terms with the crowned heads of Europe. He was personal friends with Voltaire, Rousseau, and a great many other distinguished philosophers. He was a brilliant conversationalist, was widely read, and had traveled extensively. Voltaire, the great philosopher, was quoted as saying about Saint Germain, "He is the man who never dies and knows everything." He was recognized as an outstanding scholar. He spoke German, English, Italian, Portuguese, Spanish, French, Greek, Latin, Sanskrit, Arabic, and Chinese, all with amazing fluency.

He was incredibly wealthy, but no one knew how he had accumulated his great wealth. He dressed simply but wore a great number of diamonds in his rings, watch, and shoe buckles. Saint Germain was also a great painter. Besides playing the violin, he conducted orchestras. He had an extensive knowledge of herbalism, and many people believed his physical immortality came from some secret herbal elixir. The herbal elixir, in truth, did exist, but his physical immortality actually came from the fact that he had passed his sixth initiation, or ascension.

In 1710 Madame de Gergy, the widow of the French ambassador, had the opportunity to meet Saint Germain. She said he appeared to be about forty-five years of age. She met him again in Paris fifty years later and he looked exactly the same. When she saw him she thought that he was the son of Saint Germain. He acknowledged that they had met as she remembered. Madame de Gergy is quoted as saying, "Forgive me, but that is impossible. The Count Saint Germain I knew in those days was at least forty-five years old, and you, at the outside, are that age at present. I remember seeing you there, looking just as you do now, only somewhat riper in age, perhaps, for you have grown younger since then." Saint Germain responded by saying, "I have always thought myself happy in being able to make myself agreeable to the ladies." Later in the conversation he admitted he was very old. He never admitted his secret, however, for he never wanted to endanger the true work he was doing as an emissary of the Great White Brotherhood.

Saint Germain was a master alchemist. It is said that he had the ability to change base metals into gold. He was also able to improve the quality of diamonds and precious stones so they were worth many times their original value. He had a great many diamonds and other precious jewels, including an opal the size of an egg. Saint Germain's friend Casanova actually witnessed him change a twelve-sol piece into one of pure gold. In a letter Saint Germain wrote to Count von Lamberg, he said, "I am indebted for my knowledge of melting jewels to my second journey to India."

Madame de Pompadour, consort of Louis XV, is quoted as saying, "This singular man passed being fabulously rich, and he distributed diamonds and jewels with astonishing liberality." He also had great skill as a chemist which enabled him to make cosmetics for the ladies of the French court.

One of Saint Germain's greatest claims to fame is the fact that he founded Rosicrucianism and Freemasonry in England under the title The Society of Rosicrusse Freemasons. He did this under the identity of Francis Bacon. It was this work with the Himalayan masters that was the driving force of his life.

Saint Germain prophesied the French Revolution and, in truth, was one of the main originators of it. He warned his friends in the French aristocracy of what was about to happen, but they refused to heed his warnings. It was the secret spiritual societies of which Saint Germain was the head that instigated and precipitated the revolution; these groups were much more politically oriented than most people realized.

As Francis Bacon, he tried to prepare the public mind for the democratic revolution he was nurturing through his Shakespearean plays and other writings. It was his dream to create in America a new country free of corruption, greed, and dictatorial monarchies. Saint Germain, in truth, was the father of modern democracy as it spread to the United States. He was instrumental in formulating the Declaration of Independence and the

Constitution of the United States of America as they were being written by his Masonic followers who founded this nation. Their Masonic symbols can be seen on the one-dollar bill. It is a fact that George Washington, Benjamin Franklin, Thomas Jefferson, and others were Freemasons. It is believed that Saint Germain was actually in the United States physically in order to guide his Masonic brothers. There is a famous story about the signing of the Constitution. When some doubts began to flourish, a strange man appeared on the balcony of the locked room and gave an impassioned speech which ended with the words, "Sign that document!"

In a most extraordinary letter to his friend Franz Graffner, Saint Germain made the following statement:

> I am leaving; do not visit me. Once again you will see me. Tomorrow night I am off. I am much needed in Constantinople; then in England, there to prepare two inventions which you will have in the next century – trains and steamboats. [This was written one hundred years before they were invented.] These will be needed in Germany.
>
> The seasons will gradually change – first the spring then the summer. It is the gradual cessation of time itself, as the announcement of the end of the cycle. I see it all. Astrologers and meteorologists know nothing, believe me. One needs to have studied the pyramids as I have studied them. Toward the end of this century I shall disappear out of Europe and betake myself to the region of the Himalayas. I will rest. I must rest. Exactly in eighty-five years will people again set eyes on me.

Saint Germain then spent eighty-five years with the Trans-Himalayan Brotherhood which was made up of El Morya, Kuthumi, Djwhal Khul, and perhaps others. It was these three masters, along with Saint Germain, who channeled all the Theosophical literature through Madam Blavatsky. I have an actual photograph of all four of these masters standing with Madam Blavatsky. She actually traveled to the Himalayas and stayed in Master El Morya's home. Djwhal Khul painted a picture of the ravine in which they lived in Tibet; it can be found in the book *The Masters and the Path* by C.W. Leadbeater. In the same book, Leadbeater describes a physical meeting with Saint Germain, whom he often refers to as Prince Rakoczy.

Saint Germain was later to materialize physically for Godfre Ray King in the 1930s on Mount Shasta. This was only fitting since he had discovered America as Columbus, and Godfre Ray King had been George Washington in his previous life.

Saint Germain's mission seems to have had three facets. The first was to work with individuals who had been initiated into the hidden mystery schools. Those students would then help him in his work. Saint Germain's most famous student was Cagliostro, who later founded the Egyptian Freemasonry Lodge. Another famous student of Saint Germain's was

Anton Mesmer, the inventor of mesmerism which was the precursor of hypnosis. The second facet of Saint Germain's mission involved working with the intellectual class through his plays, writings, and the army of Freemasons and Rosicrucians he was leading. The third facet of his work was the school of esotericism he ran. Even Frederick the Great of Prussia was initiated into that order.

Saint Germain lived as Francis Bacon from 1561 until 1626 when he feigned death as Francis Bacon. Then he traveled to Germany and wrote under the name Valentine Andreas from around 1626 to 1670. He is thought to have faked his death again and appeared in 1687 in Venice as Signor Gualdi. In 1710, he reappeared in Venice as Count Saint Germain. This continued until 1784 when he feigned death again and spent eighty-five years in the Himalayas. It was then that he appeared to Madam Blavatsky and C.W. Leadbeater. Later still, in the 1930s, he physically materialized for Godfre Ray King, who was later to become the channel and scribe for The "I AM" Discourses which are wonderful books that are written in a simplified form as a backlash against the extremely intellectual nature of the writings of the Theosophical Society.

The extraordinary thing about Saint Germain was the fact that his philosophical ideal of a utopian society was not just theoretical; he was able to manifest that ideal and ground it into physical reality. The French Revolution and the formation of the United States created a new social order that freed men and women from the domination and corruption of European and English royalty.

Another service Saint Germain performed, one which not very many people know about, was the King James translation of the Bible. That and his Shakespeare plays could be said to be the greatest masterpieces of the time in the English language.

At the time of Saint Germain's feigned death in 1784, Prince Charles wrote the following letter:

> He was perhaps one of the greatest sages who has ever lived. He loved humanity; he desired money only to give to the poor. He even loved animals, and his heart was occupied with only the happiness of others. He believed he could make mankind happy by procuring for them new pleasures, lovelier clothes, and colors, glorious colors that cost almost nothing. I have never known a man with a clearer mind, and at the same time he was possessed of a learning, especially in history, that I have rarely found. He had been in all countries of Europe . . . but France seemed to be the land where he lived best.

Planet Earth is very blessed to have Saint Germain still working here. He is such a gifted master that other solar systems have offered him extremely high-ranking positions within their governments, but his singular devotion to Earth has led him to choose to remain here and continue the great work he has so valiantly pursued throughout the ages.

I would like to close with this tribute, a quotation from *The "I AM"*
*Discourses*:

> To our beloved Ascended Master Saint Germain be eternal, limitless love
> and gratitude. May every human being on Earth know who beloved Saint
> Germain really is, what he has done for the freedom of mankind, and
> how great his love pours out constantly for the freedom and perfection of
> all!
>
> Beloved Saint Germain is the Law of Freedom to this Earth. He is the
> Law of the Violet Ray to this Earth!
>
> He is the power and the understanding which mankind must have of
> each one's individualized God Presence, the Mighty I AM, in order to
> complete the victory of Light which beloved Jesus came to reveal to the
> people of this world. . . .
>
> Beloved Saint Germain is the great cosmic being who is the authority of
> the cosmic law to this Earth, which means the Law of Activity of Life and
> Light in this world in regard to holding the balance of constructive
> activities for the whole system of planets to which this Earth belongs.
>
> It is the true education of life and the spiritual culture of the people for
> the whole world, for every one in the world can make the ascension by
> applying the ascended masters' instruction of the "I AM" which these
> Great Beings of Light and Perfection have given.

# 38

## *The Sleeping Prophet: Edgar Cayce*

*Why worry when you can pray.*

The Universal Mind through Edgar Cayce

The source of Edgar Cayce's extraordinary abilities lies in his past life as Ra-Ta, the great prophet and priest of Egypt. He was so gifted in that lifetime, and he built up such good karma then, that he carried much of it over into his life as Edgar Cayce.

As a child he was different from most kids. He was very interested in the Bible and he enjoyed going to church. At the age of seven or eight he had a clairvoyant experience that greatly affected his life. He was reading about the vision of Manoah in the Bible, for he loved the story of Samson. All of a sudden he heard a humming sound and saw a bright light fill the garden in which he was sitting. Looking up, he saw a figure in white, bright as the noonday light, who said, "Your prayers have been heard. What would you ask of me that I may give it to you?"

The young Edgar Cayce said, "Just that I may be helpful to others, especially to children who are ill, and that I may love my fellow man." The figure nodded and disappeared.

The next day, thinking of the vision, he bungled his classwork and was made to stay after class and write the word "cabin" on the blackboard five hundred times as a punishment for misspelling it. Later that night his tutor was angry with him for not knowing his lessons. Edgar heard a voice inside his head that told him to "sleep, and we may help you." Edgar asked to take a short break. He lay down on his bed and was guided to put his schoolbook under his pillow as he slept. He took a short catnap and when he woke up he had total recall of everything in the spelling book. However, he was no scholar, and he dropped out of school at the age of fifteen because of his inability to focus his mind. Nonetheless, he read the Bible from beginning to end each year.

As Cayce grew into adulthood his clairvoyance developed. He constantly saw fields of light and color and was able to perceive people's auras. One time he saw a woman who had no aura at all; two days later, she died. Once, without even glancing at the deck of cards, he read off all fifty-two cards in succession to demonstrate that bridge would be a bore.

Cayce began to channel the Universal Mind as a young man. It started during a rather lengthy period of time when he was unable to speak. Doctors could find nothing wrong. A professional hypnotist named Al Layne happened to be in town and Cayce agreed to be hypnotized. Once he was under, Al Layne asked his unconscious mind what was wrong with his throat. Immediately, the Universal Mind spoke through Cayce's vocal chords and said that there was a partial paralysis of the vocal chords due to nerve strain. It went on to recommend that Cayce be given a hypnotic suggestion that the blood flow to his throat increase and it prophesied that his voice would then be healed. Layne gave the suggestion and Cayce's throat became crimson red. The Universal Mind then told Layne to suggest that the circulation return to normal. Cayce was awakened shortly thereafter and was totally healed.

This began the amazing saga of Edgar Cayce. Over the next forty years he did over fifteen thousand trance readings from the Universal Mind. The first ten years he considered only physical health problems, many times to help children, as he had requested of the angel in the vision he'd had at the age of seven or eight. As people began to ask spiritual questions about the purpose of life, death, birth, God, and so on, the Universal Mind came forth with detailed understandings of the nature of the reality of unseen worlds. He spoke of reincarnation, world prophecy, future Earth changes, dreams, Atlantis, Lemuria, past lives, how to cure "incurable" illnesses, holistic methods of healing, ESP, home and family, attitudes and emotions, astrology, the Mayan civilization, Egypt, the story of creation, the story of Jesus, the human aura, and much, much more.

All of the fifteen thousand readings were recorded by his secretary and are stored at the Edgar Cayce foundation, the Association for Research and Enlightenment in Virginia Beach, Virginia. Hundreds of books have been written about Edgar Cayce and his readings, and he is considered the father of holistic healing.

Here was a man who, on the conscious level, was almost entirely uneducated and certainly had never studied medicine. He was a chain smoker and, during the early part of his adult life, didn't even believe most of the information that came through him while he was in trance. Nonetheless, he astounded doctors with his medical knowledge. Even more importantly, when people followed his often bizarre home remedies they would invariably heal. One medical authority said that he perceived Edgar Cayce to be one hundred years ahead of his time. In the field of health and spiritual information, Cayce's position was much like that of Nikola Tesla in the field of science.

Edgar Cayce was a humble man, religious and God-fearing, even though he was probably the greatest channel who has ever lived on this planet. He was guided by the Universal Mind to do only two readings a day to avoid deleterious effects on his physical body. Because of his love for people, however, during World War II he was doing seven or eight readings a day. By that time he had become world famous and was receiving hundreds of letters a day requesting readings. He would never turn away anyone who couldn't pay. His extremely selfless nature was his ultimate downfall. His own physical health failed, and he passed away at the age of sixty-eight.

The legacy of Edgar Cayce — the profundity of his abilities and the wide-ranging nature of the information he brought forth — has grown stronger and stronger with each passing year.

# 39

## *Peace Pilgrim*

*I perceived the entirely self-centered life as not
worth living. If what you're doing will not benefit
others besides yourself, it is not worth doing.*

Peace Pilgrim

P eace Pilgrim was a woman many people might not have heard of, but she was one of the most extraordinary women of the twentieth century. Many of the chapters in this book deal with great spiritual masters who are able to perform miraculous feats. This woman was not a person with unusual powers other than total love for and faith in God. In truth, these are the most miraculous powers of all, as her life clearly demonstrated.

At the age of about twenty-seven, Peace Pilgrim set out, on January 1, 1953, on a pilgrimage across the United States and the world, planning to walk until humankind had learned the way of peace. She had no money and no organizational backing. Her only belongings were a navy blue shirt and slacks and a short tunic with pockets all around the bottom in which she carried her only worldly possessions – a comb, a folding toothbrush, a ballpoint pen, copies of her message, and her current correspondence. Her only true possession was an abiding faith in God and love for God and for people.

By 1964, eleven years later, she had walked twenty-five thousand miles. It was only then that she stopped counting the miles, but she continued her pilgrimage for peace for seventeen more years after that, until her death in 1981. It is my great, great pleasure to bring to you a little bit of information about her life and her teachings.

This is a woman who truly walked her talk in every sense of the word.

By the time she died she had walked across the United States seven times and had visited all fifty states, ten provinces in Canada, and parts of Mexico.

In the last newspaper interview she gave before her death in an automobile accident, she spoke of being in radiant health. The interviewer remarked that she seemed to be a most happy woman, and she replied, "I certainly am a happy person. How could one know God and not be joyous?"

In the years before she set out on her journey, there were a number of preparations she had to make in order to become ready:

1. The development of a right attitude toward life;

2. The simplification of her life on all levels, including the purification of her physical body in terms of her diet;

3. The purification of her thinking;

4. The purification of her desires;

5. The purification of her motives;

6. The attitude each day of totally dedicating her consciousness and activities to ways in which she could be of service to others, and not forgetting the importance of a pleasant word and a cheery smile;

7. The relinquishment of self-will; she became aware of the lower and higher selves, or the self-centered nature and the God-centered nature. She dedicated her life to dying to her self-centered nature and fully living and demonstrating her God-centered nature;

8. The relinquishment of the feeling of separateness;

9. The relinquishment of all attachment;

10. The relinquishment of all negative feelings.

It was at the age of twelve that she surrendered and devoted her life to God. She spent the next fifteen years establishing these preparations in her consciousness and being before setting out on her walking pilgrimage for world peace. Her intention was to promote peace among nations, peace among groups, peace with the environment, peace among individuals, and most importantly, inner peace within the self. Peace Pilgrim believed that the last one was the most important and was the building block for all other forms of peace.

She would walk until given shelter and fast until given food. She had once fasted for forty-seven days so she knew she could skip meals and be okay. The longest she ever went without food, she said, was three days, even though she carried no money, would never ask for food, and would accept food only if it was given to her. She had total trust in the inherent goodness and Godliness of all human beings.

Her tee shirt read "Peace Pilgrim – 25,000 miles on foot for peace." The shirt often helped her make contact with people. One of her main messages was to "overcome evil with good, falsehood with truth, and hatred with love." She also believed strongly in the Golden Rule – "Do unto others as you would have others do unto you." Her life was dedicated to demonstrating these ideals, not just talking about them. One of her goals was to have the federal government establish a Peace Department and a Secretary of Peace who accepted those principles.

As her pilgrimage continued, on the spur of the moment, people would invite her to speak to their groups and share her philosophy and mission. She never accepted a penny for doing so.

Peace Pilgrim spoke of being severely tested at times, especially in the beginning. However, by looking at everything that happened as tests of her faith and opportunities to practice her spiritual beliefs, she was able to pass those tests and grow stronger because of them.

One such test occurred in the middle of the night in the California desert. A driver stopped his car and called to her, saying she should get in and warm up. They talked for a while and then he suggested that she get some sleep. She agreed and proceeded to curl up and go right to sleep. When she awoke later, the man looked very puzzled. When they began to talk, the man admitted he'd been up to no good. However, when she'd gone to sleep so trustingly, somehow he just couldn't touch her. Her innocent faith and trust in God had protected her.

Once she went hiking with a disturbed teenage boy who had a history of becoming physically violent at times. No one would walk with him alone because of this, but Peace Pilgrim offered to. Everything was fine until a thunderstorm hit. He went crazy and started to attack her. She didn't fight back but felt the deepest and most profound compassion for the poor disturbed soul that would attack a defenseless old woman. All of a sudden he stopped and said, "You didn't hit back! Mother always hits back." Peace Pilgrim later found out that he never resorted to violence again and became a useful person in society.

Another time a very large man was chasing an eight-year-old girl into a barn with the intention of beating her. Peace Pilgrim ran into the barn and stepped between the man and the girl. She looked at the poor sick man with loving compassion. He came close. He stopped. He looked at her for quite a while and then walked away. Not a word was spoken!

In Arizona she was booked by a plainclothes policeman as a vagrant and taken to jail. She said to herself, "Peace Pilgrim, you have dedicated your life to service. Behold your wonderful new field of service!" As she was put into a cell with some other women, one of them said, "Gee, you're a funny one. You're the only one to come in smiling. Most of them come in cursing." After a short time, she had all the women singing and she transformed the whole jail, even the people who worked there. Her case was dismissed. When she got her personal effects back there was a letter with them that said, "The bearer of this note has identified herself as a peace pilgrim walking coast to coast to direct the attention of our citizens to her desire for peace in the world. We do not know her personally, as she is just passing through our state, but since undoubtedly, it will be a long, hard trip for her, we wish her safe passage." It was signed by the governor of the state, Howard Pyle.

On one occasion, she was picked up by the FBI. They intensely cross-examined her, probably trying to find out if she was a Communist. At one point she was asked which she would choose if she had a choice between killing and being killed. Peace Pilgrim said that as long as her life was in harmony with God she knew that she would never have to be confronted with such a decision. The FBI agents kept badgering her and Peace Pilgrim finally said that she would prefer to be killed. The agents had a fit and couldn't understand how she could say such a thing. Peace Pilgrim explained to them that she was not her physical body, that she was only wearing the physical body. She was the being and consciousness that activated the body. She said, "If I am killed, it destroys merely the clay garment, the body. But if I kill, it injures the reality, the soul."

Another time she was asked to speak at a church service a couple of days in the future. The local newspaper advertised her talk and printed her picture. A man who belonged to the church was horrified and complained bitterly to the preacher and all his friends. Peace Pilgrim had obviously done nothing to cause such a reaction. Somehow she heard about the situation and decided to call the man. She said, "This is Peace Pilgrim calling." She could hear him gasp, for he thought she had called in anger. "I have called to apologize to you because evidently I must have done something to offend you since, without even knowing me, you have apprehension about my speaking at your church. Therefore I feel I must somehow owe you an apology and I have called to apologize!" The man was in tears before the conversation was over. They became good friends after that and corresponded by mail.

Once she was invited to stay for several days at the house of a woman who had been seriously ill. The woman had a sister who was very domineering and judgmental, and when they arrived at the house late in the evening, the sister took one look at Peace Pilgrim and her tunic and said, "You can stay tonight since it is so late, but first thing in the morning I want you out of here." She then stomped upstairs and any communication with her from that point on was impossible. When everyone had gone to bed, Peace Pilgrim wondered how she could be of service in the situation without being able to communicate. She noticed a mountain of dirty dishes, so she proceeded to wash them all, and then she cleaned the kitchen. In the morning the older sister was in tears and asked her to stay.

One day, she was invited into a tavern for some food. Many people were drinking heavily. As she was leaving, a man with a drink in his hand smiled slightly. Peace Pilgrim smiled back, greeting him warmly. The man said, "You smiled at me. I would think you wouldn't even speak to me, but you smiled at me." Peace Pilgrim smiled again and said, "I'm not here to judge my fellow human beings, I am here to love and serve." Suddenly the man was kneeling at her feet. He said, "Everyone else judges me, so I defend myself. You didn't judge me, so now I judge myself. I'm a no-good, worthless sinner! I've been squandering my money on liquor, I've been mistreating my family, I've been going from bad to worse." Peace Pilgrim put her hand on his shoulder and said, "You are God's child, and you could act that way." The man looked in disgust at the drink in his hand and then hurled it against the bar, shattering the glass. He looked Peace Pilgrim in the eye and said, "I swear to you, I'll never touch that stuff again. Never!" And there was a new light in his eyes. About a year and a half later she received a letter from someone in the town who told her that the man had kept his promise.

Another time a man stopped his car and said, "In this day and age, with all the wonderful opportunities the world has to offer, what under the sun made you go out and walk a pilgrimage for peace?" Peace Pilgrim said, "In this day and age when humanity totters on the brink of nuclear war and annihilation, it is not surprising that one life is dedicated to the cause of peace; rather, it is surprising that many lives are not similarly dedicated."

Peace Pilgrim's philosophy was to see everyone as a spark of God. She was not concerned with racial or ethnic backgrounds or skin color. All people, she said, are like shining lights. She saw all problems as nothing more than inspirations nudging people into becoming obedient to God's laws.

Peace Pilgrim's prayer was not to get rid of her problems but, rather, to have the inner strength to solve them in the way God would have them solved. That is the way to grow spiritually. Problems, hence, became opportunities, not problems at all. In that regard, she was thankful for everything that happened.

Peace Pilgrim's philosophy about anger was not to express it and not to suppress it, but rather to transform it and utilize the tremendous power inherent in it to complete all her various tasks. Edgar Cayce called this positive anger as opposed to negative anger; this way, anger is transformed into personal power.

Her belief in pacifism and nonviolence applied on the psychological level as well as on the physical level. She would never allow herself to say angry words or to think angry thoughts. If someone did an unkind thing, she would feel only unconditional love and compassion, knowing the harvest of sorrow they were bringing upon themselves because of the law of karma. Her pacifism and nonviolence also applied to the animal kingdom.

Perfect love, to her, was the willingness to give without a thought of receiving anything in return. Her simple message was this: "The way of peace is the way of love. Love is the greatest power on Earth. It conquers all things." Her philosophy was to remain in inner peace despite anything that might be going on outside of herself. She never concerned herself with the results of her pilgrimage, for she left that in God's hands.

When asked one time if she was a Christian, she said, "I am not and have never been a part of any particular faith. I am a deeply religious woman who has taken the inner way to a religious life, not the scholarly way or the way of early training. I will never say this is the only way. It is, of course, an excellent way. And people are free to choose and develop in their own ways."

Someone asked her if she ever got frustrated, and she said, "The self-centered nature feels frustration when it can't have its way. The higher nature is patient, knowing that with a proper attitude, all problems can be solved."

## Summation

Peace Pilgrim is an inspiring example. I hope this short summation of her life and teachings has inspired you as much as she has inspired me. In your short stay on Earth you have the potential to stand for something and to set a shining example for the world. Each of you has a different mission, a different way of taking that stand. What is essential is to surrender your life to God and commit yourself to your spiritual ideals with unswerving determination and vigilance. If you did that in your own unique and special way, with the commitment, faith, and devotion Peace Pilgrim demonstrated, what a world this would be! Let this be a challenge to all.

The information and quotes in this chapter come from an absolutely wonderful book called *Peace Pilgrim: Her Life and Work in Her Own Words*. The book was compiled by some of her friends from her letters and tapes after she died. If you can't find it in the bookstores, then write to the publisher at An Ocean Tree Book, Post Office Box 1295, Santa Fe, New Mexico 87501.

# Bibliography

*Anandamayi Ma, The Mother Bliss Incarnate.* Out of print.

Bancroft, Anne. *The Buddhist World.* Morristown, NJ: Silver Burdett Press, 1984.

Bernard, Raymond. *Pythagoras, the Immortal Sage.* Mokelumne Hill, CA: Mokelumne Hill Press, 1958.

Blavatsky, Helena P. *Isis Unveiled.* Pasadena, CA: Theosophical University Press, 1976.

—. *The Secret Doctrine.* Wheaton, IL: Theosophical Publishing House, 1993.

—. *The Voice of the Silence.* Wheaton, IL: Theosophical Publishing House, 1992.

—. *The Key to Theosophy.* Pasadena, CA: Theosophical University Press, 1972.

Blofeld, John. *Bodhisattva of Compassion.* Boston: Shambhala Publications, 1988.

Chaney, Earlyne. *Revelations of Things to Come.* Upland, CA: Astara, 1982.

Commander X. *Nikola Tesla: Free Energy and the White Dove.* New Brunswick, NJ: Abelard Productions, 1992.

Crandall, Joanne. *Self-Transformation through Music.* Wheaton, IL: Theosophical Publishing House, 1986.

Dalai Lama. *Ocean of Wisdom.* Santa Fe, NM: Clear Light Publishers, 1989.

—. *Path to Bliss.* Ithaca, NY: Snow Lion Publications, 1991.

Easwaran, Eknath. *Gandhi, the Man.* Tomales, CA: Nilgiri Press, 1978.

Evans-Wentz, W.Y., ed. *The Tibetan Book of the Dead.* New York: Oxford University Press, 1960.

Fuller, Jean Overton. *Blavatsky and Her Teachers.* London: East-West Publications, 1988.

Gandhi, Mohandas K. *An Autobiography.* Boston: Beacon Press, 1957.

Gonzales, Jose L. and Playfoot, Jane, eds. *My Life for the Poor: Mother Teresa of Calcutta.* New York: Ballantine, 1987.

Grattan, Brian. *Mahatma I & II*. Sedona, AZ: Light Technology Publishing, 1994.

——. *Rider on the White Horse*. Sedona, AZ: Light Technology Publishing, 1990.

Guthrie, Kenneth Sylvan. *The Pythagorean Sourcebook and Library*. Grand Rapids, MI: Phanes Press, 1987.

Hatengdi, M.U. *Nityananda: The Divine Presence*. Cambridge, MA: Rudra Press, 1984.

Hicks, Roger & Chogyam, Ngakpa. *Great Ocean: The Dalai Lama*. Dorset, England: Element Books, 1984.

Kato, Bunno & Tamura, Kojiro, Yoshiro & Miyasaka. *The Threefold Lotus Sutra*. Tokyo: Kosei Publishing Co., 1975.

King, Godfre Ray. *The "I AM" Discourses*. Schaumburg, IL: Saint Germain Press, Inc., 1942.

Lavine, T.Z. *From Socrates to Sartre*. New York: Bantam Books, 1984.

Leadbeater, C.W. *The Masters and the Path*. Mokelumne Hills, CA: Mokelumne Hills Press, 1985.

Lecky, William E. *History of European Morals from Augustus to Charlemagne*. Salem, NH: Ayer Company Publishers, 1975.

Lipski, Dr. Alexander. *Life and Teaching of Sri Anandamayi Ma*. Delhi: Motilel Banarsidass, 1977.

Lutyens, Mary. *Krishnamurti: The Years of Awakening*. New York: Avon, 1975.

——. *Krishnamurti: His Life and Death*. New York: St. Martin's Press, 1990.

Maharshi, Sri Ramana. *Maharshi's Gospel*. India: T.N. Venkataraman, 1939.

——. *The Spiritual Teaching of Ramana Maharshi*. Boston: Shambhala Publications, 1988.

——. *Self-Inquiry*. India: T.N. Venkataraman, 1990.

Mead, G.R.S. *Apollonius of Tyana*. Chicago, IL: Ares Publishers, 1980.

Moore, William L. *The Philadelphia Experiment*. New York: Fawcett Crest, 1979.

Muktananda, Swami. *Kundalini: The Secret of Life*. Out of print.

——. *Play of Consciousness*. South Fallsburg, NY: SYDA Foundation, 1991.

——. *Secret of the Siddhas*. South Fallsburg, NY: SYDA Foundation, 1978.

Murphet, Howard. *When Daylight Comes.* Wheaton, IL: Theosophical Publishing House, 1975.

—. *Yankee Beacon of Buddhist Light.* Wheaton, IL: Theosophical Publishing House, 1988.

Narayan, R.K. *The Ramayana.* New York: Penguin Books, 1972.

Nikhilananda, Swami. *Holy Mother.* New York: Ramakrishna-Vivekananda Center, 1953.

—. *Vivekananda: A Biography.* New York: Ramakrishna-Vivekananda Center, 1953.

Olcott, Henry S. *The Buddhist Catechism.* Cotopaxi, CO: Eastern School Press, 1983.

Osborne, Arthur. *The Incredible Sai Baba.* Flushing, NY: Orient Longman, Ltd., 1957.

*Peace Pilgrim: A Compilation.* Santa Fe, NM: An Ocean Tree Book, 1983.

Philostratus, Flavius. *The Life and Times of Apollonius of Tyana.* Stanford, CA: AMS Press, 1923.

Ramakrishna, Sri. *The Condensed Gospel of Sri Ramakrishna.* Hollywood, CA: Vedanta Press, 1979.

Rawson, Philip & Legeza, Laszlo. *Tao: The Chinese Philosophy of Time and Change.* London: Thames and Hudson, 1987.

Ross, Nancy Wilson. *Buddhism.* New York: Vantage Books, 1981.

Sarma, D.S. *The Master and the Disciple.* Hollywood, CA: Vedanta Press, 1944.

Sethi, V.K. *Kabir: the Weaver of God's Name.* Columbia, MO: South Asia Books, 1986.

Sinnett, A.P. *Esoteric Buddhism.* Mokelumne Hills, CA: Mokelumne Hills Press, 1969.

—. *Incidents in the Life of Madame Blavatsky.* Salem, NH: Ayer Company Publishers, Inc., 1886.

Sivananda, Swami. *Autobiography.* India: Divine Life Society, 1989.

Schiffman, Richard. *Sri Ramakrishna.* New York: Paragon House, 1989.

Stanford, Ray. *Fatima Prophecy.* Virginia Beach, VA: Inner Vision, 1987.

Sugrue, Thomas. *There is a River.* New York: Henry Holt & Co., 1943.

Tames, Richard. *The Muslim World.* Morristown, NJ: Silver Burdett, 1984.

Three Initiates. *The Kybalion.* Chicago: Yogi Publication Society, 1912.

Tillett, Gregory. *The Elder Brother*. London: Routledge Kegan Paul, 1982.

Venkataraman, Sri T.N. *Bhagavan Sri Ramana: A Pictorial Biography*. Out of print.

——. *Maharshi's Gospel*. Out of print.

Walker, Morton. *The Power of Color*. Garden City Park, NY: Avery Publishing Group, 1989.

Yogananda, Paramahansa. *Autobiography of a Yogi*. Los Angeles, CA: Self-Realization Fellowship, 1946.

——. *Man's Eternal Quest*. Los Angeles, CA: Self-Realization Fellowship, 1982.

For further information,
Dr. Joshua David Stone
can be contacted
through the publisher
or at

*We offer answers to satisfy the heart and mind*

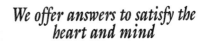

# SEDONA

## Journal of EMERGENCE!

8.5" X 11", MONTHLY
128 PGS., PERFECT BOUND
$5.95 U.S.A. / $7.50 Canada

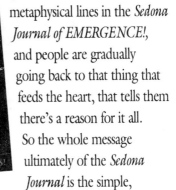

"There is something for every mental fabric along metaphysical lines in the *Sedona Journal of EMERGENCE!*, and people are gradually going back to that thing that feeds the heart, that tells them there's a reason for it all. So the whole message ultimately of the *Sedona Journal* is the simple, warm-hearted rendition of the 'truth'."

– Zoosh/Robert Shapiro

## DON'T SPECULATE . . . GET SOURCE INFORMATION!

THE LATEST COSMIC HEADLINE NEWS!
ETs, Secret Government, Earth Changes, Great Channels, PREDICTABLES Dimensional Shift, the Photon Belt . . . and More!

# ORDER NOW!

**before subscription rates are raised!**
**New Cover Price $5.95**

The one monthly magazine readers never throw away . . . helps you open spiritual doors to new dimensions of awareness.

The latest channeled information on what to do as humans and the earth move from the third to the fourth dimension — how these energies affect you and the earth.

Practical articles and features on New Age humor, healing, children's stories, ETs, UFOs, astrology, herbs, numerology, reincarnation and more!

**WHAT YOU NEED TO KNOW NOW AS YOU AND EARTH CHANGE**

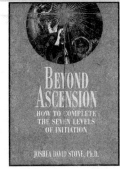

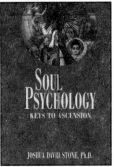

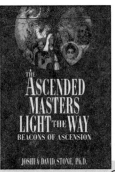
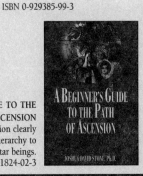

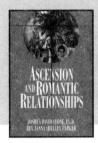

# Light Technology

## Enjoy All of these Great Books

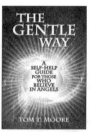
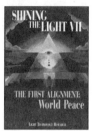

# Publishing Presents

## Plus Hundreds More!

### A New Formula For Creation

*Judith Moore*

This book brings an inspiring positive message regarding the future of our planet. Earth is experiencing the Shift of the Ages, a time marked by massive Earth changes and social upheaval. This is foretold in many prophecies, including Hopi prophecies and the biblical Revelations. They warn that raising consciousness is the only way to avert a massive cataclysm.

$16.95  Softcover, 186 p.  ISBN: 1-891824-57-0

### Living in the Heart
### *(With CD)*

*Drunvalo Melchizedek*

This is a book of remembering. You have always had this place within your heart, and it is still there now. It existed before creation, and it will exist even after the last star shines its brilliant light. This book is written with the least amount of words possible to convey the meaning and to keep the integrity of the essence of this experience. The images are purposefully simple. It is written from the heart, not the mind.

$25.00  Softcover, 120 p.  ISBN: 1-891824-43-0

### Ancient Secret of the Flower of Life *Vol. I*

*Drunvalo Melchizedek*

Once, all life in the universe knew the Flower of Life as the creation pattern —the geometrical design leading us into and out of physical existence. Sacred Geometry is the form beneath our being and points to a divine order in our reality. We can follow that order from the invisible atom to the infinite stars, finding ourselves at each step.

$25.00  Softcover, 228 p.  ISBN: 1-891824-17-1

### Change Your Encodements, Your DNA, Your Life!

*Amma through Cathy Chapman*

The first part of this book discusses what you call love. Love is the most powerful energy. The second part contains powerful techniques for working with your DNA encodements.  The third part contains what some call predictions, which are nothing more than my reading and interpretation of the energy at the time when the energy was read.

$16.95  Softcover, 303 p.  ISBN: 1-891824-52-X

### Animal Souls Speak
### *Explorer Race Series*

*Robert Shapiro*

Welcome to the footsteps of the loving beings (animals) who support you, who wish to reveal more about themselves to you and who welcome you, not only to planet Earth, but more specifically to the pathway of self-discovery. The animal world will speak through elders, since that way they can include knowledge and wisdom about their home planets. Each animal brings a wonderous gift to share with humanity—enjoy it!

$29.95  Softcover, 610 p.  ISBN: 1-891824-50-3

### Ancient Secret of the Flower of Life *Vol. II*

*Drunvalo Melchizedek*

Drunvalo shares the instructions for the Mer-Ka-Ba meditation, step-by-step techniques for the re-creation of the energy field of the evolved human. From the pyramids and mysteries of Egypt to the new race of Indigo children, Drunvalo presents the sacred geometries of the Reality and the subtle energies that shape our world.

$25.00  Softcover, 477 p.  ISBN: 1-891824-21-X

# Forever Numerology

## Includes Master Numbers 11–99!

## by Lynn Buess

In *Forever Numerology*, Lynn Buess again takes a gigantic leap for numerology with extraordinary new insights and methods of interpretation. This volume will define new standards for years to come. You will be swept through transcendent realms of light and awareness, even as Buess's solid psychological base and down-to-earth reality keep you centered right here in the present moment.

Having practiced for decades as a psychotherapist, Buess has uncovered deeply repressed blocks and negative unconscious complexes in many of his clients. In this book, he works some of his insights for recognizing dysfunction into the interpretation of numerology in the hopes of awakening new seekers to the dark side of the self. Once you recognize this dark side, you have the possibility of working it out of your life. The interpretations and experiences presented in this book are given through the symbolic wisdom of numbers.

Truly, no complete volume can be written on any subject; however, this book comes closer than ever to portraying the evolution of consciousness through the symbology of numbers. It will be of help in your journey through life and in your search for the meaning of numbers.

$17⁹⁵ SOFTCOVER 290 P. ISBN 1-891824-65-1

### Numerology for the New Age
*By Lynn Buess*

Our own vibrations or cyclical patterns are numerologically determined by our date of birth and given name. By understanding these cycles, we can learn to more effectively express our potential, human and divine. This volume concentrates more upon the experiential value of numerology than the historical.

**$11.00 SOFTCOVER 262 P. ISBN 0-929385-31-4**

### Numerology: Nuances in Relationships
*By Lynn Buess*

Welcome to a new and meaningful application of numbers in your life. This volume is written to assist you in your quest to better understand yourself in relation to another person. You will discover many new insights and avenues toward more mature and compatible interactions with others.

**$13.75 SOFTCOVER 309 P. ISBN 0-929385-23-3**

### Children of Light, Children of Denial
*By Lynn Buess*

There is a rapid and expansive awakening within the self-awareness movement that integration of self includes a harmonious dance between the light (conscious) and dark (unconscious) aspects of human nature. Lynn Buess addresses the cycle of denial that leads to so much dysfunction in our time.

**$8.95 SOFTCOVER 125 P. ISBN 0-929385-15-2**

Phone: 928-526-1345 or 1-800-450-0985 • Fax 928-714-1132
*... or use our online bookstore at www.lighttechnology.com*

# THE EXPLORER RACE SERIES

## ZOOSH AND HIS FRIENDS THROUGH ROBERT SHAPIRO

*THE SERIES: Humans—creators-in-training—have a purpose and destiny so heartwarmingly, profoundly glorious that it is almost unbelievable from our present dimensional perspective. Humans are great lightbeings from beyond this creation, gaining experience in dense physicality. This truth about the great human genetic experiment of the Explorer Race and the mechanics of creation is being revealed for the first time by Zoosh and his friends through superchannel Robert Shapiro. These books read like adventure stories as we follow the clues from this creation that we live in out to the Council of Creators and beyond.*

### ❶ THE EXPLORER RACE

You individuals reading this are truly a result of the genetic experiment on Earth. You are beings who uphold the principles of the Explorer Race. The information in this book is designed to show you who you are and give you an evolutionary understanding of your past that will help you now. The key to empowerment in these days is to not know everything about your past, but to know what will help you now. Your number-one function right now is your status of Creator apprentice, which you have achieved through years and lifetimes of sweat. You are constantly being given responsibilities by the Creator that would normally be things that Creator would do. The responsibility and the destiny of the Explorer Race is not only to explore, but to create. 574 P. $25.00 ISBN 0-929385-38-1

### ❷ ETs and the EXPLORER RACE

In this book, Robert channels Joopah, a Zeta Reticulan now in the ninth dimension who continues the story of the great experiment—the Explorer Race—from the perspective of his civilization. The Zetas would have been humanity's future selves had not humanity re-created the past and changed the future. 237 P. $14.95 ISBN 0-929385-79-9

### ❸ EXPLORER RACE: ORIGINS and the NEXT 50 YEARS

This volume has so much information about who we are and where we came from—the source of male and female beings, the war of the sexes, the beginning of the linear mind, feelings, the origin of souls—it is a treasure trove. In addition, there is a section that relates to our near future—how the rise of global corporations and politics affects our future, how to use benevolent magic as a force of creation and how we will go out to the stars and affect other civilizations. Astounding information. 339 P. $14.95 ISBN 0-929385-95-0

### ❹ EXPLORER RACE: CREATORS and FRIENDS
### The MECHANICS of CREATION

Now that you have a greater understanding of who you are in the larger sense, it is necessary to remind you of where you came from, the true magnificence of your being. You must understand that you are creators-in-training, and yet you were once a portion of Creator. One could certainly say, without being magnanimous, that you are still a portion of Creator, yet you are training for the individual responsibility of being a creator, to give your Creator a coffee break. This book will allow you to understand the vaster qualities and help you remember the nature of the desires that drive any creator, the responsibilities to which a creator must answer, the reaction a creator must have to consequences and the ultimate reward of any creator. 435 P. $19.95 ISBN 1-891824-01-5

### ❺ EXPLORER RACE: PARTICLE PERSONALITIES

All around you in every moment you are surrounded by the most magical and mystical beings. They are too small for you to see as single individuals, but in groups you know them as the physical matter of your daily life. Particles who might be considered either atoms or portions of atoms consciously view the vast spectrum of reality yet also have a sense of personal memory like your own linear memory. These particles remember where they have been and what they have done in their infinitely long lives. Some of the particles we hear from are Gold, Mountain Lion, Liquid Light, Uranium, the Great Pyramid's Capstone, This Orb's Boundary, Ice and Ninth-Dimensional Fire. 237 P. $14.95 ISBN 0-929385-97-7

### ❻ EXPLORER RACE and BEYOND

With a better idea of how creation works, we go back to the Creator's advisers and receive deeper and more profound explanations of the roots of the Explorer Race. The liquid Domain and the Double Diamond portal share lessons given to the roots on their way to meet the Creator of this universe, and finally the roots speak of their origins and their incomprehensibly long journey here. 360 P. $14.95 ISBN 1-891824-06-6

# THE EXPLORER RACE SERIES

## ZOOSH AND HIS FRIENDS THROUGH ROBERT SHAPIRO

### ❼ EXPLORER RACE: The COUNCIL of CREATORS

The thirteen core members of the Council of Creators discuss their adventures in coming to awareness of themselves and their journeys on the way to the Council on this level. They discuss the advice and oversight they offer to all creators, including the Creator of this local universe. These beings are wise, witty and joyous, and their stories of Love's Creation create an expansion of our concepts as we realize that we live in an expanded, multiple-level reality. 237 P. $14.95 ISBN 1-891824-13-9

### ❽ EXPLORER RACE and ISIS

This is an amazing book! It has priestess training, Shamanic training, Isis's adventures with Explorer Race beings—before Earth and on Earth—and an incredibly expanded explanation of the dynamics of the Explorer Race. Isis is the prototypal loving, nurturing, guiding feminine being, the focus of feminine energy. She has the ability to expand limited thinking without making people with limited beliefs feel uncomfortable. She is a fantastic storyteller, and all of her stories are teaching stories. If you care about who you are, why you are here, where you are going and what life is all about—pick up this book. You won't lay it down until you are through, and then you will want more. 317 P. $14.95 ISBN 1-891824-11-2

### ❾ EXPLORER RACE and JESUS

The core personality of that being known on the Earth as Jesus, along with his students and friends, describes with clarity and love his life and teaching two thousand years ago. He states that his teaching is for all people of all races in all countries. Jesus announces here for the first time that he and two others, Buddha and Mohammed, will return to Earth from their place of being in the near future, and a fourth being, a child already born now on Earth, will become a teacher and prepare humanity for their return. So heartwarming and interesting, you won't want to put it down. 354 P. $16.95 ISBN 1-891824-14-7

### ❿ EXPLORER RACE: Earth History and Lost Civilization

Speaks of Many Truths and Zoosh, through Robert Shapiro, explain that planet Earth, the only water planet in this solar system, is on loan from Sirius as a home and school for humanity, the Explorer Race. Earth's recorded history goes back only a few thousand years, its archaeological history a few thousand more. Now this book opens up as if a light was on in the darkness, and we see the incredible panorama of brave souls coming from other planets to settle on different parts of Earth. We watch the origins of tribal groups and the rise and fall of civilizations, and we can begin to understand the source of the wondrous diversity of plants, animals and humans that we enjoy here on beautiful Mother Earth. 310 P. $14.95 ISBN 1-891824-20-1

### ⓫ EXPLORER RACE: ET VISITORS SPEAK

Even as you are searching the sky for extraterrestrials and their spaceships, ETs are here on planet Earth—they are stranded, visiting, exploring, studying the culture, healing the Earth of trauma brought on by irresponsible mining or researching the history of Christianity over the past two thousand years. Some are in human guise, and some are in spirit form. Some look like what we call animals as they come from the species' home planet and interact with their fellow beings—those beings that we have labeled cats or cows or elephants. Some are brilliant cosmic mathematicians with a sense of humor; they are presently living here as penguins. Some are fledgling diplomats training for future postings on Earth when we have ET embassies here. In this book, these fascinating beings share their thoughts, origins and purposes for being here. 350 P. $14.95 ISBN 1-891824-28-7

### ⓬ EXPLORER RACE: Techniques for GENERATING SAFETY

Wouldn't you like to generate safety so you could go wherever you need to go and do whatever you need to do in a benevolent, safe and loving way for yourself? Learn safety as a radiated environment that will allow you to gently take the step into the new timeline, into a benevolent future and away from a negative past. 208 P. $9.95 ISBN 1-891824-26-0

# ANIMAL SOULS SPEAK

## THROUGH ROBERT SHAPIRO

Robert Shapiro is largely known as a professional trance channel, with several series of published books such as *The Explorer Race* Series, of which this is book #13; *Shining the Light* Series (8); *Shamanic Secrets* Series (3); *Benevolent Magic*, and the *Ultimate UFO* Series.

But, as he is now, he is a mystical man with shamanic capabilities well and thoroughly infused into him. He also has many unusual

Robert Shapiro

skills that he is teaching through blogs, the *Sedona Journal of Emergence* and these books. It is his intention to bring about the most benevolent change available on the planet through sharing his personal inspirations as well as his channeling, which in this book is of these wonderful beings humans call animals.

### Chapters Include:

| | | | | | |
|---|---|---|---|---|---|
| Eel | Deer | Phoenix | Dog | Myna Bird | Ant |
| Tortoise | Elephant | Chickadee | Whale | Llama | Moss |
| Frog | Rabbit | Koala Bear | Shark | Sea Sand | Overspirit |
| Skunk | Polar Bear | Spider | Gnat | Giraffe | Human Sea Elder |
| Snail | Earthworm | Cat | Butterfly | Manta Ray | Creator's Emissary |

The animal world will speak, if you prefer, through elders. This has certain advantages, since that way they can include knowledge and wisdom to a degree—not to a vast degree, but to a degree—about their home planets.

—Grandfather

### Each animal brings a wonderous gift to share with humanity—enjoy it!

Welcome to the footsteps of the loving beings who support you, who wish to reveal more about themselves to you and who welcome you, not only to planet Earth, but more specifically to the pathway of self-discovery. Take note as you read this book of what resonates, what stimulates your own memories. Use it to inspire you, to encourage you, to support you along your path toward inevitable self-discovery, and ultimately to support self-discovery in others that results in revealing the true and most benevolent heart of all beings. Good life.

—Creator's Emissary

The Explorer Race Series

**$29.**<sup>95</sup>  ISBN 1-891824-50-3
Softcover, 640 p.

Phone: 928-526-1345 or 1-800-450-0985 • Fax 928-714-1132
... or use our online bookstore at www.lighttechnology.com

# SHINING THE LIGHT SERIES

## Zoosh and Others through Robert Shapiro

### SHINING THE LIGHT IV
#### Humanity's Greatest Challenge
Includes information on Hale-Bopp, SSG, all updates since Volume III and material on the uncreating of Hitler in 1993. ✦ Negative Sirians coming to the third dimension ✦ The express bus to creatorship ✦ The poison HAARP project ✦ Luciferian traits and critical mass ✦ ETs in Brazil ✦ Comet brings light-being-filled vehicle bigger than Earth ✦ Sinister secret government under control of beings from the alternate negative future

SOFTCOVER 557P. $14⁹⁵ ISBN 0-929385-93-4

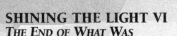

### SHINING THE LIGHT V
#### Humanity Is Going to make It!
Zoosh and others blast the cover off past events and hidden forces at work on this planet and reveal opportunities for immense growth and power. This is a pivotal time as the secrets and mysteries that have so long bewildered humanity are at last illuminated by the light of truth. ✦ Revelations about Area 51 by a rocket scientist ✦ A 75-year-long Zeta restructuring of the past ✦ Cloning: the new ethics forum ✦ Recent UFO activity in the skies ✦ The first humans and the original dark side, our shadow ✦ Angels: guides in training (30% of humans are angels) ✦ Using manifestation powers to avert man-made disasters ✦ The angel of Roswell ✦ Symbiotic spacecraft engines and faster-than-light travel ✦ The true purpose of the Mayans ✦ The SSG downs military planes ✦ The SSG realizes they need customers, not slaves ✦ Grid lines rising above the planet ✦ Homework for changing your past

SOFTCOVER 460P. $14⁹⁵ ISBN 1-891824-00-7

### SHINING THE LIGHT VI
#### The End of What Was
✦ Don't use water for fuel, or Earth will look like Mars ✦ SSG command "Don't read!" on U.S. TV sets ✦ How to aid whales caught in worldwide sonic radiation ✦ Cats as our teachers ✦ The arrival of the wisdom seekers and wisdom givers ✦ Zero point and the unified field ✦ Creator flips the switch ✦ Tunnels under Phoenix and white light in New England ✦ Oxygen-eating meteoroids ✦ Don't let the SSG draw you into a malevolent time line ✦ Kids will lead the movement to embrace outcasts ✦ Sand as crystal libraries ✦ Hacker, an SSG dupe, causes Titan 4 rocket explosion ✦ And more

SOFTCOVER 316P. $14⁹⁵ ISBN 1-891824-24-4

### SHINING THE LIGHT VII
#### The First Alignment: World Peace
✦ Don't use water for fuel, or Earth will look like Mars ✦ SSG command "Don't read!" on U.S. TV sets ✦ How to aid whales caught in worldwide sonic radiation ✦ Cats as our teachers ✦ The arrival of the wisdom seekers and wisdom givers ✦ Zero point and the unified field ✦ Creator flips the switch ✦ Tunnels under Phoenix and white light in New England ✦ Oxygen-eating meteoroids ✦ Don't let the SSG draw you into a malevolent time line ✦ Kids will lead the movement to embrace outcasts ✦ Sand as crystal libraries ✦ Hacker, an SSG dupe, causes Titan 4 rocket explosion ✦ And more!

SOFTCOVER 521 P. $24⁹⁵ ISBN 1-891824-56-2

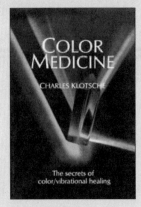

# COLOR MEDICINE
*The Secrets of Color Vibrational Healing*
## Charles Klotsche

A new dimension in holistic healing, *Color Medicine* provides a powerful technique for treating specific imbalances and strengthening the immune system. By combining aura-attuned chromatherapy with harmonious sounds, tissue salts and hydrochromatherapy, the forty-ninth vibrational technique was developed. A breakthrough, yet as old as recorded medicine, it utilizes subtle energy vibrations similar to those found in the visible spectrum. A textbook and how-to handbook, this book encompasses an encyclopedia of fascinating information, charts, diagrams and tables as well as methods of treatment and technical advice. Whether you are a holistic practitioner or merely curious, this book marks a new frontier in the world of alternative healing.

SOFTCOVER 114 P.   $11⁹⁵ ISBN 0-929385-27-6

- Does Color Medicine Really Heal?
- Color Physics: The Scientific Explanation of Color Medicine, or Vibrational Therapy
- Color Energetics: How Color Medicine Works with the Subtle Energy Fields of the Body
- Color Harmonics: The Twelve Healing Colors and Their Use

- Color Practice: Materials and Practical Techniques for Applying Color Medicine
- Color Schedule Application: Determining the Appropriate Color(s) for Relieving/Healing the 123 Major Illnesses
- Color Medicine Schedules for 123 Specific Human Disorders

---

JONATHAN GOLDMAN AND SHAMAEL, ANGEL OF SOUND

$14⁹⁵ SOFTCOVER 147 P.
ISBN 1-891824-04-X

# SHIFTING FREQUENCIES
*How Sound Can Change Your Life*

Now, for the first time, Healing Sounds pioneer Jonathan Goldman tells us about shifting frequencies—how to use sound and other modalities to change vibrational patterns for both personal and planetary healing and transformation. Through his consciousness connection to Shamael, Angel of Sound, Jonathan shares his extraordinary scientific and spiritual knowledge and insights, providing information, instructions and techniques on using sound, light, color, visualization and sacred geometry to experience shifting frequencies. The material in this book is both timely and vital for health and spiritual evolution.

**In this book, you will:**
- Explore the use of sound in ways you never imagined for healing and transformation.
- Discover harmonics as a key to opening to higher levels of consciousness.
- Learn about the angel chakra and what sounds may be used to activate this new energy center.
- Find out how to transmute imbalanced vibrations using your own sounds.
- Experience the secrets of crystal singing.
- Understand the importance of compassion in achieving ascension.

---

Phone: 928-526-1345 or 1-800-450-0985 • Fax: 928-714-1132

# CROP CIRCLES REVEALED
## LANGUAGE OF THE LIGHT SYMBOLS

*BARBARA LAMB, MS, MFL*
*JUDITH K. MOORE*

$25^{00}$

SOFTCOVER 308 P.
ISBN 1-891824-32-5

**326 CROP CIRCLE ILLUSTRATIONS**

Welcome to the world of crop circles, one of the most **TANTALIZING** phenomena in our world today. It is difficult not to be captivated by their beauty and complexity and by the questions and issues they provoke, including one that becomes more pressing everyday—what other **INTELLIGENT** life forms are out there trying to communicate with us? What are their intentions? What is the communication system between them, the Earth and humanity? Unlock the secret keys for the emergence of a new world of peace, freedom, healing and unconditional love. We are being assisted with energy as never before to **REGENERATE** ourselves and our ailing planet. Reactivate and discover your invaluable gifts and divine mission. Awaken your DNA and empower yourself! This comprehensive document reveals the deep mysteries of the crop circle phenomenon. Scientific analysis of the hoaxing controversy and high-level spiritual transmissions are combined in one masterful presentation for your use and interpretation.

# MAHATMA I & II
## *The I AM Presence*

# BRIAN GRATTAN

Awaken and realize that all of humankind will create their "body for ascension," whether they accomplish this now or later, and that this is not the exclusive domain of Christ or Buddha or the many others who have ascended—*this is your birthright.* When humans lift the veils of their unworthiness and recognize that they are the sons of God, that there is divine equality and that no one is greater than another, then you will have begun your journey in the way that it was intended. The *Mahatma* is for those who are motivated to search for the answers that can respond to their mental and spiritual bodies. No matter how contrary your current beliefs, this book contains methods for creating your spiritual lightbody for ascension and also explains your eternal journey in a way never before available to humankind.

SOFTCOVER 480 P. $19^{95}$ ISBN 0-929385-77-2

# TITLES ON TAPE
### by Brian Grattan

**BASEL SEMINAR**
10 TAPE SET (AUDIO CASSETTE), English with German translation . . . . . . . . . . .$35.00

**EASTER SEMINAR**
7 TAPE SET (AUDIO CASSETTE), English with German translation . . . . . . . . . . .$59.95

**SEATTLE SEMINAR**
12 TAPE SET (AUDIO CASSETTE) . . . . . . . . . . . . . . . . . . . . . . . . . . . . . .$79.95
Twelve one-hour audio tapes from the Seattle Seminar, October 27–30, 1994. These twelve powerful hours of meditations lead to total spiritual transformation by recoding your two-strand DNA to function in positive mutation.

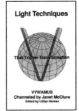